Love's Promises

Love's Promises

How Formal & Informal Contracts
Shape All Kinds of Families

Martha M. Ertman

QUEER ACTION/QUEER IDEAS
A SERIES EDITED BY MICHAEL BRONSKI

BEACON PRESS, BOSTON

Beacon Press
Boston, Massachusetts
www.beacon.org

Beacon Press books
are published under the auspices of
the Unitarian Universalist Association of Congregations.

18 17 16 15   8 7 6 5 4 3 2 1

This book is printed on acid-free paper that meets the uncoated paper
ANSI/NISO specifications for permanence as revised in 1992.

Text design by Ruth Maassen

Queer Ideas—a unique series addressing pivotal issues within the LGBT
movement

Library of Congress Cataloging-in-Publication Data

Ertman, Martha M.
  Love's promises : how formal and informal contracts shape all kinds of
families / Martha M. Ertman.
     pages cm
  Includes bibliographical references and index.
  ISBN 978-0-8070-3366-1 (hardback) — ISBN 978-0-8070-3367-
8 (ebook) 1. Domestic relations. 2. Cohabitation agreements. 3.
Unmarried couples—Legal status, laws, etc. 4. Adoption—Law and
legislation. 5. Prenuptial agreements. 6. Contracts. I. Title.
  K699.E78 2015
  346.7301'6—dc23
                                    2014038565

For my son

I give you myself before preaching or law;
Will you give me yourself? will you come travel with me?

—WALT WHITMAN

Contents

A Note from the Series Editor

The LGBT movement in the United States has fought hard to ensure that everyone has the right to enter into legal marriage. That fight continues and has made enormous strides. Still, as we all know, relationships are complicated: emotionally, romantically, financially, and legally. We also know that while marriage can tie a good many knots—particularly on issues of legal and fiscal responsibility to one another and to children—every relationship has much that is presumed, unspoken, and unimagined. Martha Ertman's achievement in *Love's Promises: How Formal and Informal Contracts Shape All Kinds of Families* is to give all couples—LGBT or heterosexual—as well as adoptive families and single parents a series of roadmaps to plan for the unexpected and the expected.

With an extensive background in contract law, Martha Ertman has provided theoretical and actual agreements that couples can enter to consciously acknowledge what they need and can expect from one another. These agreements—variously called "deals" and "contracts," depending on the relationship, presumptions, and needs of the people involved—encourage and enable couples to face their future with clear vision. By sharing her own story, Ertman shows and not just tells how contracts create and transform families.

Love's Promises is a crucial step forward for the family equality movement—which has focused significantly on marriage equality for so long—because it acknowledges that all relationships are deserving of respect, even as they have different needs and require different solutions to problems. Drawing on a wealth of case law, personal experience, an ethic of fairness, and common sense, Ertman's invaluable book forces us to radically, and productively, rethink our commonplace—often wrong—assumptions about how we love, commit, trust, and thrive in our relationships.

Michael Bronski
Series Editor, Queer Action/Queer Ideas

Introduction

The big whoop in contract law, I tell my students, is drawing a line between the kinds of promises that courts enforce and the ones they won't. But I don't tell them that contracts and the mini-contracts I call "deals" are a big whoop in my life. They brought me my family and job, and gave my son his second mother. I had no idea that contracts would be so transformative twenty-five years ago as I soaked up the law with other first-year students.

I've made a career out of teaching contracts and writing about what they bring to family law in footnote-heavy law reviews consumed by the legal community.[1] Yet it continues to surprise me that so many people, judges included, still view love and contracts as fundamentally opposite. Love is open-ended and generous, they insist, while contracts are selfish, cold, and calculating. This book challenges that myth by showing that the many contracts and deals that shape families not only exist but are also deeply beneficial. The fact is that everyone has a family—often more than one—and whether you're married or living with someone, are heterosexual or LGBT, or become a parent through sex or alternatives like adoption and reproductive technology, contracts and deals help you become and stay a family and also, if necessary, end the relationship. Recognizing this fact helps people tailor their families to match their daily lives, and ignoring it can cause a devastating mismatch between the family you thought you had and the legal reality.

Family law rules have to allow some tailoring because love comes in different packages. There is the most common model of being heterosexual and married, with kids conceived at home instead of a doctor's office. But there are alternative and increasingly popular models, which can be viewed as Plan B. Unmarried couples—same-sex or different-sex—live together, and couples as well as singles become parents through adoption and reproductive technologies. Many families are a mix of these models, like a married same-sex couple or a husband and wife who adopt.

This book argues that contracts and deals facilitate that variety by helping people create and sustain families. Moreover, family law can, should, and increasingly does recognize that fact. Once you uncover the central role of contracts and deals, you can see families in a new light. Instead of talking about "the" family as one kind of relationship honored above all others by Nature or God—marriage, heterosexuality, genetic kinship—law and society can update that black-and-white two-dimensionality to acknowledge the colorful, 3-D variety of life as it's actually lived. That means letting go of moral judgment aimed at uncommon families and replacing it with a view of variety as morally neutral.[2]

But neutrality is not an end point. Removing the clutter of moral judgment makes space for noticing the way that honoring family variety gets vital care to more people—especially children and vulnerable adults—and also supports communities. It's better, this book argues, to let people decide for themselves when, whether, how, and with whom to form their most intimate relationships than to cede that power to either church or state.

DEFINING CONTRACTS AND DEALS

"Contract" is legalese for the kind of agreement courts enforce. Courts refuse to enforce some agreements—like selling sex or babies—because they are not truly consensual or because they corrupt something sacred, such as the idea that people are different from objects. I call these not-legally-binding agreements "deals." Some deals are also crimes, like prostitution and baby-selling, but most are entirely lawful, just too small or vague to bring before a judge when they are breached. More important, the people involved never expect them to get to court. Still, they matter. Think of gambling debts from a neighborhood poker game, or agreements to take turns carpooling the kids to soccer. No one would sue if the agreements were not honored, yet these deals structure relationships. Deals can be big things, like agreeing to inseminate, or casual, implicit, daily household exchanges like "I pay the bills and you do the grocery shopping." They shape intimate relationships because they create expectations of reciprocity and grounds for changing the relationship when one person isn't holding up his or her end of the deal.

One of the biggest changes over the last few decades is that family law has upgraded a number of deals to contracts. Starting in the 1960s and '70s, both law and society began to allow people to make premarital contracts, living-together agreements, and contracts to become parents through reproductive technology. More recently, family law has recognized more open adoption contracts.

Even when courts are willing to enforce agreements, they rarely get involved because people generally keep their promises or work things out as necessary. When a relationship does fall apart, judges step in only if the person who feels injured has enough money, persistence, and tolerance for conflict to weather litigation. Sometimes, family law should upgrade agreements that it currently treats as deals to the level of contract, especially when treating them as deals suggests that a type of family is unnatural or erases the value of the homemaking work that sustains families.

What matters most is that we notice the many exchanges that define family life. This book doesn't offer a global yardstick to dictate which agreements are or should be legally binding and which mere deals. It adopts instead a more pragmatic approach that zooms in on specific contexts. Once we see the exchanges in family arrangements, lawmakers can decide which should be contracts and which are properly treated as mere deals.

DEFINING PLAN A AND PLAN B

This book also suggests new language—Plan A/Plan B—to help us think about uncommon families as exceptions to the general rule instead of unnatural or inferior. "Plan A" is what's common: more than nine out of ten kids are raised by their genetic parents, marriage is the most common family form, and most people are straight. But "common" is not the same as better. When someone veers toward the road less traveled, I call it "Plan B." Plan B covers a wide variety of uncommon families, from repro tech and adoption to cohabitation. It also improves on the usual way people talk about uncommon families ("nontraditional"; "unconventional") by replacing disdain or condescension with a matter-of-fact, morally neutral claim that society and people individually are better off when we can choose when, how, and with whom to have a family.

The morning-after pill called Plan B invokes these same values, but it comes into play only to avoid a pregnancy (and skirt barriers to surgical abortions). In contrast, my Plan B families are generally starting and sustaining relationships. Moreover, in the wide world beyond the culture wars, the term "Plan B" has long served as shorthand for working around obstacles—for example, the Plan B app that helps you find a lost cell phone and Brad Pitt's Plan B production company, formed to make the kind of movies he wants to see and star in. Since many, if not most, families are a mix of Plan A and Plan B—think of blended families and married couples who adopt—few can smugly claim a pure Plan A pedigree, and still fewer are pure Plan B.

Just as this book embraces family variety, it acknowledges a continuum of consent to the family form. Plan B can be someone's first choice, a way of accommodating a Plan B reality, a way to make the best of a terrible situation, or something in between. A couple deliberately opting not to marry may freely choose that uncommon arrangement, but choice is more constrained when one person in that live-in couple refuses to marry or a gay couple can't marry because their state forbids it. Some so-called choices border on coercion. Most birth parents would rather not place their children for adoption but are forced to by youth, illness, poverty, or the fallout from trauma. Choice, moreover, is not stable. A family may start out viewing surrogacy or adoption as a distant second-best to Plan A, yet come to see their Plan B family as meant to be. This book honors the whole range, referring to out-of-the-ordinary families interchangeably as "Plan B" or "uncommon."

Finally, the Plan A/Plan B framework reflects the law's tendency to craft a general rule for the most common state of affairs. Legal scholars call this a "default rule" because it applies to most situations. When something unusual happens, like repro tech, adoption, or cohabitation, the law carves out exceptions to fit that situation. Neither the default nor the exception is better or worse, just different.

MY LIFE IN CONTRACTS AND DEALS

Chapter 1 of *Love's Promises* is a memoir that illustrates these truths by charting my transition from single and childless to married mother. Contracts and deals allowed me to become one of three parents—all gay—raising a beloved boy named Walter.

Braiding memoir with family law serves two ends. First, it shows the emotional side of contracts and deals. Too often, economics-oriented discussions of family exchanges get dismissed as ridiculously cold, a fundamental mismatch with the warmth of family. The Beatles famously sang, "Can't buy me love," and law professor Robin West panned Judge Richard Posner's book *Sex and Reason*—an economic account of sexual regulations—for not telling a "recognizably human story." Relationship expert Harville Hendrix says that love should come without price tags because "we want to be loved and cared for without having to do anything in return."[3] The memoir elements of this book counter those claims by relating a very human story of carefully thought-out exchanges that brought love into my life, and the law part shows how exchanges also structure other families. Second, I have an essentially happy story to tell about tailoring off-the-rack rules to fit your relationships. Sad stories about rupture and disappointment already crowd library shelves and case reporters, and too little is said about the also-true tales of things working out in Plan B families.[4]

The emotional truths about love and contracts that I discovered as I found a home and family in my forties are conveyed in a series of stories pulled from seven or eight years of my life. A lot of other things happen during those three thousand days, including a bit of midlife growing up and becoming a churchgoer. My hope is that teasing out the intimate exchanges will help readers notice the contracts and deals in their own families.

Exchanges are hardly the sum total of anyone's family, because no relationship can be reduced to one thing. But they're more important than most people think. I focus on them to counteract the loud declarations in everyday conversation and legal rules to the effect that all family exchanges are pure, selfless gifts. Those assertions often mask the very exchanges they purport to deny, a masking so effective and pervasive that my argument must stand alone to counterbalance the powerful, unspoken assumptions that "family contract" is an oxymoron. Once you see the pattern, you should see numerous situations in which exchanges are camouflaged as gifts.

The biggest gift in my case was deeply contractual. Newly single after leaving a twelve-year relationship because I wanted a baby and my ex didn't, I had to figure out how I might manage to become a mom. I called Victor, a gay friend from law school, who lived across the country, and asked if he'd like to have a baby together. We negotiated what amounts to a contract: a voluntary, reciprocal exchange that courts would probably enforce. I got to be a mom, with financial and emotional backup as well as freedom to decide big things, like where to live and whom to date, and small, like how old is old enough to chew gum.

I came out in my teens and always figured I'd use a sperm bank to get the goods from an anonymous donor. But Victor, whom I knew to be a good man, provided not only good genes and money but also outstanding friendship, fashion advice, lots of laughs, and an unparalleled role model for our son.

Victor, for his part, also got a good deal. He got to be a father. At the same time, he didn't have to completely give up his city life of opera tickets, dinner parties, and bridge tournaments and knew he could rely on me to take care of the essentials of housing, food, and medical care. All told, you could summarize our deal as making me around 70 percent parent and Victor 30 percent. Women, on average, do way more child care, so our initial exchange actually echoed the one struck by many couples, tailored to account for the fact that we were friends, never lovers.

Since Victor and I are both law professors, we put our agreement in writing—a four-page contract that covers finances, the name of the baby (Walter), and even emotional stuff like our promise to support each other's romantic relationships. So far, Victor and I get along. But if we don't, or if one of us gets seriously sick or dies, those thought-out terms could well make an awful situation a lot less painful and expensive than it would be without the contract. Most important, the contract reduces the things we could fight about and therefore the chance of a drawn-out and acrimonious legal battle that would hurt Walter more than anyone.

It took a year, a posse of doctors, heaps of money, innumerable friends, and the patience of Job to get pregnant. But it finally worked. Walter came out safe and sound, with Victor holding my hand.

When our little boy was two years old, I met a sharp and idealistic lawyer named Karen. We started dating, which required new deals: Could she still jet around the country on social justice projects when I love to have dinner at home most nights? Was she up for an open-door policy for Victor's visits? These deals led to what Karen called "training rings," a rough equivalent of what business people call an "agreement to agree": not legally binding but important, showing our hope and intent to enter a legally recognized relationship down the line. Next came buying a brick colonial on a tree-lined street near good schools, complete with a mortgage and related contracts for joint bank accounts and credit cards. Then a marriage proposal and an acceptance, followed by a raft of contracts for invitations, flowers, and outfits to get married in.

But most significant was Victor, Karen, and me signing an amended parenting agreement to formally add her as Walter's other mom.

Our three-parent agreement, alongside Karen's and my Jewish wedding contract and deals about how to patch together Jewish and Unitarian rituals, all reflect the mosaic of our family.

OTHER PEOPLE'S LIVES IN CONTRACTS & DEALS

We're not the only family that's shot through with contracts and deals. Tolstoy was wrong to say that all happy families are alike, because all kinds of families have their own ways of using exchanges to create "us-ness." Agreements shape just about every stage of ordinary dating, engagement, marriage, day-to-day family life, and divorce as well as less common family forms like having kids through reproductive technology or adoption and what used to be called "living in sin."

Part I of the book focuses on parenthood and Part II on cohabitation and marriage. Consistent with my aim to recognize and even celebrate uncommon forms of family, this ordering inverts the playground chant: "First comes love, then comes marriage, then comes baby in a baby carriage." Moreover, it mirrors an increasingly common experience in American families, since fully 40 percent of babies are born to unmarried parents, according to the 2010 Census. Like many people, I was pushing a baby carriage before I found romantic love and marriage, so this structure also matches the personal story I tell in chapter 1.

Each type of family agreement gets two chapters, one focusing on basic facts and the other on legal rules. Lest we forget the breath of life animating family promises, each law chapter begins with a snippet of memoir about my experience with that kind of contract. The paired chapters then explain on-the-ground as well as on-the-books aspects of family agreements. Facts-focused chapters begin with a handful of vignettes sketching out the surprisingly long history of that type of family agreement to show that there's nothing especially new or unnatural about repro tech, open adoption, cohabitation, or marital agreements. They then conclude with a "101" section that explains in more detail how family law uses contracts to distinguish between the relationships it deems "family" and those that it refuses to recognize. Law-focused chapters, in turn, start off with a "Law as It Is" section outlining the legal rules that govern that family exchange and then explaining those rules using real-life cases. Each law chapter concludes with a "Law as It Should Be" section proposing ways that legal doctrine ought to continue its positive trajectory of honoring family exchanges.

The first family law chapters, chapters 2 and 3, show how reproductive technology contracts and deals help create one type of Plan B family. Experts estimate that the $3-billion-a-year repro tech industry brings around 40,000 babies into American families each year via alternative insemination (AI) agreements, another 6,000 more through egg sales, and as many as 1,600 new parent/child relationships through surrogacy.[5] It's entirely lawful for sperm banks to pay anonymous donors about $100 for each "sample" and for the donors to "contract out" of legal fatherhood. Family law also allows infertile couples like Diane and Ronald Johnson to become parents by paying the bank around $200 for the sperm of a man they knew only as Donor 276. Sometimes, men and women cut out the middleperson by contracting directly with each other. Family law often allows these men to contract out of fatherhood, as long as the people don't have sex or hold him out as the child's father.

But when a child's health is at stake, family law treats part of these agreements as mere deals. When Donor 276 passed on a serious kidney disease to Diane and Ronald's daughter Brittany, the California courts enforced the part of Donor 276's sperm donation agreement that made Ronald a legal dad, but modified the anonymity provision to allow the Johnsons to get medical information about the donor.

Although many experts call for increased state regulation,[6] I believe we have enough already. Existing medical and family law rules work pretty well in conjunction with consumer protection statutes that require sperm banks to test donors for diseases like HIV. Donor-conceived kids also have online resources like the Donor Sibling Registry to locate their dads and any half-siblings. Inviting legislators and judges into our bedrooms and doctor's offices may well do more harm than good, because lawmakers have an unfortunate track record of mandating sterilization, limiting access to birth control, and forcing pregnant women to have vaginal ultrasounds.[7]

Chapters 4 and 5 focus on adoption, the route that many would-be parents pursue when repro tech fails. Although virtually all states make baby-selling a crime, they also honor adoption contracts. Birth parents typically enter a legally binding agreement—a contract—to surrender their parental rights, and adoptive parents pay agencies thousands of dollars so they can formally agree to take on legal rights and duties.[8] Moreover, birth and adoptive parents increasingly enter open adoption contracts and deals that allow for continuing contact with the child. Half of the states treat these post-adoption contact agreements—known as PACAs—as mere deals because they see them as undermining ideas about what a legitimate family looks like. That's changing as family law increasingly honors PACAs (as long as they're in the child's best interest).

That change benefits people like Paul Stickles and his three-year-old son. Back in 1931, Paul couldn't adequately care for his son as a single dad, so he agreed to let his boss adopt the boy, as long as he could visit. But when the boss and his wife cut off contact, the courts wouldn't hold the adoptive parents to their promise. By 1999, Montana courts enforced birth mom Debbie Groves's agreement with adoptive parents that allowed Debbie to visit her three-year-old daughter, Laci. To conform the agreement to the girl's best interests, the court slightly modified the terms written out by the Lutheran Social Services staff. Where a birth parent is fighting the state's effort to terminate parenthood for abuse or neglect, a PACA can provide a way for a parent who's unable to care for her child to hold onto one part of that connection, though her consent is highly constrained by the threat of losing her child completely.[9]

Despite constraints like poverty, youth, and trauma on many birth parents' consent to PACAs, overall they offer more promise than peril. They can free up kids for adoption who might otherwise spend years in the foster-care system and provide adoptive kids with valuable information instead of leaving them to dig it up themselves on Facebook.

Although PACAs can generate confusion and disputes about defining a birth parent's role in the new family, research indicates that in most cases, open adoption is an improvement over the secretive, too-often shame-filled adoption procedures in years past.[10]

The second half of the book shifts the focus to adult partnership arrangements, looking first at cohabitation and then at marriage. Chapter 6 starts with a brief review of what experts in economics, sociology, anthropology, and psychology have to say about one common swap built deeply into adult partnerships: financial support for caregiving. While the template is based on heterosexual relationships, these patterns also hold true for many same-sex couples, especially if they're raising kids.[11]

Cohabitation functions as an alternative partnership when law, finances, or plain inertia get in the way of marriage. Living together has increased 1,000 percent since 1960, and the 2010 Census reports that fully 10 percent of American households were made up of cohabiting couples. Chapter 7 shows how these statistics play out in people's lives through cases about cohabitants like Flo Byrne, an elderly widow who couldn't remarry her high school sweetheart Skip Lavazzo after they reunited as senior citizens because it would have deprived her two disabled daughters of health insurance. Actor Lee Marvin couldn't marry aspiring singer Michelle Triola because he was still married to someone else, and in the 1980s, tennis legend Martina Navratilova moved in with Judy Nelson because the law didn't allow same-sex couples to marry.

Family law generally honors agreements between these live-in lovers, straight or gay, as legally binding contracts. If Martina promised to care for Judy financially in exchange for Judy leaving the life she'd led as housewife and mother to maintain their household and be Martina's companion, then courts would enforce it. Today, cohabitants can make legally binding promises in just about every state for "palimony" (or, jokingly, "galimony" among lesbians).

Yet courts still devalue the kind of tasks that Judy did for Martina like handling food, clothing, and travel arrangements, the home-making half of what I call the "pair bond exchange." A middle-aged landscaper named Howard McLane spent his $70,000 inheritance paying for his girlfriend Loretta's cancer treatments, and also improved the land on which they lived in her double-wide trailer. When Loretta died and her relatives kicked Howard out, the Florida courts treated him as "family" when it came to paying for Loretta's hospitalizations and driving her to chemo and radiation treatments, making his time and money mere "housewifely" gifts that were not compensable. But the court treated Howard and Loretta as non-family for the landscaping services, which allowed Howard to be compensated for them. This double standard is crazy. Driving to chemo and paying for those treatments is at least as important—and thus worthy of compensation—as landscaping. Family law could and should do better.

The final family law chapters—8 and 9—make a counterintuitive argument by contending that marriage is also founded on exchanges. Family law's default rules about who owns the house a family lives in—and other property acquired during the marriage—are based on the assumption that one spouse often brings home the bacon for the other to fry up in a pan. Yet both law and society also treat homemaking labor as a gift. Masking that labor as love causes limited harm in most divorces because the homemaker is part-owner of family property under the general rule of property sharing. That changed in the 1970s, when family law started allowing richer spouses like baseball great Barry Bonds to contract out of property sharing by entering prenuptial agreements. When Barry divorced his wife, a Swede named Sun, he kept all of the $43 million he earned under his six-year contract with the San Francisco Giants, and Sun got almost nothing, despite her years of caring for their homes and two children.

Some family law scholars argue that property-hoarding prenups shouldn't be enforceable. But I think that the exchange-based foundation of families makes that kind of contractual tailoring part and parcel of family life. Chapter 9 contends that the solution is for family law to recognize both Barry and Sun's sides of the pair-bond exchange. When Barry contracted out of his duty to share, he transformed their exchange into a one-way deal. Courts should recognize that the prenup undid the pair-bond exchange, which means that Barry gave up the right to treat Sun's homemaking as a gift at the very moment that Sun gave up the right to a share in the property he brought into the family. In this view, courts in prenup cases should make sure that homemaking spouses are properly compensated for the value of the time they spent cooking, cleaning, coaching table manners, attending soccer games, and other tasks that protected their families' health, happiness, and welfare.

Family law also has had to decide whether agreements about sex and religion are legally binding. On the fidelity front, the California courts refused to enforce Manuel Diosdado's written promise to move out of the house and pay $50,000 if he cheated again on his wife Donna. Chapter 9 argues that family law should honor reconciliation agreements like the one that Donna and Manuel made to patch things up after Manuel's affair.

Agreements about religion present thornier legal challenges, since they implicate constitutional doctrines about the separation of church and state. Nevertheless, courts have enforced parts of the Jewish marriage contract (the *ketubah*) and the dowry provision in a Muslim marriage contract (the *mahr*). Other agreements get treated as deals, so a court won't enforce promises to raise the kids Jewish or Lutheran. As a whole, these cases show how contracts and deals about money, sex, and religion can and do support Plan A families, despite common beliefs that contracts inevitably undermine love, trust, and other traditional family values.

HOW TO USE THIS BOOK

Students of the family, people in uncommon families, those dreaming what their lives might look like, and lawmakers and policy shapers can all use this book in different ways. Those interested in better understanding the mechanics of family life and seeking ways to increase equality between and within relationships will find a contractual framework that should help them to grapple with these complexities. People in or considering Plan B families will find practical information, inspiration, and a blueprint for one contract-centered family, as well as a few short, simple standard-form family agreements in the appendix (one of which has worked in my own family).

But the book cannot give concrete legal advice. Family law differs greatly depending on which state you live in and the particulars of your situation. Moreover, professional ethics preclude it. The best legal advice is to hire counsel who can tailor an agreement to your state law and circumstances. The appendix, supplemented by a bibliography listing websites like nolo.com ("law for all") and form books, provide a good start for anyone wishing to know how to create and modify a family in nonstandard ways. In addition, the agreements in the appendix show how straightforward the process can be and that you can include emotional terms alongside the financial ones.

Finally, professionals helping families, from lawyers and judges to social workers, will find the book useful as they work with people who are trying to get together, stay together, or separate. In particular, while most lawyers advise against including emotional language in family agreements (ours called it "mushy"), one goal of this book is to open them up to appreciating the role of deals, as well as contracts, in family life. For example, a friend of mine whose husband did almost nothing to help around the house created a list of the homemaking tasks she did each week and the time each one required. Surprised by how long carpooling, cooking, and bathing the kids took, he agreed to take on a few tasks. Having achieved that friendly renegotiation, they ripped up the list, trusting that the issues were entirely resolved. Though they'd never sue to enforce the deal, it should help them avoid acrimony on all kinds of household issues, and may even help them steer clear of divorce court. After reading this book, they also may see that putting their agreement in writing can be a loving gesture that is part of a commitment to engage in a balanced give-and-take as well as a framework for modifying the deal as circumstances change.

Seeing those links between love and contracts could work three changes in the way we see families. First, it confirms that love comes in different packages, each shaped by its own contracts and deals. That variety benefits both individuals and the larger society. Individuals get the freedom to choose and tailor their families to match their situation, while communities and society benefit from more people coming to work, school, and the supermarket with the vital social, financial, and emotional support that comes with being an "us."

Second, recognizing the contracts and deals underlying family love reveals the injustice of legal rules that value only one side of the common swap of financial support for homemaking. Instead of taking a sentimental view of caregiving as a pure gift bestowed with no thought of return, ever, we can and should see its immense value to families and compensate caregivers accordingly.

Third, these insights demonstrate that Plan B families aren't unnatural or inferior, any more than homemaking labor is less valuable than wage labor. They're just different, based on different expectations, different tastes, and differential access to the more common family arrangements. Willful blindness to that family diversity—and the many exchanges that facilitate it—causes far more harm than recognizing the complementarity of love and contracts.

A NOTE ON LANGUAGE

The mix of memoir and law in this book has required linguistic adjustments from more common modes of storytelling. On the memoir front, I've changed some names and biographical details to protect the privacy of those who appear in my personal story, and also combined some events and conversations to convey emotional truths that would have been lost had I written with a diarist's determination to record every noisy, crowded detail of the scenes portrayed. Family law chapters refer to most people by their first names to convey the human drama underlying each lawsuit and example from books, media, and movies. Using last names to discuss multiple people in the same family would be confusing, and it's infantilizing to call only the head of the family by his or her last name and the others by their first names. Scholars, in contrast, are referred to by their surnames to reflect conventions in academic discourse and their more detached stake in the topic at hand.

ONE

The Heart of the Deal

BABY TALK: SALT LAKE CITY, 2002

"Please don't tell anyone," the doctor tells us, explaining that she's the only ob-gyn in the city who's willing to inseminate single or gay women.

Victor's new home state—Texas—is nearly as red. He's taken a day off from his law teaching job to fly up from Houston so we can inseminate with fresh sperm. When the nurse calls Victor's name, he shoots up. Ten minutes later, I welcome him back with "Hey, big guy!" and a high five, gleefully sharing the sense of getting away with something. So different from the embarrassment and inadequacy that I imagine the straight couples around us feel about their fertility treatments. For gay people, simply being here is a triumph. Before the 1990s, most doctors would only treat straight, married couples.

After the insemination, Victor comes back in to chat while I lie with my heels up against the office wall. Imagining the little tadpoles splashing up against the uterine wall, he imitates Homer Simpson's "D'oh!" as if it's him ricocheting around in there.

Two weeks later, I get my period.

Only now—a decade later—can I see that I was listening for life's call, fingers itching to grab the phone to hear what it had to say. Two kinds of faith got me to the place I call home, with the people I call family: First, faith in love in its various forms. Second, faith in contracts and the mini-contracts I call "deals." Many people believe in love, even after a brutal breakup. But too few worship at the altar of contracts. This book is my effort to spread the good news: love *and* contracts saved me. But it happened incrementally—over many conversations, shared meals and confidences, and not incidentally, different kinds of agreements tailored to support different relationships.

Negotiations with Victor started just weeks after 9/11, when I called him to pop the question. After tearfully bringing him up to speed on the fact that I'd left Denver and my partner of twelve years because I wanted a baby and she didn't, I reminded him that back in law school we'd talked about having a baby together. Did he want to?

I wanted to be the primary parent, I rushed to say, but hoped we could share big expenses. Holidays and birthdays would be better still. To my immense relief, he suggested we keep talking.

Victor and his sperm both seemed like a good bet: he's intelligent, healthy, and financially sound. He's also musically inclined, while I couldn't carry a tune if it had handles. Since we were not lovers, and never would be, I never considered that he was handsome and fit, and didn't even know that his humor, kindness, and resourcefulness would make such a difference.

Our wintertime phone chats about Operation Baby landed us in a two-bedroom, one-bath Provincetown rental the following summer to see how it felt to share a refrigerator and grocery bills. Bit by bit, the baby came to seem like something—some*one*—that could actually happen.

Sometimes, we compared my suburban Boston girlhood and his Tennessee boyhood. Both of us were chubby and unpopular in grade school. Victor had fire-and-brimstone parents; my Unitarian ancestors stretched back five generations. He gave the valedictorian speech in high school; my friends and I wanted to get into the local paper's Police Notes for attempted grave robbing. He knew he was gay from the time he asked for a Barbie on his fourth birthday; I didn't figure it out until college. Yet we're strikingly similar adults: lawyers who briefly practiced before becoming teachers, worriers reassured by steady jobs, and both newly single after twelve years of being coupled. Those breakups led us both to get new jobs in new states and thus new friends, colleagues, homes, and bank accounts. Both breakups were made more manageable by the relationship contracts we had signed at our respective commitment ceremonies. Without those contracts, we'd have been legal strangers to our partners, exacerbating the financial and emotional pain of separation.

Toward the end of our summer rental, Victor casually mentioned that he was "inclined to inseminate." Counting the months on my fingers, I figured I'd be carrying by Christmas.

Eight months later, all those inseminations—supplemented by countless drugs, fertility charts, and doctors' visits—have failed to produce a joyful little bundle of cells. Turns out, when you're thirty-nine, doctors refer to your pregnancy as "geriatric," and label you infertile if you've tried unsuccessfully for six months. The full-throttle panic of having entirely reordered my life to have this baby pushes me into the office of an infertility specialist, the only one in Salt Lake City who treats single and gay people.

Of the many tests and drugs the new doc rattles off at my first appointment, only one is new to me: the hamster test. This one zooms in on whether the man is infertile by mixing up his sperm with hamster eggs, exploiting the similarity of human and hamster eggs to test whether Victor's sperm can penetrate. If it can, I have around a 10–20 percent chance each cycle, and around a 50 percent chance overall.

When I share this with Victor, his response is an uncharacteristically loud list of data about his normal sperm count: how it's actually better than average for a forty-year-old, with a good sixty million sperm, of which about 25 percent are swimmers. It's obvious we're both trying to figure out who's at fault. Have I hurt him? Will having a rodent determine whether he's man enough to father a child be one indignity too many, pushing him away and leaving me to figure this out on my own?

The man who's aced exams all his life flunks the hamster test. Victor's sperm penetrated only two of the twenty hamster eggs, meaning, the doctor says, that I'm "highly unlikely" to get pregnant by him. Victor's so silent when I tell him that I think we've lost the connection. A month later, I'm still adjusting to the news when Victor calls, ebullient, to announce, "I can get a hamster pregnant!" Baylor Medical School has redone the test, this time with fresh sperm, a weeks-long, $600 process because, the technician told Victor, "you have to call ahead of time to reserve your hamster." If I've lost a month, at least it's clear how far Victor's willing to go on Operation Baby.

The Utah doc is less game. Much as he respects Baylor's reputation, he says, and understands that the first test was a bust because the Texas techs sent too little frozen sperm, he sticks to his prognosis that it's "highly unlikely" that I'll get pregnant with Victor.

In the face of medicine's limits and fueled by equal measures of desperation and determination, I try stuff I used to scoff at: hypnosis, then Reiki, and—on the advice of a woman at work who claims to see a baby hovering in my aura—talking to that little spirit. Nuts or not, I'm a law professor, so while I light a candle on my kitchen-counter altar, I start with a warranty disclaimer, "I can't promise you I'll be perfect." Warmed by the flame's glow on the shiny gold trinkets my colleague said would attract the spirit's attention, I continue, making what contract law calls an offer: "I can promise you a safe and happy home and that we'll have a lot of fun."

As winter turns to spring and the irises in front of my bungalow reach out of the dirt, Baby has yet to accept my offer.

ADOPTION: UTAH AND PROVINCETOWN, 2003

Adoption emerges as Plan B once I locate the underground railroad of attorneys and social workers who help gay folks skirt Utah's anti-gay-adoption law. Some child does seem to be waiting for me, in some other woman's belly if not my own, because three babies cross my path even before my criminal background check is complete. Baby Number One arrives in the first few days of June, via a college pal, followed a couple of weeks later by Baby Number Two, ushered into my sightline by another friend. Other people quickly step in to parent those babies, but Baby Number Three comes close to being my destiny.

She arrives in my voicemail box in late June, delivered by yet another friend, who tells me about a pregnant lesbian in Utah looking for a gay couple to adopt her baby. That baby stays in play just long enough for me to have a long interview with the birth mom, which ends with her saying that she wants a couple, not a single lesbian. Hanging up the phone feels like the first step of giving in to the barriers separating me from motherhood.

OVERNITE MALE: FROM SEATTLE TO PROVINCETOWN, 2003

A year after Victor said he was "inclined to inseminate," I'm again in a Provincetown rental, while he's teaching summer school in Seattle. While I'm beginning to seriously entertain the possibility that our crazy plan will remain on the drawing board, Victor has been doing his homework. Over lunch with a friend, he finds out about one last option. A kit called OverNite Male sold by the University of Illinois Andrology Department allows Victor and me to inseminate with fresh sperm despite the three time zones separating us, courtesy of FedEx and a medium of sugars and proteins that keeps those little swimmers alive for twenty-four hours. "It worked for my friends," Victor enthuses, adding that it's just $25 plus FedEx charges.

Two weeks after an insemination all alone in the living room, using Victor's FedEx'd sperm, I take a drugstore pregnancy test, reminding myself that it's better to be pregnant with hope than with nothing. When the two long-awaited parallel purple lines emerge on the plastic stick, I want to cry out and hold it over my head like an Olympic athlete.

Instead, as if the stick were the baby, I gently carry it out to the living room and lay it on a clean paper towel so I can keep checking that it says what I think it says while I call Victor.

He doesn't pick up.

But I told him I was just about to take the test.

Maybe he missed it by one ring and will call right back.

Silence.

At 1:00 a.m. — 10:00 p.m. Seattle time — the phone wakes me from a sound sleep. When I exclaim that I'm pregnant, Victor screams with delight and says that this is the best news he's ever had in his whole life.

As he explains that he didn't get my earlier call because he left his phone at home by mistake, I roll my eyes but don't chide. An intuition, not fully articulate, holds my tongue: *Victor's your friend, not your partner.*

You're getting away with something by having a baby as a single person with a kind, reliable, talented man who will be a father but not boss you around. Don't push it.

Even then, I had a sense that that quick and quiet middle-of-the-night interaction with Victor clarified a key aspect of our deal. But only years of honoring the deal brought the knowledge that our deal works well because it honors two pleasures. The first is the mischievousness of friends on a grand adventure, a zing coloring just about every moment. The second, best described as "belonging," comes with feeling part of something bigger than myself. From the very first phone call, my deal with Victor has been shaped by these twin pleasures, which muzzle any impulse to nag.

But Victor was and remains his own person, with his own view of our deal, as I discover a month into my pregnancy. Our parenthood negotiations included plans to buy a three-family house in Provincetown and spend the summers together. We'd each have an apartment: Baby and me in one, Victor in another, and a tenant up top. Yet one August afternoon, I get a voicemail from Victor gleefully reporting that he's bought a one-bedroom apartment in Seattle with a loft for Baby and me and already has a German photographer to rent it during the winter months. What is he thinking? He's supposed to spend summers with Baby and me, in P'town. He says that there's plenty of room and explains that we could go back and forth between Provincetown and Seattle, so he can teach summer school. Either he's unilaterally changing our deal, or I misunderstood it.

"Victor, a baby can't sleep in a loft," I laugh, shooting for light instead of bitter. Will this be our first fight? With my ex, I would have veered right down Acrimony Ave. But friendship—even a coparenting friendship—calls forth more gratitude than entitlement, as if not getting into your friend's body disciplines you against getting under his skin. Plus, I want to love better the next time, with less whining and more laughter. If I get a next time.

Finally, Victor seems to get it. But instead of engaging the question directly, he says that he has to go out and will call back later. When we finally do talk, I've let off steam debriefing with friends who assure me that I'm not crazy.

A space—comfortable, not cold—lies between Victor and me as we talk it through. Unwilling and unable to pinch one another as lovers do, we find a mid-ground in short order. We'll mostly spend summers in Provincetown to-gether, but make sure there's time for him to teach for a few weeks in Seattle.

A year later, Victor will sell that apartment. His Seattle friends, I'll learn, relish saying that they really knew Victor was whipped when he sold it. I listen carefully to Victor's laugh at the joke, relieved to hear in its verve and volume the message that he must still feel he got a good deal. But only living under that deal and others will fully refine his role as Dad instead of donor, and therefore the contours of my sort-of-single motherhood.

Lest I end up totally isolated with a screaming baby, I spend the first month of pregnancy busily shoring up connections, the very opposite of Victor shielding his independence. Packing up the car for the drive back to Salt Lake City, cataloging possible pregnancy complications that could spell disaster, I take comfort in the many friends coming to Baby's and my aid. One helps me pack, another accompanies me on the 2,500-mile drive. But the picture in the photo album is of Victor and me on the weathered gray front porch in Provincetown. I'm on the right, coquettishly posed for the camera, and he's turned three-quarters toward me, almost like a beauty queen. His arms circle my lower back and belly and the folds of his sand-colored silk shirt flap a little in the breeze. We're both in shorts, laughing at the mischief of posing as a sort-of couple, yet also soothed by the luxury of belonging to this family-in-the-making.

When I left Denver two years earlier, I stepped off the tightrope of intense couple-ness, leaving a life defined by working, living, and playing with the woman who is now my ex. After a lonely, panicked, sickly year in free-fall, I landed with a job, house, and new friends in Utah, as well as a summer life in Provincetown. I bounced instead of crashing only because a net of love caught me. Not romantic love, but love arising out of neighborliness, friend-ship, family, and combinations thereof. All that love sustained me during a pregnancy marked by solitude, high blood pressure, and higher anxiety. But it really paid off after the baby was born.

COMING OUT: SALT LAKE CITY, 2004

In the early 1980s, when I came out, stepping out of common ways of lov-ing required me to redefine family, not least because my parents, despite being Unitarian, were hardly poster children for Parents and Friends of Lesbians and Gays. Years later, helped by history's embrace of gay people, they opened their hearts.

Still, a few months into my pregnancy I'm afraid to tell them that I'm having a baby with a gay friend. Can I bear it if my parents think it's as sad or strange as they found my college buzz-cut? Fortunately, my mother's response is, "What thrilling news! And surprising! We're very happy for you." Victor's parents are also game, though his mom needs an explanation of how you get pregnant with reproductive technologies. Even then, she keeps asking if we're going to get married.

Now that it's officially a go, Victor and I have to transform our talk about the terms of our contract to words on the page. Lawyers generally use templates rather than start from scratch, and I score one from a sociologist who studies Plan B families, who in turn got it from a lesbian and gay guy who had two kids together.

Truth be told, I want a mix of Plan A and Plan B. Victor's my friend, a lot like a brother. The contract I write reflects our hope that each of us will find sweethearts, as well as the plan for Victor to split big expenses like daycare and college, visit once a month during the school year, and spend summers with Baby and me in Provincetown. I also build in clauses for therapy if we don't get along and for mediation outside of court if we need help to act like decent human beings. We also promise to support each other's romantic relationships—a deal that a court could never enforce. The romance clause gets tested when I start dating an ER doctor during my eighth month of pregnancy, and Victor hooks up with a reproductive anesthesiologist in Houston. Fortunately, we like each other's doctors. The Houston anesthesiologist even sends me flowers with a note saying that "a good epidural can be a good friend."

On my due date Victor, another friend who's acting as a birth coach, and I all head to the hospital. As we're settling in, the ER doc I'm dating stops by, wearing a hot-pink Free Martha T-shirt—a picture of Martha Stewart behind bars. When two nurses come in, I introduce everyone and specify each person's role: my baby daddy; my date, the ER doc; my friend, the birth coach. One nurse sneers, "Whatever," but the other asks whether any of us live together, her friendly voice matching my playful lilt.

We don't, I confess. There's an awkward silence, during which I look around, noticing the gaps between us. Despite this army I've assembled, I'm still single, more or less. A saucy introduction revealed, instead of masked, the shifting—and perhaps shifty—family configuration that this baby's about to join.

Twenty-five hours later, I'm considerably less jaunty. Baby's head is too big, and by nightfall I'm slipping in and out of consciousness. The ob-gyn suggests I either nap for a few hours or have a C-section.

Suddenly, we're in the operating room. Someone's bent the one-coach-per-birth rule and both Victor and my friend come in, decked out in matching green scrubs. She stands at my head, rubbing my temples while Victor holds my hand. Down by my feet, my doctor's saying that it won't hurt but will feel like I'm being pulled up to the ceiling by my stomach. I drift in and out, not feeling a thing.

Then I hear the baby's first declaration, a quiet, wet eruption of breath. I manage, "That sounds like a duck," and Victor says, "No, a lamb," using the endearment he often bestows on close friends and lovers. Someone says that Victor should come meet the baby, but he doesn't drop my hand. He doesn't even get up. Instead, I hear him say, "Martha and I will meet the baby together."

Next thing I know he's carrying Baby Walter into the recovery room, careful but moving quickly to touch Baby's cheek to my skin as soon as possible, just like the baby books recommend. When Victor lays him on my chest, I finally see this boy of mine, noticing first the crown of black hair that makes him look like an eight-and-a-half pound monk and then his surprisingly clear blue eyes. Meeting the curl of his tiny fingers gripping my little finger—like a pinky promise—I bring his open mouth to me. Victor snaps a picture, capturing me looking like a farm animal, flushed, exposed in heart as well as body and surprised at the camera, or maybe the whole business.

Even drugged, I know to resist Victor's suggestion to use that pic on a baby announcement, so the photo we send shows Baby Walter all by himself, looking quizzically at the camera, bundled up in the standard-issue pink-and-blue hospital blanket.

RITUALS: PROVINCETOWN, 2004

Six months later, Victor and I are on the right side of figuring out how to dose Infants' Tylenol and divide up middle-of-the-night feedings. As if to show off these accomplishments in the place where Victor accepted my offer and I finally conceived, we're back in Provincetown, pushing a stroller en route to the naming ceremony at the other end of Commercial Street. Walter's a catalog baby, happily cooing and looking around, finally past the nonstop crying that dominated his first three weeks. It could be that the tricks we used finally worked, from jiggling him on my lap and making shooshing noises to mimic the soundtrack of the womb to watching Almodóvar movies *en famille.* But the story I like to tell is that he wailed in shock that he got us instead of the parents he expected when he put in for a Utah birth.

He's about to get inducted as a Unitarian, about as far as a baby can get from being Mormon. Unitarian child dedications bless and welcome kids into the church community, but don't cleanse them of original sin because Unitarians don't believe in it. Victor's people are Christian, and he sang in a Christian rock band in high school, so I'm surprised and a little disappointed that he doesn't want a christening. Half-seriously I ask whether we should, just in case there's a petty dictator ruling the universe, doling out eternal goodies only to those bestowed with magic words and a splash of water. He responds, "Whatever God is, God will protect him and love him."

Walter's also protected by a passel of family and friends who have schlepped from far and wide to confirm Walter's place among them. It's a trick, clarifying that Victor and I are an "us" without slipping into the ill-fitting fiction that we're a couple.

The naming ceremony's contract-like promises help tailor the terms of our deal. Where some religions are creedal—requiring belief in, say, the divinity of Christ—Unitarianism is covenantal—defined by promises to dwell together in peace, seek the truth in love, and help one another. Accordingly, the minister elicits a series of promises from godparents, grandparents, Victor and me, and finally our people in the pews, to formalize the us-ness of our arrangement within the larger us-ness of family and friends.

Deal #1: The Godparents

Walter is blessed, the minister says, by the care of his godparents' friendship. She also reminds those dear friends that they helped Victor and me become the people we are, as well as helping Walter go from an idea to reality. When asked to pledge their support for us and for Walter, they reply in a ragged chorus, "We do."

Deal #2: The Grandparents

I just about hold my breath when she turns to the grandparents, asking them to share their wisdom with Walter and to support both him and us, and wonder if all four of our parents will really embrace our weirdo family. But they stick to the script, answering, "We do," without hesitation.

Deal #3: The Parents

Then she turns to us, just as Walter departs from his script and begins to fuss as if sensing the attention of a hundred eyes. When my jiggling doesn't work, Victor takes him with a conspiratorial smile suggesting that he too feels that we're in a play. Like a narrator, the minister starts off by clarifying that we've never pledged ourselves to one another in love, yet here we stand ready to pledge to raise Walter together in the loyalty, admiration, and trust of friendship. When we get to our lines—"We will"—we're smiling as much at the tremendous fish squirming in Victor's arms as the odd parallel between this and a wedding vow.

Deal #4: The Congregation

Finally, the minister turns to the pews, asking everyone whether they too will strive to love and cherish Walter and us, in times of struggle as well as gladness. As scripted in the order of service, fifty voices promise that they will, also pledging to build a community in which Walter "will grow old surrounded by beauty, embraced by love, and cradled in the arms of peace."

STORYTELLING: PROVINCETOWN, 2006

Two years later, Victor, Walter, and I have called on just about all those promises, getting advice from bathing to teething to dating with a baby in tow. Walter's toddling by the time we're settling in for our third Provincetown summer à trois. Victor's got a new love interest, a tall Texan who visits for two weeks. The ER doc has cut me loose, explaining that while she loves Walter, our arrangement is just too out there. The rejection hits hard—will

I ever find romantic love?—but it does free me up to plot a move to DC, where I have two brothers and a shot at a job because there are about a thousand law schools nestled among the nation's lawmakers. I haven't landed a permanent gig, so in August I'll head down there for a one-year position.

That all feels very far in the future as Victor and I resume our summer routine. He comes down mornings with his coffee, and we chat and tag team to get Walter ready for daycare. As usual, deals lend structure. One of us does drop-off at daycare, and the other picks him up. At the end of days spent on legal research, we take turns making dinner, and clear houseguests with each other to avoid overcrowding. It's not a negotiated tit-for-tat, usually, but instead an easy back-and-forth.

One week, Victor does both drop-off and pick-up because I've made another contract, one that'll change everything. I pay $500 to take a memoir-writing class at the Fine Arts Work Center.

Midway through the class, I read a paragraph about taking pictures of Walter in our back yard, voice shaking from the exposure of sharing my intimate life with strangers. Reading the words, I imagine the teacher's feedback. Will he, a gay man, praise my ingenuity at having a baby with Victor, or my marvelous way with words? When I finish, he says that he's thinking of who he can set me up with in DC.

REGARDING KAREN: WASHINGTON, DC, 2006

"Why do you love these boxes so much?" I ask.

Karen and I are strolling through the Smithsonian's cavernous Joseph Cornell exhibit. Compelling as these eerie little shadow boxes are, it's Karen who catches my attention. Falling into step beside her, I stop when she stops, surreptitiously watching her lean in to examine first a box populated by a cockatoo and watch faces, then another with broken stemware. Before answering my question about what she loves about these boxes, she pauses a good thirty seconds, totally still other than the pupils of her eyes, which open like a camera's aperture. It's the first glimpse she's afforded me into her inner world, a welcome complement to the sharp outer shell of spiky salt-and-pepper hair topping pointy features. Finally, she says, "I don't have words to express the way I feel about these boxes of things that don't seem to go together."

I love that answer. My life is a box with things that don't seem to go together. Lesbian, gay man, baby. I've made a career of writing about love and contracts, two things that most people would say definitely don't go together. Plus, it's a relief to hear her express passion for something other than work.

Later, tapered fingers circling a margarita glass at a hip Mexican place across from the museum, she's back to work, getting my thoughts on a program that links law schools with lawyerly projects for the public good. One plan—working to make Mississippi the social justice state—makes me wonder how firmly she grasps reality. But instead of quibbling I tell her that law professors would jump at the chance to be part of something bigger than themselves.

She insists on picking up the check, upping the ante from our usual Dutch-treat format. Is she lifting a corner of the veil that's hung between us?

Until that afternoon, Karen's and my conversations largely steered clear of matters of the heart, though I did hear on our second non-date, tucked into the dark corner of a vodka bar she steered us to after a fund-raiser, about how she'd left Los Angeles in her early forties, leaving behind the safety of a long relationship, friends, and family. Determination marked every word as she described one Eastern European gig, then another, then receded as she told me how everything had changed when her mom got sick and passed away, leaving her stroke-victim dad on his own. Her chin tipped back up, voice clearer as she declared that she didn't give up on her new life, opting instead to go part-time at work so that she could spend a week in LA every month, helping her dad. Matching her midlife-crisis story with my own of leaving Denver to build a new life in Utah didn't land us in each other's arms, but may have laid the foundation for that exchange about Joseph Cornell, and the one over margaritas. In any case, something shifted.

A December Saturday not long after that museum date, Karen invites me to a dinner party at her little jewel box of a townhouse, where the fact that we're not dating doesn't keep us from slipping into the role of cohosts. I serve as sous chef, then help serve, clear, and fill wine glasses. Finally, I offer to stay and help with the dishes. She tells me that Thanksgiving was her mom's favorite holiday. They always hosted, and played the Dictionary game. Ertman dinners, I counter, aren't complete until someone's whipped out a reference book to find out Shakespeare's dates or whether Pluto is really a planet. All that talk of postprandial reference books cues up an imagined future of bookish family traditions with Karen. I think, *I want that for Walter*, and kiss her.

Suddenly there are no words, or even images, just surprise and pleasure at her returning my kiss. No wondering, even, what happens next, until we pull apart. I'm smiling but she looks serious, even sad. Trying to dispel the ghost of whatever is pulling her away from me, I joke that it's not a funeral. She agrees, kissing me again.

Karen kissing me back opened the door to other reciprocities.

First, an employment contract. Monday morning, the University of Maryland calls to ask if I'd like to apply for a job teaching law. As I'm being grilled by the university's hiring committee, I'm struck by how much this is like dating. As with Karen, I want them to imagine a life with me down the hall. It must have gone well, because they invite me back for a day-long interview. By interview day, Karen and I have been dating all of six weeks, but already she's in deep enough that she drops Walter off at daycare so I can leave early. Fifteen hours, half-a-dozen small meetings, and a job talk later, I stumble through the door and find her half-awake and waiting, as if we lived together.

Come March, the University of Maryland finally proposes, and I accept the job on the spot. While that contract undergirds my relationship with Karen every bit as much as her returning my kiss, four months into the game, Karen and I are still at the deal stage of romance. We work out an agreement to have dinner together—with Walter—two or three nights a week. Though I wish we were moving faster, more deals have to pile up before we make legally binding contracts for moving vans or joint credit cards.

By late spring, Karen's using the phrase "unfolding" when I ask where we're headed. I'd like something more certain, but "unfolding" is a big upgrade from her midwinter report that "no path was blocked." Part of that unfolding happens when she gets an award for twenty years of tirelessly protecting underdogs, giving a talk titled "Never Give In to Cynicism." We're so early in our dating trajectory that the talk's earnestness is just as surprising as the news of her desire to include us in her life, conveyed through the invitation for Walter and me to join her.

TRIAL RUN: PROVINCETOWN, 2007

Victor embraces Karen from the word go, and Walter also seems to give the thumbs-up for folding Karen in from the first time she comes over for dinner. That night, listening contentedly to her read *Curious George*, he rests his slipper-clad foot against her leg on the yellow loveseat as if it was a regular routine. Three or four months into our dating, just shy of his third birthday, he even gives her a special name, "Gaty," the only name he's ever bestowed on any of the many friends and family who cycle in and out of our house. We can only guess how to spell it, but that only matters if Karen sticks around until he learns to write.

Provincetown provides a place to make that call, just as it did in 2002 when Victor and I decided to inseminate. We four spend July in the house Victor and I bought: Karen, Walter, and me in the first-floor apartment and Victor upstairs. Over dinner, she, Victor, and I speculate about directions that Victor's relationship with his boyfriend could take and place a moratorium on toilet training talk at meals, taking turns policing infractions.

After a week or two, Victor starts shooing Karen and me out the door after dinner, saying he'll put Walter to bed so we can stroll up and down Commercial Street. One evening, Karen suggests we get "training rings." We poke our heads into every jewelry shop the entire three miles of Commercial Street, but I don't know what we're looking for. Playful Lucite? Serious gold? Expensive jewels? I don't know whether she's suggested engagement or a more informal arrangement. Were we making a business deal instead of a love match, those training rings would be like an "agreement to agree." The ones we pick also nod to hard-won wisdom gleaned from the ghosts of relationships past. For me, the urge to merge into a respectable (read Plan A) family model led to a life in Denver that all but foreclosed having a life of my own, just as Karen's long-delayed departure from LA left her with persistent wanderlust. The handmade silver rings that adorn our middle fingers have little holes punched here and there, which I hope will let in air and remind us to allow our connection take the shape that fits each of us.

The fact that our deal isn't legally binding doesn't reduce it to fluff. Having both come out in the 1980s, neither Karen nor I came of age expecting law to honor our loves. Like most same-sex couples exchanging rings that summer of 2007, we expect that the law will come into our intimate lives in the form of contracts: designating one another as beneficiaries on a retire-ment account, say, or signing powers of attorney to make financial or medi-cal decisions for each other. While it'll be a pain to cobble together our own version of legal rights and obligations, the upside of this necessary invention is the freedom to think and talk through what legal bells and whistles match the emotional state of our union.

By Thanksgiving, we're negotiating what to look for in a house.

All those deals lead to lots of contracts: a mortgage, a joint credit card, joint AAA and sports club memberships, and paying a contractor to add a full bath and kitchenette to the basement so that Victor has a room of his own on his frequent visits. Those first months after moving in together, Karen is still calculating what she's lost—the freedom to travel, more than anything else—and won't know all that she's gained until months of meals, cleanups, baths, and decisions about Walter's health, education, and man-ners have piled on one another to make us a family.

A bunch of little deals help us get there. I unpack the kitchen because I'm the one who cooks more, while she unpacks the living room because she cares more about how everything looks. Once we're ready to tackle the garden, and have set up joint finances through a common bank account, we tacitly agree that I'll tend garden while she makes sure we pay our bills on time.

Other agreements balance Jewish and Protestant rituals. Karen doesn't come to church with Walter and me, but she always asks over lunch how it was. One Sunday, I tell her that the sermon extolling the benefits of honoring the Sabbath made me wonder about lighting her grandmother's Shabbat can-dles on Friday nights. Those candlesticks in our dining room, I learn, graced the sideboard all of Karen's childhood without ever getting lit over challah at a Shabbat dinner. "If Walter's going to be bar mitzvahed, he should know these prayers," I say.

Somewhere along the line, I realize that family happens incrementally. Spiri-tual people talk about faith as a practice, and see praying the rosary, meditat-ing, or attending services as gestures toward salvation, enlightenment, or just living fully, loving well, and letting go. Similarly, Walter's birth made me a biologi-cal mother, but only changing, feeding, loving, and worrying about him made me a mom. And Victor became a dad instead of a donor through kitchen-sink baths and middle-of-the night feedings and then later via early-evening phone calls on those many nights when he wasn't with us. Karen, likewise, negotiated her spot in our family constellation over time, as I did in hers.

But that realization itself took time. Indeed, during our year of dating, then the first of living together, Karen's grief over the loss of her parents was strong enough to make me question whether she had it in her to embrace a new family. Once she said that the world went from color to black and white when they died. Another time, my complimenting her crooked smile made her face crumple, a response I decoded only later as flowing from her inheriting that smile from her mom and the compliment coming on her mom's birthday. Nevertheless, inspired by her injunction not to give in to cynicism, I decide to give it a shot.

PROPOSAL: WASHINGTON, DC, 2008

The plan—not shared even with Victor—is to pop the question on a night away from home, an in-town vacation made possible by Victor's offer to come for a weekend to hang out with Walter. On Karen's work trip to Ukraine last spring, a jaunt I could join only because Victor offered to "batch it," as he likes to say, with Walter for five days, I'd snagged a small silver ring, inscribed "keepsake" in Cyrillic. Hammer in hand down in the basement, I craft a wordless proposal, in honor of her opening up a world beyond words to me, starting that afternoon in the Cornell exhibit.

The little house I build combines odds and ends from our house, our parents' houses, and our history. The wood's left over from the drawers that we had made to provide more storage space under our bed, and the walls are papered with a map of DC. It's furnished with unmatched sherry glasses— one from each of our parents' houses—and peopled by plastic parrots to reference both the cockatoo in the Cornell box and the birds' habit of mating for life. After gluing on colored glass windows and shellacking it when Karen's out of the house, I hide it in the garage. If she notices that my hammered fingernail turns blue, she doesn't say so. By the big day, the box is wrapped up in a wooden tangerine crate and tucked into the trunk of the car.

As she unwraps it in the hotel room, I lose my nerve. Instead of baldly proposing, I tell her it's a riddle. After closely inspecting my amateur attempt at a Cornell box, she slips the silver ring from a plastic parrot's throat, looks up, eyes as open as they were at the museum, and asks, "Marry me?"

MAKING IT LEGAL: WASHINGTON, DC, 2009

Once we establish the wedding's basic infrastructure—when, where, the guest list—we turn to the marital infrastructure.

As lawyers, Karen, Victor, and I realize that off-the-rack legal rules treat Karen as a stranger to Walter. But we can alter that through a contract in which Victor and I agree to share parental rights and duties with her. We also appreciate the limits of that contracting, since a judge could refuse to enforce any agreement that seems contrary to Walter's best interests. Finally, like many midlife fiancées, we know that the best intentions don't guarantee happy endings. So the addendum I write up to Victor's and my parenting agreement folds Karen in as a third parent but also spells out what happens if she and I part ways.

The lawyer's little conference room, plastic blinds drawn against the summer heat, suddenly feels like sacred space as Karen and I sign with blue pens, having dutifully proven that we are who we say we are by showing the notary our licenses. These contracts make us an "us" in many ways: silencing any butthead arguments Victor or I might make that Karen's not a parent and clarifying that if something happens to me, Walter should be spared other changes. We're also patching over gaps in the law created by the rapidly changing marriage equality map. On the night I ask Karen to marry me, DC, where we live, doesn't extend marriage equality to gay couples. But by the time we sign all these documents it has recognized same-sex marriages performed in other states, and by the end of the year it will recognize in-District marriages. By the time we celebrate our fourth wedding anniversary, the feds will also recognize us as married.

EMPTY SEATS: WASHINGTON, DC, 2009

The ghost of Karen's parents hovers over every wedding issue, big and small. We sift through possibilities for marking their absence: mentioning it; an empty chair. One way to include her mom, at least, is the invitation.

Sitting in front of Karen's computer, trying on and rejecting options, I notice a calligraphed teal and green message from her mom that hangs over her desk. "Love" appears at its center, interlocking the Beatles' line "all you need is love" with the Emily Dickinson couplet that inspired it: "That Love is all there is, / Is all we know of Love." Unearthing it from a box of her mom's artwork while she packed up her townhouse had brought forth a torrent of tears, resurrecting the still-fresh grief.

"Why don't we use that?" I ask and get a nod and tears in reply, assent in the language of that world without words that I'm coming to understand.

CHOOSING OUR RELIGION: BOSTON, 2009

Whether and how to include religion in the wedding requires more deals. Karen's Judaism is largely cultural, expressed through Passover Seders—using a pacifist, feminist Haggadah—that focus on the release of all people from all kinds of slavery. As a Unitarian who's just barely become a person of faith, I'd like to have a minister officiate. So our patched-together ceremony is officiated by both a Unitarian minister and a cantor. The Unitarian elements are pretty standard, like guests pledging to support this marriage by answering very loudly "We do!" as they did at Walter's naming ceremony, but the Jewish elements require some tweaking.

First, the *ketubah*, or Jewish wedding contract. We check the egalitarian, interfaith boxes when we order it from a Judaica store. Otherwise, the text seems pretty standard, promising love and respect. Framed by a bright design of simple images like grapes and the occasional Star of David, it calls to mind home and hospitality as much as Judaism. Plus the design leaves room for extra signature lines enabling the cantor, my sister, my college friend, Karen's brother and cousin, and, of course, Victor, Karen, and me all to sign off on our marriage.

The other two traditions are less obviously contractual but also signal consent. While a Jewish bride traditionally circles the groom seven times to indicate his centrality in her world, we two brides instead circle Walter. As the minister calls him up from his seat alongside the tall Texan and Victor, I'm struck by how handsome father and son look in the matching seersucker suits that Victor picked out, accented with red and purple checkered

Vans. Shy at first, Walter works his way toward us, beaming below his sandy bangs. Before we circle him ring-around-the-rosy style, Karen gives him a little ring, and the minister says a few words about how Walter's getting even more love as Karen joins our family.

But I don't cry until we get to the Seven Blessings that form part of Jewish weddings. We've hollowed out that tradition, too, substituting new content by inviting seven people to speak whatever blessing they like. My parents' approval, which I could hardly have imagined during my stormy coming-out years, comes in the form of the same Shakespearean sonnet that they read at my brothers' and sisters' weddings, the one that starts "Let me not to the marriage of true minds / Admit impediments. Love is not love / Which alters when it alteration finds." The last line brings a fresh wash of tears in response to their embrace of my Plan B family by changing a word—a crime in my family, since we worship reference books. Instead of saying, "If this be error, and upon me proved / I never writ, nor no *man* ever loved," my dad's quavering voice, emphasizing the change to "no *one* ever loved," wholeheartedly consents to our marriage.

On Karen's side, an uncle speaks, accompanied by his partner of thirty-five years, followed by an octogenarian cousin who quotes Harriet Tubman to invoke the spirit of social justice that shaped Karen's childhood. Victor alone uses the traditional language of the Seventh Blessing, but adjusting the text to address "bride and bride," before he passes on his own wish for us, "that you may know greater and stronger love, compassion, joy and connection to all, including all who have preceded you and passed on, and all who are here."

POSTSCRIPT: WASHINGTON, DC, 2009

Thanks to newspaper wedding announcements, Walter starts kindergarten famous, and Karen and I don't have to explain on the playground that we're spouses, not sisters. But within a few weeks, that easy comfort gets tested at the park.

As usual, Walter's tearing around with other kids. This time they're being led in a fierce game of tag by a wiry girl whom I've just learned has two dads. When I get a chance, I lean in to tell Walter this news, which he brushes off.

But the sturdy blond boy behind him is nonplussed. He snaps his hand at Walter's arm, exclaiming, "Two dads?!" clearly expecting a response.

Walter doesn't respond, just keeps on running.

As soon as the blond boy catches up with Walter, he whaps him again on the arm, crying out more loudly this time, "TWO DADS??!!"

Again Walter blows him off and keeps running.

Finally, the blond boy grabs Walter's sleeve, forcing him to stop and answer the urgent query, put yet again. Hovering at the sidelines, I'm wondering whether I should jump in, explain that love comes in different packages and give a few examples of Plan B families, when Walter finally responds. Apparently, he's picked up a generous habit that Karen and Victor share, finding one sliver of a statement to agree with and pretending that it's all that's been said.

"You're right, it is unusual. Usually, it's two moms," Walter says easily, looking directly at his interrogator, barely waiting for the blond boy to take in his answer before sprinting away. The boy looks a little stunned, then grunts, either conceding the point or just giving up as he takes off after Walter.

Walter, it seems, can convey an idea much more succinctly than his mother. Though I wrote this book in part to protect him by nudging the world just a little toward embracing Plan B families, he's doing fine on his own.

PART I

Plan B Parenthood

Family relationships can be either vertical—meaning between adults and kids—or horizontal relationships between adults. Since the rights and duties of parenthood differ markedly from those that come with partnership, half of the legal chapters in this book address parenthood and the other half explore partnership.

I start with children for two reasons. First, parenthood before partnership upends smug certainties that there's only one way to form a family, a truth evidenced by the many people—myself included—who become parents before establishing life partnerships. Second, tackling Plan B parenthood at the outset faces head-on the concerns about baby-selling that permeate any discussion of how far the language and norms of exchange reach into families. Highlighting the family-friendly exchanges built into reproductive technology and adoption demonstrates that these agreements help form and define thousands of new family relationships across the United States every year and also that family law is increasingly waking up to this reality.

TWO

Basics of Reproductive Technology Agreements

IMMACULATE CONCEPTION

"If it won't kill the sperm, it probably won't kill you," Victor says.

We can't know that this insemination will be our last, because this time it'll take. All we know is that the odds are against us. The scientists who sell OverNite Male say it's "impossible" to get pregnant unless we centrifuge out the magic fluid that keeps sperm alive for twenty-four hours so it can shoot across the country from Seattle, where Victor's teaching, to Provincetown, where I'm hunkered down for the summer. They won't even tell us the medium's secret ingredients, but Mr. Majored-in-Chemistry figures it's probably just proteins and sugars, none of which should harm me. Getting a centrifuge on the Cape would mean getting a new doctor and doing new intake procedures—HIV tests, hormone tests—and I'd rather take my chances with the medium than lose the last month that I'm thirty-nine. So we take the double risk.

After playing his part in this drama one summer night, Victor calls to tell me everything went well. He added his sperm to the medium and screwed the top on super-tight, he says, before putting the container in the little styrofoam box and paying extra to get it to P'town by noon. He adds that I'll need scissors to cut off all the tape he's wrapped around it.

Later, lying in bed, I address my thank-yous far and wide: To Victor, for honoring my request to use extra caution—and tape—and for giving me the details, knowing crazy movies about leaky jars and sticky packages would play in my head; to him finding out about OverNite Male from his friends and researching it; to OverNite Male and the andrologists who figured out how to send fresh sperm so we could keep inseminating when Victor's three time zones away; and to FedEx, which makes possible this crazy collage of friends, family, and commerce. Finally, to love itself: friendship love, love of knowledge, and love of life.

When the FedEx truck pulls into my clamshell drive the next morning at eleven thirty, I bound across the lawn to greet the driver, probably looking like a golden retriever eager for a treat. I'm especially happy because this morning, a kit from the drugstore showed that I've ovulated for the first time in six months.

When I cut open the package with the scissors I've got at the ready, it's dry. So are the small plastic container and its gray foam bedding. The sperm left Victor's body in Seattle at around 4:30 p.m. to meet the 5:00 p.m. FedEx deadline, so with the time change, it's been eighteen hours. I lower the blinds and head for the couch, lying in the now-familiar position, heels propped high on the wall. Gingerly picking up the syringe I got at the drugstore, I pull out more than 5 ccs, guessing how much is the active ingredient that could jump-start a life.

———

SIX STORIES OF PLAN B BABY-MAKING

While OverNite Male is among the more obscure ways to conceive a child, all kinds of men and women contract around limits imposed by luck or biology when Plan A—husband and wife making babies in the privacy of their bedroom—doesn't pan out. Plan B parenthood takes two main forms: reproductive technologies and adoption. I'll get to adoption in chapters 4 and 5. In these two chapters, the focus is on alternative insemination (AI), with a brief mention of surrogacy and in vitro fertilization (IVF)—stops for many people on the road to adoption. The six stories here show the long history of reproductive technologies, the thousands of people who take this Plan B route to parenthood every year, family law's use of contracts to define the uncommon families that it recognizes, and ultimately the benefits of letting people decide for themselves when, whether, how, and with whom to have children.

Reproductive Technology in the Biblical Sense

Sarah, who was infertile, told her husband of many years, Abraham, to "go in unto" her maid, Hagar. The child born of Abraham and Hagar's union, Ishmael, grew up to become an Islamic patriarch. Another biblical couple, Jacob and Rachel, similarly "employed" their maid Bilhah to carry a child sired by Jacob.

But not every wife can happily send her husband to sleep with another woman. Moreover, it is a crime today to force your maid to sleep with the man of the house, though some maids cut their own deal with the boss. Mildred Baena, who kept house for California governor Arnold Schwarzenegger's family, got him to put $65,000 toward a house for her and their love child.[1]

Modern Surrogacy

If these biblical couples had lived in the 1980s, they might have sought out Noel Keane, the attorney who matched surrogates with infertile couples. Doctors Bill and Betsy Stern took that route in 1985. Keane brokered their surrogacy contract with Mary Beth Whitehead, a married mother herself, to conceive and bear a child. Most surrogacies happen privately, like Plan A baby-making, but courts got involved when Mary Beth refused to give up the baby. Newspapers around the globe followed the case, publicizing the new reproductive technologies. Ultimately, the New Jersey Supreme Court refused to enforce the surrogacy contract, declaring that "there are, in a civilized society, some things that money can't buy."[2] Nevertheless, the court awarded custody to the Sterns and allowed Mary Beth occasional visits with her child over the years.[3] To this day, newspapers note the case's anniversary. In 2007, when Baby M turned twenty-one, she happened to be an undergraduate at the same university where I was teaching. A few of my Contracts students, taken with our class discussions of *In re Baby M*, friended her on Facebook. She and her friends met up with my students at a local watering hole, where they all toasted her birthday.

Baby M was also the child of Noel Keane's imagination. In the 1970s he founded Infertility Centers in New York, California, and other states to broker surrogacy agreements, earning him the nickname "father of American surrogacy."[4] You could say that surrogacy's other parent was the convergence of legal, technological, and social innovations that made having kids more of a choice than it was in the 1960s and '70s. Noted constitutional law cases like *Griswold v. Connecticut* and *Roe v. Wade* let people decide for themselves when and how to create a family by decriminalizing birth control and abortion, and other cases struck down rules that punished pregnancy outside of marriage.[5] The Pill made birth control simple, clean, and reliable. The women's movement made social and economic space for women in higher education and the workforce, and the zero-population growth movement urged everyone to have fewer children. As parenthood became more of a choice than a mandate, many women exercised that choice. Putting off having children until they established careers, many found that their eggs' expiration date had come and gone.[6]

Keane, an observant Catholic who described his groundbreaking surrogacy business as "making my stand on the side of people who want to create life,"[7] may not have supported the rights to birth control and abortion that paved the way for surrogacy. But surrogacy was just as controversial. At first, mainstream newspapers like the *Detroit Free Press* rejected Keane's classified ads looking for surrogates, so he turned to less discriminating college newspapers like the *Michigan Daily*, which printed his ad: "Childless husband with infertile wife wants female donor for test-tube baby." The ad generated national newspaper coverage, free publicity that Keane took full advantage of in numerous media interviews (including the first of five appearances on the hugely popular *Phil Donahue Show*).[8] Those TV shows trumpeting surrogacy as a method of Plan B baby-making got Bill Stern's attention and led him to hire Keane to broker the surrogacy agreement that brought Baby M into the world, the courts, and breakfast-table conversations.

Yet Baby M was no test-tube baby. The first test-tube baby, Louise Brown, was born in 1978, the product of doctors fertilizing her mother's egg with her father's sperm in the lab, then implanting it back in her mother's womb. The process remained highly experimental well into the 1980s. Harvard law professor Elizabeth Bartholet weathered invasive and expensive infertility treatments for the better part of a decade, culminating in three IVF cycles, only to finally realize that in those early years "the chance of an IVF patient over forty getting pregnant and keeping the pregnancy [was] near zero."[9] Even with today's improved IVF techniques, only 1 percent of forty-five-year-old women can have a baby conceived with their own eggs and only 5 percent of forty-three- or forty-four-year-old women can.[10] Dr. Betsy Stern was forty-one when she and Bill decided to start a family, making it unlikely that her eggs could support a pregnancy. Instead, Baby M was conceived by a doctor inseminating twenty-six-year-old Mary Beth Whitehead with Bill Stern's sperm, per agreements signed by the Sterns and the Whiteheads.[11]

The legal nightmare created by *Baby M* and technological advances in in vitro fertilization rendered "traditional" surrogacy nearly obsolete, the dinosaur of reproductive technology agreements. Today, fully 95 percent of surrogacies are gestational, meaning that a surrogate carries a child to whom she has no genetic relationship because another woman has donated the egg.[12] Angela Bassett—famous, appropriately, for starring in *What's Love Got to Do with It?*—became a mother at forty-eight after she and her husband hired a surrogate who gave birth to twins. Likewise, at forty-four, Sarah Jessica Parker became a mother via surrogacy. A *Desperate Housewives* plotline in 2006 concerned a love triangle involving the characters Gaby and Carlos Solis and their surrogate, Xiao-Mei. Surrogacy was common enough that ABC News dubbed it a "Hollywood Surrogate Trend."[13]

The Price of Eggs

The popular press lionizes celebrity surrogacy and the few surrogacy cases that make it to court. But court cases are rare because people generally give and get what they expect and make sure that they're in a state like California that honors gestational surrogacy contracts. Occasionally, a couple commissions a traditional surrogacy or unwisely does it in a state like New Jersey that doesn't recognize even gestational surrogacy contracts.[14] Much more common is the situation of Susan, a twenty-four-year-old divorced mom who "donated" her eggs for $5,000 so that she could pay for both car insurance and Christmas presents for her three-year-old. While she came into the baby business for money, she came out enriched by the satisfaction of having helped a couple have a child. She explained the way that exchange—each getting and giving something—contributed to making it an essentially positive experience:

> The thing that just melted me and still does to this day—I don't know who these people were; they don't know who I am—when I went in for the [egg retrieval], the office staff was great, and my recipients had dropped off a gift. It was a children's book. In it, she wrote a note: "You have no idea what you've done for us." At that moment, it became everything about this couple that is just so desperate to have a child that they'll do this.

Yet Susan's emotional involvement did not splash over into a thwarted desire to be part of their family or friends. She did not even want to know whether the couple had a boy or a girl with her egg. But Susan did want to know "that they did receive a gift from this, that they didn't just give and give and not get anything back."[15]

The recipient couple in another egg "donation" also saw exchange as a way to honor the emotional significance of helping someone create a family. Melanie Thernstrom wanted to be sure that the woman she called her "fairy god-donor" got something in exchange for giving Melanie and her husband, Michael, the chance to be parents. Rather than resisting or regretting having to pay one woman for eggs and two others to gestate their children, Melanie and Michael welcomed the chance to make "the relationship feel more reciprocal" through these payments. They knew the value of what the women were doing, having weathered six rounds of failed IVF and Melanie's medical condition that endangered a fetus's health. In a way, that payment brought the surrogates into Melanie's extended family, so it made sense to have them attend the kids' first birthday party. Exchange is built into all close relationships, in Melanie's view: "That's what friends and family are for . . . an obligation for mutual assistance is part of the nature of the relationship." [16]

Melanie, like many women, would have preferred Plan A babymaking with, as she put it, "the fun, free tools," and Susan probably would prefer to have enough money to support herself and her son without selling eggs.[17] When reality—in the form of biology for one and finances for the other—blocked Plan A, contracts provided an alternative. Rather than pine away for their first choice, both women embraced Plan B.

Plan B takes many forms. IVF brings the most babies into American families each year but rarely raises problems for family law because the egg and sperm usually come from the married couple who raise the child. Alternative insemination, the next most common way to create a Plan B baby, in contrast, has required family law to determine who the legal parent is. (Like some other family researchers, I call it "alternative" insemination instead of "artificial" because "alternative" better conveys the message that coital reproduction is not the only natural method of becoming a parent.)[18] Because AI affects thousands more families than egg donation or surrogacy, it will be my focus, with occasional sidebars on other kinds of reproductive technology agreements.

Early American Alternative Insemination

Alternative insemination is nearly as old as America. In 1785, Dr. John Hunter performed the first documented AI to impregnate the wife of a London linen merchant with her husband's sperm. A century later, in 1884, Dr. William Pancoast performed the first documented insemination using donor sperm. The woman thought it was her husband's sperm, which is just as well, since some legal commentators of the day saw donor insemination as adultery. Before long, it was not unusual to remedy a man's infertility—due to a low sperm count or slow swimmers—by inseminating his wife with sperm from an anonymous donor. By the 1940s US doctors routinely, if quietly, inseminated the wives of infertile men with samples collected from medical students. When those babies were born, no one knew that they were conceived with assistance unless the parents chose to disclose it. Most kept it a secret, largely for social reasons, but also, perhaps, because up until the 1950s some courts still treated those children as illegitimate products of adultery.[19]

Alternative Insemination Today

Family law has since clarified that those kids are legitimate by allowing a donor to contract out of legal fatherhood and another man to contract into being a dad by consenting to donor insemination.

Legality has allowed assisted reproduction to become a $3 billion-a-year business that brings over 100,000 babies into American families every year. Many of these babies are conceived via AI, because it is much simpler and cheaper than IVF or surrogacy, making it an option for most middle-class people.[20] Thousands of lesbian couples have used AI to have kids. Not being able to combine their genes, they pick the donor from a cryobank catalog, often one with qualities that mirror the nonbiological mother's. They can even inseminate at home, thawing out the sperm that arrives via FedEx, stored in liquid nitrogen. If that doesn't work, they can have doctors do the insemination. After one child is born, a couple often conceives a second with sperm from the same donor.

Single straight women also appear on sperm bank customer lists. Like many women in their thirties who want children but haven't found Mr. Right, a woman named Abby got profiles from a sperm bank. She sat down with a close friend and a glass of wine to evaluate their education, height, weight, and health histories. There was no partner to match, so they could pick anyone, and joked about one donor's narcissism in designating the donation of his Ivy League sperm as "the greatest act of charity."[21] A single straight friend of mine whose boyfriend could not commit to parenthood enlisted her sister to review donor profiles. Both scientists, they looked for what they dubbed "hybrid vigor" by balancing their French ancestry with a donor from the other side of the world. Both Abby and my friend bought donor sperm, contracts made possible by the donors' agreement with the banks years before to sell their sperm for around $50 a sample, which they probably used to cover tuition and living expenses.[22]

Reproductive Contracts at the Fringes

Some people, as an alcoholic friend puts it, have "portion problems," a tendency to go overboard. The son of Republican presidential candidate Mitt Romney hired surrogates to become the father of six.[23] IVF increases the likelihood of twins, triplets, and higher levels of multitude; those crowded conditions in turn increase the chance of a child suffering from health challenges.[24] Nadya Suleman, already a thirty-something single mother with six children, bore octuplets in 2009, conceived through IVF. That earned her tabloid fame, a reality TV show, and the nickname "Octomom." But the news that she now had fourteen children and was single and on public assistance generated a public outcry. The California Medical Board revoked the medical license of her doctor, Dr. Michael Kamrava, for his extreme departures from usual practices, like implanting up to twelve embryos in women undergoing IVF, three or four times the usual number.[25] That censure shows the atypicality of Suleman's situation and also the medical community's willingness to police doctors and patients who do not know when to stop.

Recognizing these extreme stories as outliers helps us see that as a general matter, reproduction agreements seem to do more good than harm. Consider a story about selling breast milk, a side-product of reproduction. Two months after nineteen-year-old college student Desiree Espinoza gave birth to a baby girl, she found that her body produced enough milk for triplets but her bank account was nearly empty. Through a website called Only the Breast, she found other new mothers near her Phoenix home who were willing to buy enough of Desiree's milk at $2 an ounce that she could buy the dress in which she married her twenty-two-year-old baby daddy, baby clothes, medicine, and a new computer for classwork. Enough people want to buy and sell breast milk that the literal mom-and-pop founders of Only the Breast have established sister sites in the United Kingdom and European Union.[26]

Like other Plan B arrangements, breast-milk contracts and deals are nothing new. Ancient Roman legal records even report a wet nurse suing to be paid for her services.[27] In short, there's nothing especially novel, or even unnatural, about contracting for reproductive goods and services. While problems arise, as they do in common modes of reproduction, existing legal and medical systems manage to address them.

REPRO TECH 101

Assisted reproduction exchanges are Exhibit A in this book's case for links between love and contracts. They created more than a million American families in the past half-century alone.[28] That number has led family law to carve out an exception to the general rule of parentage to allow people in most states to contract out of legal parenthood by selling their gametes, and the buyers of the eggs or sperm to contract into the rights and duties of parenthood. Contract, in short, operates as a line dividing the relationships that the law designates as "family" from the biological ties between legal strangers.

To fully appreciate these agreements, it helps to have an overview of the immense and complex baby-making business.

Vital Statistics

Between 10 and 15 percent of the adult population experiences infertility.[29] It may be biological, like a man's low sperm count, a woman's blocked fallopian tubes, or anyone's genes for a debilitating kidney disease that you would not wish on your worst enemy, let alone your own children. Social factors, like being single or gay, can also get in the way of common methods of conception. Consequently lots of people, for lots of reasons, use reproductive technologies, and the numbers are increasing.[30]

While precise numbers are hard to come by, alternative insemination with sperm from either anonymous or known donors brings around 30,000–40,000 babies to American families annually. Egg sales and gestational surrogacy bring forth many fewer babies (around 9,000 from egg donation each year, and 1,600 from surrogacy). IVF, in contrast, brings over 62,000 American babies into the world each year, but, as I've said, it creates few legal questions because generally people use their own gametes to conceive.[31]

Back in the 1980s, when I was in college, things were different. We joked about turkey-baster babies and repeated funny, ribald stories of gay men helping lesbians have kids by masturbating into baby-food jars, putting the jars into potholders to keep warm, and dashing over to the friends' home, where the mothers-to-be waited, turkey baster in hand.[32] (Becoming one of those wannabe mamas myself years later, I would learn that turkey basters are way too imprecise for insemination because they quickly spill the tablespoon or so of liquid containing those millions of sperm. Instead, a syringe from the drug store does the trick.)

Internet Sperm Sales

The 1980s also ushered in the age of AIDS. Before then, most sperm-donation programs were small, offering fresh donations from local medical students for infertile couples. A few commercial sperm banks offered frozen sperm, but this was far less desirable since the lower pregnancy rates, due to the damage done to all but the hardiest sperm by freezing and thawing, paled in comparison with the conception rates achieved with fresh samples. But once researchers realized that a man could test negative for HIV three months after his exposure to the virus, everyone had to start freezing samples in liquid nitrogen and storing them for six months so they could test the donor again before using his sperm for insemination. By the late 1980s commercial sperm banks could compete with medical school sperm banks by offering a much more varied "inventory" and providing much more information about donors' looks, education, personalities, and health histories.[33]

In the summer of 2002, as Victor and I were talking about whether to have a baby together, sociologist Rene Almeling was busy collecting data on the brisk business of reproductive technology. Her book *Sex Cells* documents exchanges of thousands of vials of sperm and hundreds of eggs that year, including the following:

- One major sperm bank had 125 donors and distributed around 2,500 vials of sperm each month, while a smaller one had just 30 donors and sent out around 400 vials each year.
- A major egg bank had 465 donors on its website and 100 active matches that summer, while a smaller one had 123 donors and 23 active matches.[34]

A quick visit to the sperm bank or egg agency website puts life into these dry numbers.

If you go to the site of Egg Donation, Inc., in Encino, California, and enter a search request looking for an egg donor like me—tallish, white, and college-educated—you might pull up the file of Brittany, aka Donor #45583, an open-faced blonde with a 3.45 college GPA, an IQ of 132, and no serious illnesses in her family (though she did have her appendix removed). She's twenty-three years old, 5' 10", 135 pounds, has blue eyes, a fair complexion, and is from Irish, German, and Italian stock. She works in human resources and plans to get her master's at the University of Michigan. She describes herself as "a very outgoing, independent, driven, goal-oriented woman. I know exactly what I want out of life. I live for a challenge. I don't want to wake up one day and wonder where my life went so therefore, I live it to the fullest." She wants to donate eggs, she explains, because "I myself do not want children but would love to help a couple acquire their dreams by becoming a parent [sic]." A mountain of small details creates a vivid picture: she doesn't sleep with stuffed animals or believe in life on other planets, but she does believe in fate, miracles, and an afterlife. She describes herself as "100% hopeless romantic," has gay friends, and her favorite character on *Sex and the City* is Samantha.

Replicating Victor

One day that summer, I took a break from drafting a law review article called "What's Wrong with a Parenthood Market?"[35] to see if I could find someone like Victor by visiting the California Cryobank website. Punching in a search with his characteristics brought up a healthy, white sperm donor who's good at math and music. No serious illness, and other women had gotten pregnant using his "sample." Average height—5' 9"—and thin at 135 pounds, he had English, French, Irish, and Polish ancestry. While there was no picture, he described himself as fair-skinned but not freckled, with a "Roman nose" and "large, wide-set eyes." He was sharp—a 3.96 GPA in college and 4.15 in graduate school for chemistry—and musical, shown by his guitar playing. He sounded like someone I'd like: a vegetarian who went for spicy foods, an active mountaineer who also meditated and engaged in environmental activism. He had enough of a sense of humor to list his favorite animals as cats, marmots, and ostriches and was sufficiently self-aware to describe his personality as "calm, relaxed and easy-going, but quite focused. . . . Intelligent and sharp-tongued with a good sense of humor. Adventurous. Unsentimental." He wanted to donate sperm, he said, because "I feel that I have been lucky enough to come into the world with a good set of genetic material; and, as a result, I should offer my help to people who want to have children." His message to the families receiving his sperm was "Everything that is born must die. Make the most of your time here on Earth." The California Cryobank staff described him as "witty, interesting, outgoing . . . always looks a little mischievous; alert and observant."[36] For a small fee, I could have ordered a more extensive donor profile, a facial features report, and even an audiotape of his voice.

No wonder lots of single straight women reviewing sperm-donor profiles fall for their donors, even carrying around the donor's baby picture as if they actually were family.[37] However, that relationship is usually entirely one-sided, because the two people never meet. Melanie Thernstrom, the infertile woman we encountered at the beginning of the chapter, departed from this general rule by flying to California with her husband, Michael, to take their would-be egg donor out to brunch. Where many a straight woman buying sperm fantasizes about *being with* the donor, as if he were the boyfriend who stayed around just long enough to get her pregnant then evaporated into thin air, Melanie focused on how she would like, in a parallel universe, to *be* this donor. In the *New York Times Magazine*, she described how the woman she would come to call her "fairy goddonor" immediately felt like "the one":

> She grew up in Los Angeles, where I had lived as a child. . . . She was literary, but she worked in an area of science, which overlapped with an interest I had recently developed. . . . She was the same height and weight as I and also had long straight hair. . . . She was athletic and played tennis and surfed, as I imagined I would have done, and would still do if only I didn't suffer from the chronic pain condition that I wouldn't have if I were her—and wouldn't then pass on to my children.[38]

The fantasy was that the egg donor was just like Melanie, only better.

High Emotion but Low Litigation Rates

With emotions running so high, and strangers making babies after connecting on the Internet, you'd expect to see hundreds of cases about reproductive technologies clogging courthouse dockets. Amazingly, given that repro tech brings tens of thousands of babies into American families every year, a search for cases after 1990 pulls up just over a hundred cases. The most common seeks to list the intended parents on the birth certificate, a dispute with state administrators instead of a contest over parental rights or duties. A couple of dozen disputes do involve parenthood in sperm donation, and about the same number of cases involve embryo or gamete disputes during a divorce. The least common—about a dozen in each category—concern gestational surrogacy/egg donation, or disputes with fertility clinics.[39] The paucity of cases, I suspect, indicates that for the most part reproductive technology contracts and deals work out pretty well for the people involved. When law does get involved to resolve disputes, family law rules that are shaped by contractual thinking provide much of the legal doctrine. The remainder of the chapter describes the fairly limited legal rules that govern AI. Consistent with widely held beliefs in the sanctity of family decision making, family law often lets men and women contractually create families, meddling only when necessary to protect vulnerable parties.

Limits on Parenthood-by-Contract

Federal and state regulations aim to protect people's health and safety by requiring gamete banks to screen donors for diseases. Moreover, the medical profession has adopted ethical guidelines to protect donors, kids, and gamete recipients, and donor-conceived families have created online donor sibling registries that connect donors, legal parents, and the kids conceived through repro tech contracts. As a whole, these legal, medical, and social mechanisms protect reproductive technologies as a route to parenthood as well as people's health and welfare. Because lawmakers cannot prevent parents from teaching their kids a foreign language any more than they can outlaw birth control, it makes sense that they also, for the most part, keep their laws off of repro tech matters.[40]

Consumer Protection

Most of the federal and state law regulating reproductive technologies focuses on safety and other aspects of consumer protection. Clinics must keep records and screen donors for diseases like HIV and genetic anomalies.[41] The Centers for Disease Control require fertility doctors to report their IVF success rates and publish that data to provide infertile women with accurate information about their odds of becoming moms that way.[42] Finally, fifteen states protect equal access to reproductive technologies by requiring insurance companies to cover some aspects of infertility treatment.[43]

The Ban on Baby-Selling

The second major legal rule explains why so many people mistakenly think that family law does not allow parenthood-by-contract. Law forbids outright baby-selling. At first glance, this ban, imposed by virtually all states, seems to outlaw the contracts for eggs and sperm I have been talking about, since gametes, combined, become zygotes that in turn can become babies.

But eggs and sperm are not babies, any more than an acorn is an oak tree. Baby-selling statutes generally apply only to adoption, situations like the arrest of impoverished twenty-three-year-old Nicole Uribe-Lopez for giving her five-month-old baby to Irene and Jose-Juan Lerma for $1,500.[44] The New Jersey anti-surrogacy opinion in *Baby M* speculated that the traditional surrogacy agreement between Mary Beth Whitehead and the Sterns might also be criminal, since it required Mary Beth to consent to Betsy Stern adopting Baby M. Following that case, some states did criminalize commercial surrogacy.[45] But most states do not see gestational surrogacy—the most common form of surrogacy by far—as baby-selling, and no state prohibits or even limits alternative insemination.

Judicial Denial of Parenthood-by-Contract

Family law sometimes decries the very idea of parenthood-by-contract. A Massachusetts court announced in 2004 that "parenthood is a status conferred by law and not one that can be conferred by private agreement."[46] In that case, the court refused to legally enforce a woman's oral promise to help raise her ex-partner's donor-conceived child. The case illustrates Justice Oliver Wendell Holmes's quip that hard cases make bad law. One woman in the couple (I'll call her Reluctant Girlfriend) was dead set against having a child in light of her abusive childhood and history of depression. The other was determined to become a mother. They disagreed vehemently. But one day Reluctant Girlfriend finally gave in and agreed—orally—to go along to get along. She even helped pick out a donor from a sperm bank. The couple had split up by the time the baby was born, and the mom wanted Reluctant Girlfriend to pay child support. The court held that she did not have to because, it said, "'parenthood by contract' is not the law of Massachusetts."[47]

That is not the whole truth. Massachusetts, like many states, does recognize parenthood-by-contract by allowing sperm donors to contract out of being dads, and the spouses of women who are insemi-nated to contract into it.[48] I think the court reached the right result—Reluctant Girlfriend is not a parent—but for the wrong reason. It could have said, as other states do, that Reluctant Girlfriend can only "contract" into legal parenthood by either signing a formal written promise or living with the child for a period—maybe six months or a year—acting as a mom through midnight feedings, baths, diaper changes, and daycare drop-off and pickup.[49] A known donor can also contract back into fatherhood in some states, as long as he signs a dad contract with the child's mother.[50]

Medical Ethics

The medical community, perhaps more than lawmakers, has taken the initiative to protect the interests of the men, women, and children involved in repro tech.

The American Society for Reproductive Medicine, or ASRM, has published ethical guidelines on a variety of topics like limiting the amount egg donors get paid, limiting the number of children sired by each sperm donor, disclosing medical errors, informing donor-conceived children of their situation, and providing infertility treat-ments to gay and single people.[51] It's hard to determine compliance with some of these rules, such as the guideline that each sperm do-nor sire no more than twenty-five children per population area of 850,000, because there's no central recording of babies born through donor insemination. While one study of clinic compliance with adver-tising guidelines reported significant gaps between the rule and actual practices, another study found that clinics complied with ASRM's guidelines capping egg prices at $5,000.[52] Fortunately, donor families themselves have filled some gaps left by medical and legal regulations.

Online Registries

The Donor Sibling Registry, AnonymousUs.org, and the *Confessions of a Cryokid* blog provide lots of information on donors and half-siblings.[53] This social universe is so big that law professor Naomi Cahn calls it the "donor world."[54] If the goal is to provide crucial medical information, sperm banks already give recipients twenty-page, three-generation health histories and screen donors pretty well for diseases. The fact that so few people have sued sperm banks provides strong evidence that this self-help information system works pretty well in conjunction with the consumer protection rules and ethical guidelines.[55]

The Kids Are Mostly All Right

In 2010, *The Kids Are All Right*, starring Annette Bening and Julianne Moore as a lesbian couple raising kids conceived with donor sperm, garnered four Oscar nominations and won two Golden Globe awards. The plot revolved around the women's teenage son wanting to meet his donor. The mothers initially embrace this handsome, earthy man (a literal embrace for Moore's character), but by the closing credits, the original Plan B family has been reestablished. The final scene looks like a Norman Rockwell family dinner: kitchen lit up in the darkened evening like a stage for us to see them in this typical family tableau. The donor sees it too, standing—literally—outside that family, gazing plaintively through their kitchen window. Viewers and commentators accepted the film's invitation to value this family for its ability to do what families do—connect and stay connected—through challenges from within and without. One reviewer noted, "It's like it could be any family."[56]

Of course, no family situation is perfect, and many donor-conceived kids would like to know more about their donors. A teenager named Colton Wooten eloquently described his longing to connect with his donor dad in a 2011 op-ed for the *New York Times* titled "A Father's Day Plea to Sperm Donors."[57] He knew what his mother remembered from reading the donor's profile, way back in 1992: a medical student, with brown hair and olive skin, the child of an Italian mother and an Irish father. Colton wrote this piece, I imagine, hoping that the article would finally lead him to his biological dad so he could find out more information such as what he looks like, whether there are any half-siblings, and any medical issues he should be aware of.

Stories like Colton's are nearly absent from case law, since most cases involve disputes between adults and institutions. That leaves the children, who are most vulnerable and the very reason there's a case at all, to express their views in the "donor world" of websites and pieces like Colton's essay. We must, therefore, keep their voices in mind as we explore the repro tech cases in the next chapter.

THREE

Legal Rules of Reproductive Technology Agreements

PARENTS BY CONTRACT

"Why would you put that stuff in front of a judge?" the lawyer asks me.

"To keep it away from a judge," I respond. The lawyer I hired to review the coparenting agreement I drafted for Victor and me looks at me blankly, eyes dropping briefly to my VW-sized belly under the short black dress that's gotten me through the whole pregnancy, then down to my cowboy boots, before she looks back up, as if wondering how all these disparate elements landed in her conference room at the same time. A year ago, she was coaching me on how gay folks manage to adopt in Utah, but now I'm the one instructing her on the benefits of including emotional terms in our coparenting agreement.

She's crossed out about half the document, first the preamble's recital of "the spirit of love, cooperation, and mutual respect that has developed over the course of our 15-year friendship" and then the clause in which we promise to support each other's romantic relationships. The one that bothers her most is a dispute resolution clause that acknowledges that Victor and I, as an "opposite-sex gay couple raising a child together," are likely to face "misunderstandings and difficulties along the way in what we trust and hope will be an otherwise rewarding and loving relationship."

I start by saying that the couple reference is a joke, meant to acknowledge the Plan A and Plan B hybrid we're cobbling together and remind us of the sound of our shared laughter, should we ever fall out. "We're talking to ourselves as much or more than to a judge," I explain, since we'd reread this document if we had a serious dispute and, as lawyers, we know more than most about the uncertainties and expense of litigation. Unconsciously brushing my hand across my huge belly, I tell her that if Victor and I manage to keep a sense of humor about ourselves and this whole business, it seems less likely that we'll all end up miserable, in court, harming the kid most of all.

Still quizzical, and suggesting I add in a provision for regular child support payments, the lawyer grudgingly concedes that "all that mushy stuff" probably won't hurt, but she isn't sold on it.

————

LAW AS IT IS RE ALTERNATIVE INSEMINATION AGREEMENTS

Contrary to what the expert said, putting emotional terms into our coparenting agreement has helped steer my family around conflicts, perhaps because we've kept our promises. Shortly after I send Victor a receipt for summer camp fees, he shoots me a check for half the cost. Little things, like Victor spending Thanksgiving with his partner in Texas, and big ones, like him signing the documents that make Karen a third parent, are all undergirded by our original promises to support each other's relationships. Law, fortunately, has not darkened our door, though the knowledge of which provisions could be enforced and which cannot shapes the way we see the terms—formal and informal—of our contracts and deals.

Every year thousands of other men and women also contract into and out of legal parenthood. A diagram outlines the rules governing those agreements, first setting out the general rule that dictates who's your daddy under family law, then an exception and an exception to the exception that family law has carved out to let men contract into and out of legal fatherhood through reproductive technology:

> *General Rule:* Genetic dads = legal fathers. This is the rule for more than nine out of ten cases.
>
> *Exception:* Genetic dads can contract out of legal fatherhood by selling their sperm to sperm banks.
>
> *Exception to the exception:* A genetic dad—like Victor—can agree to help a woman conceive through alternative insemination (AI) and then contract back *into* legal fatherhood by agreeing with the mom that he'll be a dad instead of a donor.

Another general rule presumes that a husband is the legal father when his wife has a baby. Marriage and genetics can both supply the general rule of fatherhood because in the vast majority of cases married women use their husband's sperm to get pregnant. If a baby does arrive courtesy of an affair or a sperm bank, then an exception to either rule may dictate who's the legal dad.

Living under an exception is a little like having type AB+ blood. Only 4 percent of Americans are type AB, compared with 45 percent for type O. Yet the Red Cross has to plan for that 4 percent, just as family law has to figure out how to deal with uncommon family arrangements. Since the early 1970s, family law has recognized baby-making via alternative insemination, and in recent years it has begun to recognize other variations as well.

Most people manage to work things out without resorting to the law. One boy, Griffin, is being raised by forty-something Carol Einhorn and her college friend George Russell, who provided the other half of Griffin's genetic material. George stays over half the time, a coziness made easy by his twenty-year friendship with Carol. They chat over dinner, and George helps by putting Griffin to bed. It is a long-term exchange, with each person giving and getting something back. When disagreements arise, like Carol's mom snubbing George's boyfriend, they work it out.[1] Of course, not every situation works out so smoothly, as lesbian mothers Sandy Russo and Robin Young discovered through years of custody litigation in the early 1990s with Tom Steel, a gay sperm donor who had become a part of their daughter's life.[2] Difficult as that was for the people involved, those judicial decisions benefited other Plan B families by providing guidance for people like Carol Einhorn and George Russell, which decreases the likelihood of a courtroom battle. Sociologist Judith Stacey's book *Unhitched* describes these and other uncommon agreements that underlie families like mine. She observes that people living Plan B lives are "at once freer and more obliged than most of the rest of us to craft the basic terms of their romantic and domestic unions."[3] The agreements between gay parents that she documents, which she describes as "thoughtful, magnanimous, and child-centered," must help them function as a family, because most of them were still intact and functioning smoothly when she checked in with them a decade after her initial research.

I could fill this chapter with things-work-out-fine stories.[4] But I focus on four legal cases because those rules shape all families, including the vast majority that never takes a dispute to court.

Case #1: The Package Deal of Sex and Fatherhood in *Kesler v. Weniger* (2000)

Love makes a family, a popular bumper sticker declares, but love-*making* makes a legal father. My first case story illustrates the general rule that the surest way for men to contract into legal fatherhood is to have sex with the mother.

Conrad Weniger found out the hard way that the general rule that genetic fathers = legal fathers applies when two people have sex to conceive. Conrad conceived a son, Scott, with Susan Kesler toward the end of their fifteen-year extramarital affair.[5] He stayed married throughout the affair and tried to evade child support obligations by arguing that Susan promised not to ask him for financial support. According to Conrad, he was just helping a friend have a baby. Susan's version, which the court described as "a slightly more romantic affair," highlighted their year-and-a-half cohabitation, Conrad's presence at Scott's birth, and his participating as dad at Scott's baptism. The court believed Susan, poking fun at Conrad's story of "15 years of compassionate but clinical assistance."[6] It held Conrad to the general rule, treating him as a legal father and ordering him to pay $330 a month in child support until Scott grew up.[7] This result must have made a huge difference for Susan and Scott, as well as for Conrad and his wife. But the case's greater impact is on other people.

Once a case is published in the legal database, a dispute between two people guides the outcome in future cases. *Kesler v. Weniger* confirms the general rule that genetic dads are also legal dads if they have sex to conceive a baby, despite any side deal that he is just a sperm donor. When men and women in Conrad and Susan's situation ask courts to decide whether the man has to pay child support, the court finds its answer in the rule of *Kesler*. It would treat *Kesler* as "precedent," which means that one court decision influences future ones. It might even quote the court's declaration that Conrad has to pay child support because "this is not a case of an anonymous clinical donor or a sperm bank. While science has enabled all manner of assisted conception, variations of which continue to evolve, we decline to recognize a category of 'artificial insemination by intercourse.'"[8] This general rule—that sex leads to fatherhood—applies more than nine times out of ten because sex is the most common way to become a parent.

That's fair, according to family law. When men like Conrad protest that the general rule unfairly rewards conniving women who promise they are just in it for the sperm and then turn around and sue for child support, family law calmly responds that the law's job is to be sure somebody pays for children's food, clothing, and vaccinations. If Conrad wanted to avoid that he could easily have worn a condom or, simpler still, stayed home with his wife. As the next case shows, Conrad also had a third option.

Case #2: The Sickly Sperm Donor in *Johnson v. Superior Court* (2002)

If Conrad Weniger really meant to be just a donor, he and Susan could have had a doctor do alternative insemination, which would have allowed him to contract out of legal fatherhood as long as they did it after breaking up. Most sperm donors are anonymous. Ronald and Diane Johnson found their donor through the California Cryobank (CCB) in 1988.[9] CCB promised the Johnsons that Donor 276 had been screened for infectious diseases and "reasonably detectable genetically transferred" abnormalities.[10] That screening, supervised by two doctors, involved lab tests for diseases, physical exams, and an in-person interview. Although that process revealed that Donor 276's mother and aunt both suffered from kidney disease, CCB nevertheless approved him. It even sold 320 vials of his sperm before withdrawing him from the list of donors because, as it later told Diane, "new information on his family members . . . indicates that he is at risk for kidney disease."[11] Unfortunately, Brittany Johnson, conceived with Donor 276's sperm, also had kidney disease. The Johnsons sued CCB for providing that tainted sperm.

Before we find out who Brittany's legal dad is, and who foots the bill for her medical treatments, let's take a look at the web of contracts and deals that shape the relationships.

CCB and Donor 276's Contract

Donor 276 came to the CCB in 1986, perhaps answering an ad in a college newspaper or free weekly magazine that joked, as some sperm bank ads do, that donors could "get paid for what you're already doing." To get accepted, he needed to be fairly tall, good-looking, healthy, and well educated (because that's what sperm bank customers want), on top of having an exceptionally high sperm count (the bank needs this so that enough swimmers survive freezing and thawing). Since banks invest a lot of time and money screening and testing donors, they also prize responsible donors who keep their promise to donate for a year so that the banks don't run out of their samples. Only 10 percent of men applying to be donors satisfy these stringent requirements.[12]

CCB promised to pay Donor 276 $35 per donation (about $75 in 2014 dollars), and he, in turn, promised to donate once or twice a week for a year. As of 2002, sperm donors received $50 to $100 per sample, 50 percent more if they agreed to be contacted by the children after they turned eighteen.[13] The extra money that banks pay donors to be "open," as CCB calls it, and that recipients pay to buy sperm from open donors, shows the value of donor identity. Donors value their anonymity, so they demand more money per donation to give it up, and parents, for their part, value the prospect of contact, so they pay extra for the donor's agreement to be contacted down the road.

In the 1980s, however, CCB didn't sell sperm provided by open donors. Donor 276's contract with CCB contained his promise never to try to discover who got his sperm, and CCB, in turn, promised that the donor's identity "will be kept in the strictest confidence unless a court orders disclosure for good cause."[14]

CCB and the Johnsons' Sperm Purchase Contract

The judge in *Johnson* did not say precisely how much the Johnsons paid, but the average in 2002 was $175–$215 per vial, which, in 1986 dollars would be around $106–$130.[15] The contract also included CCB's promise that it screened its donors for genetic diseases and the Johnsons' promise they would "not now, nor at any time, require or expect [CCB] to obtain or divulge . . . the name of said donor, nor any other information concerning characteristics, qualities, or any other information . . . whatsoever concerning said donor." CCB even promised to destroy all records relating to Donor 276, "it being the intention of all parties that the identity of said donor shall be and forever remain anonymous."[16]

CCB didn't keep either promise. First, it retained its records from interviewing Donor 276, and initially sent the Johnsons a doctored version. Eventually, CCB released the complete file, which showed that the bank approved Donor 276 even though it knew about his genetic predisposition to kidney disease.

At the end of the day, the Johnsons settled the case.[17] That money mattered to them, since it must have covered some of Brittany's medical expenses. But what matters most about the case for the rest of us is how it illustrates parenthood by agreement, including which parts of sperm sales are contracts—legally enforceable—and which are merely deals that courts won't enforce.

Repro Tech Riddles

The *Johnson* case answers two family law riddles:
When is a father not a father? and
When is an anonymous donor not anonymous?
The answers show the central role of contracts and deals.

Riddle #1: When Is a Father Not a Father?

A father is not a legal father when he contracts out of fatherhood through a sperm donation contract. Donor 276 entered a donor contract, so the Johnsons sued him to get medical information, not child support. Ronald was the legal father, per his dad contract. Decades before, California had decided to enforce both donor and dad contracts.

Back in 1964, when Folmer Sorensen and his wife separated, Folmer claimed he didn't have to support their six-year-old donor-conceived son. Folmer had signed an agreement consenting to the insemination, instructing the doctor to select a white male donor and promising not to seek out the donor's name. Folmer also was listed as the father on the birth certificate, and treated the boy as his own. The California Supreme Court said that Folmer was the legal dad and had to support the child, laying the legal foundation for California to become a reproductive technology center. He was a dad, according to the court, because he had consented to the insemination, while the anonymous donor was not a "natural father," because he "was no more responsible for the use made of his sperm than is the donor of blood or a kidney."[18] Essentially, Folmer contracted into legal fatherhood, because, according to the court, "without [his] active participation and consent the child would not have been procreated."[19]

Sorensen coincided with seismic social and legal changes, among them US Supreme Court cases that legitimized kids born out of wedlock.[20] Lawmakers rushed to rewrite statutes that defined who was, and was not, a legal parent. In 1973, a national organization known by its clunky acronym NCCUSL (short for the even clunkier National Conference of Commissioners on Uniform State Laws) published the Uniform Parentage Act (UPA), a model for states to use as they updated their family law rules. The UPA sets out the general rule outlined at the beginning of this chapter as well as the exception for sperm donation. Some states adopted the UPA, while others did not—a common event, since states are largely free to fashion their own legal rules. By the late 1990s, new technologies like IVF and gestational surrogacy made the 1973 UPA seem to some experts as outdated as a leisure suit, so NCCUSL updated it in 2002. Today, about two-thirds of states follow a version of the UPA, either rules that resemble the 2002 UPA or the 1973 version. Both versions of the UPA provide clear answers about legal parenthood when a married woman is inseminated, though ambiguities remain for parenthood when the woman is unmarried. It gets more complex in the rest of the states, which either have no statute or have statutes that differ from both UPAs.[21]

California's version of the UPA also makes the donors' identity and medical information confidential unless a court finds good cause to open the files.[22] That brings us to the second riddle.

Riddle # 2: When Is an Anonymous Donor Not Anonymous?
An anonymous donor is not entirely anonymous when the child inherits a serious illness. The *Johnson* case carved out the anonymity provision of AI contracts, treating that one provision as a mere deal but enforcing the rest of the terms, like Donor 276 being just a donor.

The court used surgical precision to limit the anonymity promise, allowing the Johnsons to collect medical information about Donor 276 but also keeping his name and other identifying information confidential. Its ruling, it explained, made sure that family law still provided "a vehicle for obtaining semen for artificial insemination without fear that the donor may claim paternity," and also allowed men to donate semen "without fear of liability for child support."[23] Courts' ability to demote one part of a parenthood agreement to a mere deal shows that contractual views of family allow for flexibility, especially to protect an important public interest like a child's health.

Johnson and the UPA show that parental rights are bought and sold every day through entirely legal contracts. The next two cases show that family law can also honor sperm donation agreements between friends like Victor and me. Because different people want different things, we'll see that some friends make donor contracts, while others make dad contracts.

Case #3: The Friendly Sperm Donor in *Ferguson v. McKiernan* (2007)

Joel McKiernan and Ivonne Ferguson met in 1991 through their work at Blue Cross/Blue Shield. Once their friendship turned romantic, they were lovers for a couple of years. Their relationship was turbulent, partly because Ivonne was married. Though she eventually left her husband, she and Joel didn't last. In late 1993, a month after they broke up for the last time, they were still close enough that Ivonne asked Joel to help her have a child. He initially refused, saying that marriage wasn't in their future. But she persisted, and he eventually agreed on the condition that she wouldn't pursue him for child support. She reassured him that she could raise the child herself, saying that she would rather have him donate than buy sperm from an anonymous donor.[24] Neither promise was in writing.

Ivonne's loose relationship with the truth further complicated the case. During their affair, she told Joel that she was using birth control, when in fact she'd had her tubes tied in the early 1980s. Later, after they broke up, she asked him to sleep with her again so she could have a child, all the while knowing that the tubal ligation made coital conception impossible. She also lied to her fertility doctor by listing her soon-to-be ex-husband's name on medical forms, and having Joel pose as the husband at the clinic, a ruse made necessary by the doctor's policy of only treating married women.[25] When the twins Tyler and Travis were born, Ivonne listed her ex-husband as the father on the birth certificate.

Joel, for his part, contributed to the situation's complexity by entering the agreement knowing that Ivonne still had feelings for him and staying in such close contact during the pregnancy that he sometimes slept on her couch. He also came to the hospital when she went into premature labor, and brought her and the boys home from the hospital. Joel stayed in touch until the twins were about six months old, eventually telling his parents that he was their father.[26]

Only when Joel moved to another state, met another woman, married her, and had a baby with her did he fully vacate Ivonne and the twins' lives.

We wouldn't know about Ivonne, Joel, and the twins if everyone had kept their word. But Ivonne exhausted her savings by footing the attorneys' fees when her oldest son ran afoul of the law.[27] When she happened on Joel's new address through a work project, she decided to pursue him for child support.

Family law's job is to clean up messes like the situation between Joel and Ivonne. As with anonymous sperm donation, contract principles do a good bit of that work by policing the line between donor and dad. The UPA rule discussed earlier lets donors contract out of legal fatherhood as long as a doctor performs the insemination. Just as Donor 276 in *Johnson* contracted out of legal fatherhood by selling his sperm to the California Cryobank, Joel "sold" his sperm to Ivonne in exchange for her promise not to hold him financially responsible for Tyler and Travis.

Contract law recognizes that not all exchanges are for cash, like when you trade in your car as part of the price of a new one. The Pennsylvania Supreme Court enforced Joel and Ivonne's contract because it was a mutual exchange: she got sperm, and he got freedom from legal fatherhood. The court invoked a "commonsense distinction between reproduction via sexual intercourse and the non-sexual clinical options for reproduction that are increasingly common," concluding with solid legal support for families created through repro tech:

> The inescapable reality is that all manner of arrangements involving the donation of sperm and eggs abound in contemporary society, many of them couched in contracts or agreements of varying degrees of formality. An increasing number of would-be mothers who find themselves either unable or unwilling to conceive children in the context of marriage are turning to donor insemination to enable them to enjoy the privilege of raising a child.[28]

Joel and Ivonne's donor contract, the court concluded, was legally binding.

Relational Contracts vs. One-Shot Contracts

Contract scholars would view Joel and Ivonne's dispute as a disagreement about whether their arrangement was "relational," meaning long-term and complex, or "one-shot," meaning a single interaction between people who then go their separate ways. Dad contracts, by definition, are relational because they presuppose years of complex and, everyone hopes, mostly amicable interactions. Contrast that with Donor 276's agreement with the California Cryobank. The contracts between Donor 276, the sperm bank, and the Johnsons were entered expecting very limited, short-term interactions.[29]

A one-shot sperm donation contract is a bit like a one-night stand. A man provides a good genetic profile, hands it over in a jar, and gets genetic immortality without ever having to change a diaper, let alone pay for college or lie awake at night worrying about that no-good daughter-in-law's fondness for lunchtime martinis. A more prosaic one-shot contract occurs when you buy a Slurpee at the 7-Eleven. You give the store $3.00 and get the drink and 7-Eleven gives the drink and gets $3.00. Like all contracts, it's a two-way street. Similarly, like all contracts, it's consensual. That voluntary reciprocity may well explain why family law so often uses contract principles to police the line between donors and dads. Joel and Ivonne, consenting adults, freely agreed to let Joel contract out of fatherhood in exchange for Ivonne getting to birth and raise the twins. Family law should override their exchange only if it causes sufficient harm to the people involved and/or society more generally to justify the state departing from its usual posture of deferring to family decision making.

Case #4: Contracting Back into Legal Fatherhood: *In re Sullivan* (2005)

The fourth and final case of this chapter illustrates the cutting edge of the trend toward contractual freedom in families, which has led some courts to honor families like mine. Like most baby-making—and many business contracts—we only know about Sharon Sullivan and Brian Russell's arrangement because one of them had a change of heart.

At first blush, Brian and Sharon's situation resembles Victor's and mine. Both gay, Sharon "wanted badly to conceive a child," the *Houston Press* reported, "and he was willing to oblige."[30] So they negotiated an exchange. Like Victor and me, they signed a formal agreement promising to raise a child together as gay friends in two different households. Both quasi-couples agreed that the guy would be listed as the dad on the birth certificate. But the similarities end there. Brian and Sharon barely knew each other, having met through a hairdresser, while Victor and I had been friends for fifteen years and even roommates for a couple of summers. Sharon had a girlfriend who'd be a second mom, while Victor and I were both single. They weren't lawyers, so they—or at least Sharon—seem not to have fully understood what they were signing.

Things started off smoothly: Sharon got pregnant after just two inseminations. But at nine weeks, they discovered that the baby had no heartbeat, so she had to terminate the very-much-desired pregnancy. Rather than weather the ordeal with Sharon, Brian jetted off to a romantic Paris getaway with his boyfriend. They kept inseminating, but Sharon wanted to rework their agreement. They swapped drafts of a new agreement that would include her girlfriend and demote Brian to donor status but never signed it. Nevertheless, they kept inseminating, and Sharon got pregnant again. During the following months, negotiations broke down so severely that Brian's lawyer wrote to her lawyer, "It would be appropriate for Mr. Russell to attend the birth of his own child. Please ask Ms. Sullivan to communicate with Mr. Russell as soon as possible when the child's birth is imminent."[31]

Sharon apparently did not want Brian in the delivery room. She had a baby girl, in March 2004, without telling him.[32] He responded by filing suit, asking the court to declare him the baby's dad. The legal question was whether he had "standing," meaning the kind of direct interest that allowed him to claim paternity. The answer is more complex than you might think.

As we have seen, most states let sperm donors contract out of legal fatherhood, though the statutes are often silent about parenthood

when the woman is not married or they inseminate at home instead
of in a doctor's office. By the time Brian and Sharon were in court,
Texas, like a good number of other states, had updated its version of
the UPA rule to more clearly state that "a donor is not a parent of a
child conceived by means of assisted reproduction."[33] If Brian was a
"donor" according to this new provision, then he was out of luck.
But if he was not, he could try to enforce his agreement with Sharon.

The Texas Family Code defined "donor" as "an individual who
provides eggs or sperm to a licensed physician to be used for assisted
reproduction," regardless of whether the donor gets paid. Usually
those donors are strangers, like Donor 276 in *Johnson v. Superior
Court*. But here the legal question was whether men who contract
out of legal fatherhood via alternative insemination could also contract *back into* being legal dads.[34]

The case was so important that the court asked the Texas Attorney General to consider how Sharon and Brian's agreement squared
with the Texas Consitution. The AG emphasized that the Lone Star
State had a policy of "facilitating" the purchase and sale of sperm
and eggs. Because Brian and Sharon's agreement was, in the Attorney
General's words, "mutual" and "voluntary," it, like other mutual,
voluntary agreements, could be legally binding.[35] The Texas Court
of Appeals ruled that Brian deserved his day in court to try to prove
that he and Sharon had entered a dad contract. Sharon gave up, and
they settled the case, agreeing to raise their daughter together, more
or less.[36] For our purposes, the part of the case that matters most is
that Texas allowed men like Brian to contract out of being legal dads
through AI, then back in by explicitly contracting with the moms.

Perhaps worried that its decision seemed to openly acknowledge
family law's recognition of parenthood-by-contract, the Texas court
slipped in a footnote at the end of the case clarifying that it took "no
position on the validity" of the coparenting agreement between Brian
and Sharon.[37] Yet the only way that Brian could be a dad under Texas
law was through that coparenting agreement. The court's footnote
seems to reflect the same partial truth as the Massachusetts' court
declaration noted in chapter 2 that "'parenthood by contract' is not

the law."[38] As we've seen in *Johnson* and *Ferguson*, parenthood-by-contract is the law in most states—including Texas and Massachusetts—because they adopted the UPA rule letting donors contract out of parenthood and the spouses of inseminated women to contract into it. The trick to finding a legal rule is to read a whole set of cases and statutes together. Some judicial statements are merely what lawyers call "dictum," or sidebars. You need to see the larger pattern, taking care to avoid becoming what law students call a "victim of dictum."

LAW AS IT SHOULD BE RE AI AGREEMENTS

Sharon and Brian's daughter, like Brittany Johnson and Tyler and Travis Ferguson, are all children of choice. Their moms and dads used agreements to create families when the road well traveled was closed to them. A person's view of uncommon methods of baby-making probably depends on how much he or she thinks that law should protect people from harmful choices. If the Pope dictated the laws, all kinds of reproductive choices—from abortion to AI—would probably be banned.[39] But I think it is wrong for government bureaucrats—regardless of whether they claim to speak for God—to say that there's only one natural form of family. Nice as they may be, I do not want Congress or state representatives in my bedroom or doctor's office. If legislatures do get involved in reproductive technologies, they should expand contractual freedoms as California and the District of Columbia have by explicitly allowing a mother's partner or a known sperm donor to contract into legal parenthood by signing a formal agreement. Those new rules should also recognize that actions—like living in a parent-and-child relationship for a year—can speak as loudly as words on the page.

New Directions in Alternative Insemination

Option 1: Let It Be
Other scholars agree that family law should honor people's choices to make whatever family arrangements they choose, as long as health and safety are protected. Berkeley law professor Marjorie Shultz argues

that family law ought to "support developments that extend and en-
hance individual purpose and choice" unless "compelling reasons"
require government intervention.[40] Harvard law professor Glenn
Cohen has suggested that family law ought to interfere in donor insemination only if it would similarly meddle in people's conceiving
through sex.[41] But that's a minority view. The much louder call is for
states to meddle in Plan B parenthood.

Scholars Seeking Government Oversight

A number of law professors, political scientists, economists, ethi-
cists, and journalists would limit donor anonymity, limit payment
for gametes and gestation, cap the number of children each donor
can sire, or have government oversee fertility clinics to keep them
from taking undue advantage of people desperately hoping to have
kids.[42] While these calls for increased regulation largely have failed to
produce results, some states have enacted new regulations. In 2011,
Washington passed a law allowing children conceived with donor
sperm or eggs to find out their donors' full names and medical histories. But even that law honors families' privacy and choice by making
kids wait until they're eighteen to access the donor database and allowing donors to opt out of being identified.[43]

Many European governments make decisions for their citizens
about when, whether, and how to create family through reproductive technologies, perhaps because socialized medicine increases
government control over medical treatment generally. England
eliminated anonymous donation and sets sperm and egg prices very
low.[44] France—which began recognizing same-sex marriage in 2013
—doesn't allow unmarried or single people to use alternative insemination but does let unmarried straight couples access AI. As of
mid-2014, Germany limits AI to married couples and doesn't allow
same-sex couples to marry.[45] People skirt these barriers by traveling to
other countries, like Denmark. Abby, a single, forty-one-year-old British lawyer, conceived her son, Oscar, with gametes from the Danish
sperm bank Cryos after failing to conceive with the limited selection
of sperm produced under British restraints. Cryos is the biggest sperm

bank in the world, thanks to Danish laws allowing anonymous donation as well as Danes' reputation for height, health, and good looks. It has lured would-be mothers from sixty countries with its slogan "Congratulations, it's a Viking!"[46] Technology greatly facilitates this reproductive tourism through websites for reviewing donor profiles, electronic payment with credit cards, and overnight shipping in liquid nitrogen so that sperm can rocket across the planet. People access these technologies, and the sperm itself, through contracts.

Some people argue that Plan B families don't deserve the kind of privacy, dignity, and autonomy that Plan A families generally enjoy.[47] But proponents of government meddling in family formation fail to notice the implications of letting government make our most private decisions.

If we forbid anonymous sperm donation, reasoning that all kids deserve to know their genetic parents, then we should also forbid closed adoption and genetically test all children to ferret out the ones conceived in extramarital affairs. While urban legend holds that as many as 10 percent of children are products of the mother's extramarital affair, a 2006 study suggests that mandatory genetic tests would unpleasantly surprise around 2 percent of husbands.[48] If we forbid sperm banks from touting their donors' genetic superiority, fearing eugenic consequences of breeding designer babies, we ought also to ban in-person attempts to select especially accomplished mates, like the monthly Ivy League Singles Socials in Washington, DC.[49] I suspect that the people who invite the state into other people's bedrooms and doctor's offices would be a lot more shy about handing over their most private decisions to legislators and judges.

Venerable constitutional law cases reach the same conclusion. After a brief romance with eugenics in the early twentieth century, the Supreme Court decided that the government can't forcibly sterilize people it labels "feeble-minded," "promiscuous," or "habitual criminals." Along the way to this conclusion, though, the Court in 1927 famously justified state-sponsored eugenics by declaring, in *Buck v. Bell*, that "society can prevent those who are manifestly unfit from continuing their kind . . . Three generations of imbeciles is enough."[50]

Even assuming that the government had the right to sterilize people, it got the facts wrong in that case. Carrie Buck, the teenager forcibly sterilized, was no imbecile, nor was her child. She did well in school before her foster family took her out in sixth grade to work, and her daughter's intelligence was normal.[51] By 1942, the Court reversed course by striking down Oklahoma's Habitual Criminal Sterilization Act because it interfered with chicken thief Jack Skinner's "basic liberty."[52]

Too often, the government tries to prevent people in minority populations from becoming parents. States have pressured poor, often African American and Native American, women to use Norplant, a long-lasting contraceptive, as a condition for receiving welfare.[53] Arkansas and Florida tried to ban gay people from becoming foster parents or adopting.[54] Scholars such as Marsha Garrison, Mary Lyndon Shanley, Debora Spar, and Michael Sandel, who would increase state regulation of reproductive technologies, ignore or downplay the possibility of majorities using these laws to bully minorities. They hold up other countries as models for limiting payments for sperm and eggs or forbidding donor anonymity, without mentioning that these same regulations often fence out gay and single people. Naomi Cahn flags this danger and argues for states to abandon "outdated" models of ideal families that exclude gay couples, but she has more faith in lawmakers' friendliness to gays and single women than I do.[55] In 2012 alone, legislatures enthusiastically limited reproductive choices by resisting insurance coverage for birth control and mandating nonconsensual vaginal probes of pregnant women, and in 2014, the Supreme Court allowed the religious owners of the craft store Hobby Lobby to deny contraceptive coverage to their female employees.[56]

The government should be invited to limit reproductive choices only when those choices pose dangers that outweigh the harm done by government meddling.[57] No reputable data establishes specific ways that families created through reproductive technologies hurt the people in them so much, or society more generally, that family law should put them out of business. Consequently, we should stick with the private mechanisms we have, which do at least as good a job as government bureaucracy would to protect donor-conceived kids, their parents, and the donors.

Option 2: Clarify Parenthood-by-Contract Statutes

I may be wrong in thinking that allowing legislators to get involved in baby-making decisions will result in invidious discrimination. A few legislatures, given the chance, have done the right thing by clarifying the rules governing parenthood-by-contract in repro tech cases. In 2012, California changed its rule to explicitly allow a known donor to enter a dad contract with the child's mother. That statute requires that the mom and would-be dad sign a written dad contract before the child is conceived.[58] The District of Columbia follows a similar rule.[59]

It makes sense to require a signed document, because otherwise the well-established Plan B rule that sperm donors are not dads would be eroded. Contract law generally requires big agreements—for land, say, or those lasting more than a year—to be in writing, and signing on to parenthood is among the biggest commitments a person can make.

The DC parentage statute also provides two ways for a partner or wife to be recognized as a legal mom of a child conceived by alternative insemination. First, she can contract into a marriage or domestic partnership, which creates a presumption that she is a legal mom to kids that her wife or partner bears. Consistent with freedom of contract principles, that couple can also agree that only the birth mother will be the legal mom, though evidence of non-parenthood has to be clear and convincing.[60]

The second way for a wife or partner in DC to become a legal mom is through a formal parenthood contract. That agreement must be in writing and signed. But even if a couple like Sharon Sullivan and her partner do not sign a formal agreement, the partner can still be a legal mom if they all live together, holding out the child as both of theirs.[61]

Private agreements play a different role in adoption. That makes sense because adoption usually involves a child from an unplanned pregnancy, the very opposite of ultra-planned parenthood through reproductive technologies, which justifies a different set of legal rules that reflect the social and emotional context. Nevertheless, as chapter 4 shows, adoption law relies more heavily on contracts and deals than most people realize.

FOUR

Basics of Adoption Agreements

INTERVIEW WITH A BIRTH MOTHER

"Is this a good time to talk?" I ask, sounding like I'm trying to get something out of her. I am. I want her to give me her baby, little guessing that I'll manage to get pregnant myself before long.

We talk for a few minutes, me asking her age (twenty-two), how the pregnancy has progressed (fine), trying to be friendly and sympathetic. Wondering if I'm breaching protocol, I ask her name.

"Conni with an 'i,'" she responds, definitively.

Over the next two hours I find out that she and her now ex-girlfriend wanted to have this baby together but broke up over what Conni calls her anger management problems. She had sex with a friend to get pregnant and can't keep the baby because a battery arrest disqualifies her from working at her old job as a security guard. She's living with her dad, who thinks that she's too immature to be a mom.

"Ooooooh," she coos, as I explain that I'm a professor and could provide love, stability, and flexibility. Interrupting myself, I ask what's happening on her end and find out that she's opening a purple onesie from her aunt.

As I resume describing myself over the rustle of tissue paper, she interjects, "That's all really impressive, but I don't need this baby to be with someone super rich. What I want is to live near, for the baby to know me and even call me 'Mom,' and maybe I can be friends with the two women who adopt her."

"Mom," I echo. "Have you talked to other people who might adopt your baby?"

"Yeah," she says. Two women from Chicago told her that the windy city has a great gay pride parade, that they could all march together, and that she could live there near them. They even promised to name the child Taynan. When I ask where she got the name, she proudly reports that she made it up.

"I know that I can't make them do it," she finishes a little more quietly.

I don't tell her that courts enforce some adoption agreements. Could I promise to name a child Taynan, when I'm set on either Beatrice or Walter? If I did, I'd have to keep my word, having made a career of championing family contracts. Conni's next words cut off all other thoughts.

"Maybe you and I could get together. Wouldn't that be weird? If I gave you the baby, and then we fell in love, I could still be the mother."

I flash on a future with Conni and her anger management problems and say that it sounds like she's inclined to go with the Chicago couple.

"Why would I choose a single mother? I'm a single mother. Besides," she continues, "I'm still hoping I can figure out a way to get my dad to let me keep it."

————

NINE STORIES OF ADOPTION

While Conni's circumstances are unique, her shopping around for adoptive parents and negotiating terms for post-adoption contact are commonplace in domestic adoption. Just a generation ago, birth parents had no say in who raised their kids or visits after the adoption. Yet contracts and deals have long played a role in adoption, with adoptive parents and agencies dictating the terms. Today's adoption contracts and deals can reflect the desires of birth parents and adoptees as well.

Contractual adoption sounds like an oxymoron, especially when you consider that virtually every state forbids baby-selling. But those statutes apply only to a narrow set of situations that look like an overt exchange of cash for a baby. It's entirely legal, we'll see, for the adoptive parents to pay an agency "fees" for services like the home study, and to pay the birth mom's medical and legal expenses and even, sometimes, her living expenses. Most important, adoption generally requires that the birth parents make a legally binding agreement—a contract—to surrender their parental rights and duties, and also that adoptive parents contract into the care and feeding of those children.

The real question is how openly we acknowledge the role of contracts in adoption. Legal economists like Elisabeth Landes and Richard Posner have fully embraced contracts, suggesting that adoptive parents could pay higher fees to induce birth mothers to choose adoption over abortion. Most others, like University of Michigan law professor Peggy Radin, bristle at open acknowledgment of the contractual nature of adoption because, she argues, "conceiving of any child in market rhetoric harms personhood."[1] This chapter proposes a middle path. Family law should more openly acknowledge the role of contracts in adoption, while also recognizing that a civilized society ought not to compare kids in foster care to "unsold inventory stored in a warehouse," as Landes and Posner did in 1978.[2] By uncovering the contracts already lying at the very foundation of every adoption, we can consider how law and society can and should shape the terms of those agreements in ways that protect everyone involved.

When adoption was "closed"—social work lingo for secret and often shameful—the terms of adoption contracts were more favorable to adoptive parents. That's changing as family law increasingly honors post-adoption contact agreements, or PACAs, such as what Conni was bargaining for. That's good, because the traditional rule too often gives people like me—or the couple in Chicago—too much power over birth moms like Conni and the children.

Since open adoption, like all of us, carries features of its ancestors, I start by exploring its long and often-surprising history.

Plan B of Biblical Proportions

Adoption dates back to biblical times. When Moses was just three months old, his mother sent him down the Nile in a papyrus basket to save him from Pharaoh's decree to kill Hebrew baby boys. Baby Moses might have drowned had Pharaoh's own daughter not fished him out of the river. Like many adoptive parents, she gave him a new name that meant "drawn out of the water," a name that some theologians see as a sign of his destiny to draw the Jews out of Egypt. His situation also prefigures open adoption, in that Moses's birth mom stayed in his life by getting hired to be the baby's nurse.

The story lives on through today's safe haven laws, which are also called Baby Moses laws. These statutes allow parents to surrender their newborns in safe places like hospitals and fire stations if they can't raise them, without risking liability for abandonment.[3] Relinquishing a child is nobody's Plan A. But when poverty, isolation, illness, trauma, or youth force birth parents into Plan B, Baby Moses laws can steer them away from routes leading toward child abuse, neglect, or abandonment in a public restroom or dumpster. Viewed through a contract lens, the state forgives a birth parent for abandoning her infant if she leaves the baby at a safe place. Though not ideal, the arrangement is safer for the baby and protects the new mom—who's already in a crisis—from a criminal prosecution that hurts her and helps no one. Yet the very feature of Baby Moses laws that protects women and children—anonymity—can harm birth parents who'd benefit from counseling about their options and birth dads who might not even know about the adoption.

Fair or not, the widespread enactment of Baby Moses laws exemplifies the larger pattern of law using contracts and deals to help people work out alternative arrangements when the usual routes are blocked. As with reproductive technology, the terms of those agreements have changed over time.

Early America

Kids have always needed a safe haven when they lost their parents to war, death, separation, desertion, illness, or poverty and also, until recently, when they were born to single women. At any stage of history, better-off families have had more and better Plan B options than poor ones.

Take President Andrew Jackson. When his dad died just a few weeks before he was born, his widowed mother and her sisters teamed up to fill the gap. Then cholera claimed his mother in 1781—orphaning Jackson at fourteen—requiring those aunts and uncles to step up their support. If Mrs. Jackson's sisters had been too poor to take the family in, or if Andrew's parents hadn't married, Andrew's mother might have had to abandon him at an almshouse or foundling asylum. The few jobs available to colonial women didn't pay a living wage, and insurance and public assistance didn't exist yet, nor did many private programs. Andrew might not have survived an asylum childhood: conditions there were so abysmal that infant mortality rates ran as high as 80 or 90 percent. Even if he had, he'd have had to work hard to earn his meager rations and may have remained illiterate. At twelve or fourteen, he'd have been apprenticed out to a family for domestic or farm work. Then, when he turned eighteen or twenty-one, he'd have been loosed on the world armed only with a little money, clothes, a new Bible, and perhaps some cattle.[4]

The Birth of Modern Childhood

Today that bleak scenario sounds like child abuse. But law only began to worry about child labor—and provide free public schools—in the mid-nineteenth century. Before then, most kids helped support their families, often through indentured servitude or apprenticeships, which meant that only the privileged few got an education. Until 1865, enslaved children toiled alongside adults in fields and households, and even after Reconstruction, many African American children worked instead of attending school. Gradually, reformers changed childhood into a stage of life focused on school instead of wage labor, which in turn led family law to start helping the most vulnerable children—orphans and kids whom even family law called "bastards"—by providing them loving and permanent homes. The earliest child labor laws—passed in Massachusetts in 1836 and

1842—merely required children under fifteen to attend school three months a year and banned them from working more than ten hours a day. A century later, these reforms finally ripened to the first federal ban on child labor, the 1938 Fair Labor Standards Act.

Modern Adoption

My mother happened to be born at a good time to be adopted. In 1930, a private adoption agency in Evanston, Illinois, called The Cradle placed her with a devoted middle-aged couple of Danish descent. By then, Illinois, like most states, had followed the lead of Massachusetts by enacting an adoption law that protected children's best interests. The 1851 Massachusetts statute required a judge to determine that the adoptive parents were "of sufficient ability to bring up the child, and furnish suitable nurture and education," and also made the child a permanent member of that family instead of a servant.[5]

The laws of supply and demand also have governed adoption. According to Princeton sociologist Viviana Zelizer, until the end of the nineteenth century a buyer's market determined the fate of orphans and other kids whose parents couldn't raise them. In effect, the high supply of children and low demand for them so lowered their price that many birth mothers—especially unmarried and poor women burdened by the shame of a non-marital pregnancy and hampered by deficient education and barriers to women's employment—had to pay people known as "baby farmers" to take the children off their hands. In the hands of the baby farmers, that low value translated to low survival rates. Children lucky enough to survive were put to good use, getting hired out for farm or domestic work.

That situation had changed by the 1930s. According to a 1937 magazine article, "The baby market is booming . . . the clamor is for babies, more babies. . . . We behold an amazing phenomenon: a country-wide scramble on the part of childless couples to adopt a child."[6] Technologically, the advent of safe infant formula, accomplished at The Cradle a few years before my mother arrived on their doorstep, reassured adoptive parents across the country that they could provide adequate sustenance.

But larger social changes more powerfully spurred demand among would-be adoptive parents. The value of children underwent a transformation, from economic value for the work they could perform to sentimental value associated with the newfound innocence of childhood. As an adoptive father told *Good Housekeeping* in 1927, "Talk about children owing their parents anything! We'll never be able to pay what we owe that baby."[7]

Market rhetoric in adoption, in short, is nothing new. In the early twentieth century, babies were commonly offered for adoption through newspaper classified ads. For example, the *Boston Globe* printed this query: "Who wants to take a little girl, three years old, the picture of health and a smart, handsome child? Only those who can give a comfortable home need answer."[8] Other ads were more blunt ("For Adoption at Birth, Full Surrender, No Questions Asked.").[9] This practice became widely controversial only when the idea of childhood as a vulnerable period spent in school instead of work had taken firm root in American law and culture, producing reforms like social workers vetting potential adoptive parents.

These reforms left undisturbed the contractual framework of adoption. Adoption professionals just masked the role of money in adoption by relabeling the payments made by adoptive parents, a masking that continues to this day. Although all states now forbid obvious baby-selling, a loophole allows adoptive parents to pay "adoption expenses." Some states let adoptive parents pay for the birth mom's living expenses during the pregnancy as well as medical and legal fees, while others make it a criminal offence for adoptive parents to pick up the tab for the birth mom's maternity clothes, unless they have a doctor's note certifying that she is too sick to work.[10]

Birth moms generally surrender their kids only if they're too poor, sick, or young to care for them, so depriving them of those funds is not only cruel but also defeats the purpose of the ban on baby-selling by pushing them into black market adoptions that pose far more risks than paying for maternity clothes. The lawmakers who voted to paint birth parents into that corner can't possibly have considered the situation from their perspective.

The Silent Treatment

Although today's adoption policies need improvement, fifty years ago the situation was far worse, especially for birth moms. In 1967, during her junior year of high school, a girl named Claudia got pregnant by a thirty-one-year-old Cape Verdean man she met in a life-drawing class. Her parents shipped her off to St. Mary's home for unwed mothers in Dorchester, Massachusetts, where nuns expressed their "palpable" disapproval by giving all residents false names to cover their shame.

For a few days she got to hold the baby she named Raina, reveling over her "tiny heart-shaped mouth, big dark eyes, beautiful reddish-brown skin, and tons and tons of black hair." But on the third day, Claudia remembers, her parents arrived to take her home:

> I got in the backseat. . . . [M]y dad's way up there driving, totally white-knuckled, and I'm looking out that back window at the hospital. And seeing the view of the hospital getting smaller and smaller and smaller, I flipped out—it was total, 100 percent, ripped terror, wailing, screaming, crying—and nobody said a word. My mother didn't even turn around.[11]

It was, Claudia explains years later, "the beginning of being invisible," because no one in her family ever mentioned the adoption again, even just to ask how she was.[12]

In the 1990s, Claudia finally reunited with Raina and found out that she'd been adopted by "dark-skinned" Italians who lived about a mile down the street. Raina knew that she was adopted but not that her birth father was black. In Claudia's case, as for many other birth mothers and adoptees, openness was the only remedy to profound injuries inflicted by losing a child in the midst of all that secrecy and shame.[13]

If Claudia got pregnant today, she'd have more options. She might have been able to keep the child. If she opted for adoption, she might have selected a biracial couple as birth parents. She might have gotten pictures and letters as Raina grew up, and perhaps even had phone calls or visits. That adoptive family would still be Raina's parents, but the child could also know where she came from.

Listening to Birth Parents

By the 1970s, birth moms began to band together to bring about these changes. Organizations like Concerned United Birthparents (CUB) provided emotional support to birth moms and to women considering adoption, as well as information and support with searches and reunions. Individual birth parents also began to press adoption agencies, lawmakers, and judges to listen to their views. But the laws of supply and demand may have provided the biggest catalyst for social and legal change in adoption.

Starting in the 1970s, several phenomena contributed to a rapid drop in the supply of infants available for adoption. Increasingly, women could get birth control and legal abortions. More single women could keep their children because they could get jobs that paid enough to support them. Unmarried moms could collect child support from their kids' dads once family law finally recognized non-marital fathers as legal fathers. Poverty was less likely to force a woman to relinquish her child for adoption as federal welfare programs extended, if modestly, their coverage to more poor, often unmarried, women and their children. Rises in non-marital births and divorce decreased the stigma of single motherhood. On the other side of the equation, demand for children to adopt went up as more women delayed childbearing while they established careers, leaving them less fertile when they got around to building a family. This short supply of infants, coupled with high demand, drove up the "price" of babies.[14]

Agencies began to sweeten the deal for birth parents by offering open adoptions, a big upgrade from the culture of shame and secrecy. Openness took two main forms. First, birth parents got to select the adoptive parents from portfolios submitted to the agencies. Then after the adoption, they often got information about the kids via letters and pictures, phone calls, and even, increasingly, in-person contact.

Those changes reframed the way both law and society viewed adoption. Instead of designating birth moms as sinful or mentally unstable and adoptive parents as rescuers, adoption moved toward moral neutrality. As the director of Lutheran Social Services put it in her influential 1983 book *Dear Birthmother*, "Every parent is real in a unique way" and "No parent is better or worse."[15]

Adoptable Children

Just as some parents were once deemed better than others, some children used to be viewed as more worthy than others. Early twentieth-century Americans' growing willingness to see children as little angels instead of little laborers did not restrain adoptive parents from requesting characteristics as if ordering from a catalog. Race was at the top of the list. A 1909 *New York Times* article on orphan asylums concluded that "every baby who expects to be adopted . . . ought to make it a point to be born with blue eyes," and a 1907 article in the *Delineator* treated "adoptable" as a synonym for "white" by reporting that "a two-year-old, blue-eyed golden haired little girl with curls, that is the order that everybody leaves. It cannot be filled fast enough."[16]

Children with disabilities were also excluded from the category "adoptable." Fortunately, my mom's sole defect was overlapping toes, or her adoption agency might have dispatched her to an institution, their practice with the babies they dubbed "congenitally diseased" in the agency's early years.

Only after World War II did agencies finally embrace the idea that all children are adoptable. The discrediting of eugenics in the wake of Nazi horrors, the civil rights movement, and increased demand all contributed to this change. Agencies also began to treat children of color as "adoptable," changing the face of adoption. By 1948, a *Child Welfare* article could report a "growing conviction" among adoption professionals that "the color of a child's skin, the texture of his hair, or the slant of his eyes in no way affects his basic needs or the relation of his welfare to that of the entire community."[17] Although a 1951 study reported that nearly half of American adoption agencies still rejected disabled children, by 1955 the president of the Child Welfare League of America could laud a "new trend" toward placing children with disabilities or family histories of mental illness.[18] Unfortunately inequalities persist. Though programs like Oregon's

Operation Brown Baby started in 1957, and 30 percent to 50 percent of babies adopted through The Cradle today are African American or multiracial, African American children remain more likely than whites to languish in foster care instead of getting adopted.[19]

Suitable Parents

Before the 1950s, adoption law and policy also discriminated against would-be parents to prevent interracial and interfaith families. My mom's adoption file includes a letter from The Cradle's charismatic founder, Mrs. Florence Walrath, who explained that she picked Danish parents to raise my mom because "we believed that you sprang from the same race as your adoptive parents, and your inherited characteristics would make you thoroughly congenial." The Cradle even managed to match hybrid ethnicities. In 1935 *Time* magazine reported that Al Jolson—a rabbi's son famous for his blackface performance in *The Jazz Singer*—and his Irish-Catholic wife, Ruby Keeler, adopted a seven-week-old boy who was "half Jewish, half Irish" through The Cradle. To underline the point that adoption could mimic genetic parenthood, the article described Jolson as "a dark Semitic-looking man" and quoted Ruby cooing, "I think he takes after Al a little, with that dark hair."[20]

In 1972 transracial adoption again became controversial when the National Association of Black Social Workers came out against placing African American children with white families. They reasoned that "only a black family can transmit the emotional and sensitive subtleties of perception and reaction essential for a black child's survival in a racist society."[21] The tide turned again in 1980s and 1990s, as the War on Drugs pulled more kids away from their parents than agencies could place with families of any race, leading Congress in 1994 to ban racial grounds for delaying or denying an adoption.[22]

Class also influenced "suitability." In the early twentieth century, when many single mothers had to surrender their kids for adoption, law and society allowed other single people to adopt those children. Joan Crawford was between husbands in 1940 when she adopted Christina (who would later make the star infamous as the mother from hell in *Mommy Dearest*). More prosaically, a 1948 study of single people adopting described a woman it called Gertrude R., a social worker, who fostered three children in the 1940s, taking them at around eighteen months so she could "train them into [her] own ways."[23]

Sometimes the law mistook spinsters for singles. In the 1920s, for example, University of Pennsylvania professor Jessie Taft adopted two children, Everett and Martha, and raised them together with her life partner, Virginia Robinson. Joint adoption as a couple would not have been possible in a legal regime that saw a same-sex relationship as a crime. As late as 1997, journalist Jesse Green sat at the back of the courtroom watching his partner, Andy, adopt their son, Lucas, closeted for fear that the judge wouldn't let them adopt together.[24] States like California and New York had begun just a decade earlier to start allowing same-sex couples like Annie Affleck and Rebecca Smith both to be legal moms to their daughter, Nancy.[25] Slowly, the law has come to realize that kids need homes and loving families, rather than families that take a particular form. Today, more than half of US states allow gay couples to adopt, married or not. Throwbacks do persist. Mississippi, for example, bars gay couples from adoption, and Utah fences out people who live with someone they're not married to.[26]

Beyond Secrecy and Shame

Having rejected the shame and secrecy of the closet themselves, it's hardly surprising that gay people are among the leading advocates for open adoption. Sex columnist Dan Savage embodies that pairing: he made the leap from sexual openness in his syndicated column *Savage Love* to personal openness through memoirs about marrying his boyfriend, Terry, and adopting their son, DJ. His description of the birth mom, Melissa Pierce, conveys better than any I've read the emotional price birth moms pay for adoption and the respect that adoptive parents owe them. Melissa was, he says, "a nineteen-year-old street kid with long brown hair, a lip piercing, and half a dozen tattoos" who picked Dan and Terry because "the first couple she chose, a straight couple, didn't want to do an open adoption with a homeless teenager who admitted to drinking during the early stages of her pregnancy." Dan, Terry, and Melissa sat in a recovery room at the hospital, taking turns, he says, "holding our son, a tiny infant who would quickly grow into a charismatic, blond-haired, blue-eyed skateboarder." They'd wanted an open adoption, negotiating "pictures a few times a year and the occasional visit" so that Melissa would be part of DJ's life. But before Dan, Terry, and DJ could become a family, Dan remembers, they had to "take [DJ] from his mother's arms as she sat sobbing on her bed." He describes that moment as "the hardest thing I've ever done in my life. . . . You know what a broken heart looks like? Like a sobbing teenager in a hospital bed giving away a two-day-old infant she knows she can't take care of to a couple she hopes can."[27]

Dan and Terry did their best to give Melissa something in return. Beyond sobbing themselves and giving her a bracelet engraved with the name she'd chosen for the baby, they gave DJ Melissa's last name, the most traditional way to dub someone "family." Melissa, like other birth moms who place their kids with gay male couples, also gets to remain the only mother in the picture.

The law is starting to do better by birth parents like Melissa and adopted kids like DJ. Kids deserve to know about the reasons their parents relinquished them, and know basic facts about their genetic relatives. Birth moms deserve reassurance that the kids they let go of with so much anguish are doing all right. Adoptive parents should have access to medical and social information to help their children form an identity that incorporates biological as well as social kinship.

ADOPTION 101

Vital Statistics

Adoption is considerably more common than our first example of Plan B parenthood, reproductive technologies. While reliable statistics are hard to come by, about two and a half times more children are adopted than are conceived by alternative insemination each year. That translates to over 2 percent of kids under eighteen, or between

120,000 and 150,000 adoptions a year. The numbers get really big when you realize that for every adoption, adoptive and birth families also are deeply affected. According to one estimate, fully 60 percent of Americans have been personally touched by adoption, meaning that they themselves, a family member, or a close friend is adopted, has placed a child for adoption, or has adopted a child.[28]

Adoption rates fluctuate greatly. They increased in the early twentieth century as society came to see children as needing protection instead of a paycheck, then peaked in the 1950s and early '60s as American culture increasingly prized homogeneity of family form. Access to birth control and abortion rights changed that. In 1972, the year before the Supreme Court recognized abortion rights in *Roe v. Wade*, nearly 20 percent of white single mothers placed their babies in adoptive homes. By 1995 that rate decreased to 1.5 percent, and has since dipped to about 1 percent. Black mothers, in contrast, have never relinquished in high numbers. Before *Roe*, barriers to placing black babies and willingness of extended kin networks in the African American community to take them in translated to only about 2 percent of black single mothers surrendering their infants for adoption. Since then the number has dipped to nearly zero. (One reason that any black newborns are adopted is that single African American women have higher birth rates than single white women.) By the late 1980s, a hundred wannabe adoptive parents were chasing every healthy infant available for adoption, according to one estimate.[29]

Many people think of adoptions by strangers as typical, but they account for only about a third of US adoptions. The rest are stepparent adoptions (meaning that a biological parent's new spouse adopts that parent's child) and adoptions out of foster care.

But while the foster care system houses half a million children at any given time, only a tenth of them—around fifty thousand—get adopted each year. That's partly because they're older, averaging age six or seven years, and 80 or 90 percent of them have special needs. They might shuttle through foster care for three years while the state tries to reunite them with birth families, then another year and a half before their adoption becomes final. Most come from poor families, because middle-class kids are more likely to have family friends and relatives who can take them in. Nearly two-thirds are children of color, around 45 percent African American and 14 percent Latino. Only 38 percent are white, though 61 percent of American children are white.[30]

These raw numbers tell only part of the story. Rhetoric used by lawmakers, adoption professionals, and adoptive families also matters.

Parenthood-by-Contract

Scholars speak of law's "expressive function"—its ability to speak both to the parties in a particular case and to the wider society. This expressive function can lead lawmakers to make grand pronouncements about absolute rules that actually have exceptions. Recall from chapter 2 the Massachusetts Supreme Judicial Court's decree in the case of the woman I call Reluctant Girlfriend. The court treated her oral promise to coparent as a deal because, it declared, "'parenthood by contract' is not the law of Massachusetts."[31] That's only a partial truth. True, both law and society blanch at treating kids as items of commerce. But family law in Massachusetts, as elsewhere, routinely uses contracts to sever and create parenthood in the adoption as well as the repro tech arena.

According to Berkeley law professor Joan Hollinger, a leading expert on adoption law and practice, "Bargaining is intrinsic to a transfer of a child by a birth parent in exchange for a promise by adoptive parents or an agency to support and care for the child."[32] Over time, as we've seen, birth parents have gained more bargaining power in the negotiations. Many, like my birth-mom-for-a-moment Conni, want pictures and letters to reassure them that their child is growing up safe and sound, as well as phone calls and in-person visits.

That contact agreement can prevent an agency from breaking its promise to place the child with the adoptive parents selected by the birth mom. Amanda Woolston was an adult when she discovered that the couple that adopted her in 1986 wasn't the one that her birth mom had chosen, and also that the agency had withheld information and a teddy bear that her birth mom had left for Amanda. Not surprisingly, that same agency put up roadblocks when Amanda tried to find her birth mom.[33] Other agencies have done much worse, letting children languish in foster care or institutions after promising the birth parents that the children would be placed with families. While these broken placement promises matter, they have not garnered much legal attention, perhaps because there's little a court can do when an adult adoptee like Amanda finds out that the agency lied.

Anatomy of Adoption

Adoption is not entirely contractual. A driving force behind post-adoption contact agreements (PACAs) is status. Though family relationships are generally a mix of status and contract, the contract terms change, while the status is fairly fixed. Law can erase a social relationship like marriage by granting a divorce, but it's powerless to undo the genetic tie between sisters, brothers, and parents. You could say that there's no such thing as an ex-sister, at least biologically speaking. Birth parents, accordingly, can contract away only part of their parenthood: the rights, duties, and privilege of raising a child.

A list of the five elements of an adoption process shows the interplay of status and contract by designating contractual elements in italics and status elements in bold type:

1. Birth parents generally must *consent* to terminate their legal ties to the child;
2. Birth parents often *select* adoptive parents, after *negotiations* about things like religion, education, and post-adoption contact;
3. The child gets a new birth certificate, officially creating a new **status** relationship that replaces the old one;
4. The records remain closed during the child's minority to protect this new **status** from competition or confusion regarding biological **status**; and
5. The new family is **permanent** and cannot be undone.[34]

Each of these elements is subject to exceptions. The first two—consent and negotiation—don't hold true for many foster-care placements. Birth parents who contest the claims of abuse and neglect that justify a court terminating their parental rights may agree to an open adoption arrangement only to prevent the termination.[35] They're likewise not involved in selecting the adoptive parents. The fifth element—permanence—doesn't apply to situations where a court undoes an adoption that was induced by fraud. Nevertheless, most adoptions involve adults agreeing to sever one family relationship and create another in its place.

The very centrality of contract, coupled with anxiety about baby-selling, may explain the gift rhetoric that runs through most discussions of adoption. Birth mothers are said to "bestow" or "surrender" their children to new parents, "solicitation" is deplored, and most states prohibit finders' fees. In 2005, an Austin TV station ran a series of adoption stories called "Gift of Love." Evangelical Christians often call adoption the "gift of life," a dual reference to discouraging abortions and rescuing, as a member of the Christian Alliance for Orphans put it, "at-risk children who will be sharpened as Arrows for God, and launched back into society to proclaim the Good News of Jesus to the world."[36]

That gift rhetoric may be so big and fluffy because it takes a lot to cover up the big role that contract plays. Adoption generally involves money changing hands. When Columbia University law professor Patricia Williams adopted a brown-skinned baby who arrived at her house in a little blue knitted beanie, the agency charged her a "special" rate—half off—that applied to "older, black and other handicapped children," a policy that seemed to her like a "two-for-one sale."[37] The Cradle today charges $33,900 for domestic adoption. If black or multiracial parents adopt a multiracial child, the fee is reduced to $16,500 to increase choices for a birth mom who wants to place her child with parents of color. Its fee for "medically fragile" children is $7,500, and $12,500 for siblings of children already adopted. The Barker Foundation, in contrast, bases its fees on the adoptive parents' income, starting at $9,000 and going up to $22,500. Reputable adoption agencies like The Cradle and the Barker Foundation don't charge birth moms any fees, and provide them counseling and services so that they can make the best decision for themselves and their children. If they decide to keep the child, they don't have to reimburse the agency or would-be adoptive parents.

Other agencies employ high-pressure tactics. According to a *Boston Globe* article, in 1983, an unmarried Mormon woman named Peggy Hayes sought counsel of her ward bishop, Mitt Romney, about her pregnancy. He told her to surrender her child to LDS Social Services—the adoption arm of the Mormon Church—and that she could be excommunicated if she refused. The message, Peggy said, was "'You will not be saved. You will never see the face of God.'" Another technique is accusing birth mothers who change their minds of breaching faith with the agency or adoptive parents, as when, in 2005, an adoption agency director in Utah raged at a birth mother having second thoughts in the midst of labor, "You can't do this. You made a deal."[38]

Some agencies pressure the birth mom to keep her promises but don't hold themselves to that high standard, a one-sidedness dished out as punishment for a birth mom's sin. A number of these stories come out of Bethany Christian Services, the largest adoption agency in the United States, with 2011 revenues of nearly $75 million generated by one hundred offices in more than thirty states. When twenty-one-year-old Carol Jordan got pregnant in 1999, she called Bethany, which offered her free board and medical care in a single mothers' home, only to deposit her with a "shepherding family" of home-schooling evangelicals hundreds of miles away from the friends and family who could help her decide whether to keep the baby. Only adoption personnel were present at the birth, and when Carol expressed doubts about relinquishing her baby, one told her brusquely that she was on her own if she kept the baby and another said she'd end up homeless and lose the child to foster care. Carol caved and used her last $50 to buy a bus ticket home, where she promptly lost fifty pounds in her grief. When she called Bethany to use the counseling services she'd been promised, the shepherding mother answered the phone and told her sharply, "You're the one who spread your legs and got pregnant out of wedlock. You have no right to grieve for this baby."[39]

Bethany's outsized impact on domestic adoptions justifies a closer look at the agreements it makes with adoptive parents. In addition to promises to pay for placement services common to all agencies, Bethany has adoptive parents sign a "Statement of Faith." It's hardly surprising that a Christian adoption agency seeks out "sincere and committed Christians" to adopt, but it is astounding that the largest adoption agency in the nation—secular or religious—asks adoptive parents and staff to sign a statement that starts out "I believe that the sovereign, triune God created the world," and then declares fidelity to beliefs like "God instituted marriage as a life-long covenant between one man and one woman," "all people . . . live in a world permeated by sin," and "in all matters of faith and life, the Scriptures of the Old and New Testaments are the final authority."[40] Fundamentalist biblical interpretations lead to indicting unmarried mothers and letting men off the hook, an approach that many progressive Christians reject, as do many Jews, atheists, and agnostics.[41]

The Next Generation of Adoption

Right or wrong, the control exercised by adoption agencies may be a thing of the past as the Internet changes adoption practices. With a few keystrokes, a birth mom, adopted teenager, or even grade school adoptee can access all kinds of information. That transfers much of the gatekeeping function away from agencies and into the hands of birth moms, adoptive families, and adoptees themselves through social media like Facebook, search engines, blogs, chat rooms, webinars, and online photo listings.

Like other shifts in adoption practices, the web presents both dangers and possibilities for easing the losses on which adoption is grounded. One birth family contacted a thirteen-year-old adoptee on Facebook, without the adoptive parents' knowledge. In another case, an adult adoptee located her birth family in just four days through census and genealogical websites, tracking down her birth parents' names. This woman, who had thought herself alone in the world, discovered eight brothers and sisters, three of whom she contacted.[42]

These self-help options can skirt legal and agency rules. According to a 2012 report by the Donaldson Institute, the premier adoption think tank, "It is no longer ethical for those who assist in adoption—even in intercountry adoption—to promise secrecy or anonymity to anyone."[43] Fortunately, openness is what most people want, though there's a big range between the openness of having basic biographical information about the birth and adoptive families and spending holidays together. Today only 5 percent of infant adoptions are completely closed, 55 percent are fully open, and the remaining 40 percent are mediated, with information being shared through the agency. The Donaldson Institute report concludes that this contact, in its various forms, "can be, and usually [is] positive."[44]

An Inside View of Birth and Adoptive Families

The British novelist Jeanette Winterson wrote from an adoptee's perspective, first in the 1985 novel *Oranges Are Not the Only Fruit*, which centered around her adoption by a terrifying Pentecostal mother, and years later in a memoir about her actual childhood and finding her birth mother. Upon meeting her birth mother, Winterson found gratifying physical similarities like narrow hips and an "ease we both have in our bodies," as well as character traits like optimism and self-reliance.[45] She also took comfort in knowing that she was conceived in love and that her birth mother was neither a drunk, a slut, nor dead, as the woman she refers to as "Mrs. Winterson" had insisted.

Other adoptees say that those touchstones can help them come to terms with the experience of adoption, develop positive feelings toward their birth mothers, and, when the relationship proves close, benefit from having an additional supportive adult in their lives. Winterson, however, reports that reconnecting with her birth mom left her feeling "warm but wary," mindful that rediscovered parents are no more "instant family" than adoptive kin. The only certain thing, she says, is feeling pleased that her mom is safe.[46]

Birth parents, too, want to know that the kids are all right. Amy Seek, who wrote about the "awkward choreography" of being the birth mom to a boy named Ben, said that the difficulty of being the kind of mother "who surrendered her child but is now back to help him build a Lego castle" is balanced out by "the comfort of seeing my son with his family, whom I can no longer imagine him or myself without."[47]

Once people grieve the losses inherent in adoption, an upside can emerge. According to law professor Annette Appell, adoptive parents who know their children's birth parents are less likely to demonize or fear them. Amy Seek similarly observes that open adoption prevents the birth mother from being "powerfully absent," as she is in closed adoptions. Consequently, Ben's mom can joke to Amy that a benefit of open adoption is that "at least you know what the birth mother is doing, that she's busy at school and not conceiving a plot to steal her child back."[48] The adopted son of actor Dan Bucatinski and his husband, Don, can chat with the boy's birth mom on his fourth birthday and happily thank her "for carrying me in your womb!"[49]

Keep these stories in mind as we turn to law in the next chapter. It focuses on post-adoption contact agreements that went to court, not the hundreds of open adoptions that never fall apart because the people involved kept their promises, more or less. Nevertheless, the law throws a long shadow, even in families that never end up in court.

FIVE

Legal Rules of Adoption Agreements

POST-PARTUM PRESSURE

"Fatherhood is a big responsibility," the somber young man informed Victor.

Victor has to remind me of this line years after we've left the hospital. But even then, struggling through a post-C-section morphine haze to nurse eight-pound Walter without letting any weight rest on my belly, I wondered why so many functionaries were barging into the hospital room, day and night. The motivations of the ones selling baby pictures are obvious, but it's less clear why the social worker keeps reappearing. They must all want a look at the spectacle of a gay man and lesbian who had a baby, we joke. It's especially funny that the social worker keeps coming back to ask Victor whether he's up to being a dad, as if forgetting his answer the minute he walks out the door. But neither of us is laughing when someone wants in at the very moment I undertake the arduous process of getting into street clothes for the first time since I checked into the hospital.

Inching across the linoleum floor to protect my still-sore midsection is hard enough without that insistent knocking. Victor pops his head out the door to ask whoever is out there to come back, and the refusal he gets turns his voice monotone and insistent. As I struggle to get an elastic waistband up over my hips and waist without brushing the wound, he's forcibly keeping the intruder out by leaning on the door, palms flat and fingers splayed, leaving his post only when I'm finally dressed. All through my long, shuffling trek back toward the bed, we exclaim over this persistence. What could he possibly want so badly?

Later, we'll laugh about the earnest young man in the video that the social worker finally drags Victor to see in a little dark room down the hall. "It's clearly for teenage boys," Victor reports when he gets back, shaking his head at the difference between that situation and our middle-aged, very planned parenthood.

A decade later, writing this book helped me finally figure out what that social worker wanted. Telling Victor one day that I'd discovered Utah's reputation as an adoption mill, courtesy of laws that make it much easier for birth parents to relinquish parental rights than in most states, he reminds me about that video. Now the persistent guy who seemed like a harmless rubbernecker—or incompetent—looks more malevolent. His real motivation may well have been to get that non-marital child out of our family and into a nice Mormon one. What I'd thought of as Plan B for everyone might have been Plan A in the Utah hospital's operating procedures for unwed parents.

Fortunately for the peace and tranquility of the maternity wing, that social worker never asked me to give Walter up.

LAW AS IT IS RE OPEN ADOPTION AGREEMENTS

While adoption laws differ from state to state, it's possible to map out general patterns in post-adoption contact agreements, or PACAs. As with reproductive technology, I'll discuss both the general rule and its exceptions. But unlike repro tech, the rules in this area are changing so quickly that the exception may come to swallow the rule.

A General Rule and an Exception

General rules and exceptions operate at two levels. In the country as a whole, the general rule applies everywhere, while some states also allow people to contract into an exception.

Adoption rules, simply stated, provide:

> *General Rule:* Adoption completely severs the relationship between birth parents and the child.
>
> *Exception:* Birth and adoptive parents can contractually agree to post-adoption letters, e-mails, calls, or visits.

Adoptive parents anywhere can make informal agreements to let birth parents stay in their children's lives. The question here is whether those agreements are legally binding contracts, or merely the nonbinding agreements that this book calls "deals." If a PACA is just a deal, then adoptive parents can restrict or forbid communication for good reason, bad reason, or no reason at all.

As of 2013, about half of the United States enforces PACAs as legally binding contracts. These laws, nearly all passed since the 1990s, reflect the larger pattern charted in this book that family law increasingly allows people to decide for themselves who is in the family circle.

A Brief History of Openness in Adoption

While early forms of adoption like placing a child in a foundling asylum were often hush-hush to cover up the shame of an illegitimate birth, few people thought of adoption as completely replacing the birth family until the twentieth century. Until then, the people and agencies charged with placing children generally focused more on finding work or an institution for them than on finding loving and permanent homes. Today adoption advocates call permanent placements "forever families," a phrase evoking a safe and sunny future for kids. Conceiving of adoptive parents as "forever families" can also be backward-looking, erasing the first families through a legal fiction that "forever" also includes the child's life before adoption.

Minnesota headed the pack. In 1917 it was the first to require judges to investigate a child's adoptability and adoptive parents' suitability and also to protect children from stigma by eliminating the word "illegitimate" from birth certificates.[1] Other states followed suit, incrementally obliterating birth parents from the public record. By 1948, nearly every state issued entirely new birth certificates for adopted children, literally papering over their origins.[2] All that confidentiality was supposed to shield people from harm: birth moms and adoptees from the shame of bastardy; adoptees from shocking information like abuse and criminality in their natal families; and adoptive parents from the stigma of sterility. Initially, those beneficiaries could still access those records. But in the decades after World War II, adoption historian Ellen Herman explains, confidentiality "calcified into secrecy," so that even adult adoptees couldn't discover their origins.[3]

You can chart these legal changes through my mom's 1930 adoption. Illinois didn't issue a new birth certificate when she was adopted, but The Cradle created a certificate-like document that listed her new name, birthday, and that she was delivered to the adoption agency nine days later. When she was fifteen years old, a new rule made adoption records confidential, and Illinois later started issuing new birth certificates for adopted children.[4] By 1960, about half the states sealed their records, and by 1990, nearly every state had followed suit, a silencing that adult adoptees and birth parents have managed to overcome in only eight states. In 2010, Illinois, like a handful of other states, opened up its records to allow adult adoptees to access their original birth certificates.[5]

But that's just law, and just relating to birth certificates. For people who want to know, many adoptees and birth families have enough information to find each other without accessing the state's records. The difficulty is that this social openness leads many birth mothers to believe that the law has also opened up to allow emotional and social ties to survive the adoption while half the country still clings to the fiction that adoption can and does completely erase birth families from the picture.

The following four cases show how the legal rules play out in real life families. Alongside legal details like writing requirements we'll encounter stories that convey the emotional toll on birth moms, adopted children, and even adoptive parents when law treats a PACA as an "empty promise," as one adoption professional put it. For a good number of birth moms and adoptees, enforcing that promise can help salve the pain that some adoptees and birth moms experience as a "permanent wound" or "black hole."[6]

Case #1: The General Rule of Disappearing Birth Families: *Stickles* (1931)

After his wife, Mathilda, died, salesman Paul Stickles still managed to spend one day a week—Sunday—with their three-year-old son, Paul Jr., and to check in frequently with the relatives who cared for him. Like most of the country in 1929, Paul must have worried about keeping his job. So his boss Albert Reichardt's offer to adopt the boy may have seemed like an offer he couldn't refuse. Paul may also have figured that it'd be a net gain for the boy, since the Reichardts promised to give the boy "comforts, advantages, and an education," while still allowing Paul to visit out of respect for Paul's "natural ties" to his son.[7] Perhaps Paul trusted those promises, since he'd known Albert for twenty-five years. In any case, Paul accepted the offer. But just four months later the Reichardts broke their promise, cutting off all contact.

Paul took his case all the way to the Wisconsin Supreme Court, a monumental feat in the Depression. He lost. The court held that adoption "destroys the parental relationship . . . and creates a new relationship between the child and its adoptive parents."[8] Paul lost his relationship with his son, and his son lost ties with the man he'd known as his dad his whole life.

Analytically, contract also lost out to status. As noted in chapter 4, up to the early twentieth century, parents routinely contracted their children out to farm, domestic, or industrial work. But the growing view that childhood was a special, protected status developed along-side a trend toward homogenization of family form. Nuclear families emerged as the dominant model, largely replacing households made up of extended kin, boarders, servants, apprentices, and often slaves. Adoption adjusted to fit that new conception of family by crafting rules to make an adoptive family mirror a blood family as closely as possible.

In the *Stickles* case, the Wisconsin Supreme Court declared that "adoptive parents can no more barter away their rights in their adoptive child or modify its status by contract than could a natural parent."[9] It treated parenthood as an all-or-nothing proposition, a status you could contract into and out of but not modify to recognize any variations patched together in the wake of unexpected circumstances like the Depression or Mathilda Stickles's death. It allowed Paul a bit of freedom of contract, observing that he had "voluntarily contracted away his rights," but not the freedom to modify the terms of the adoption agreement to reflect the fact that little Paul Jr. still had a biological dad in addition to the adoptive parents who took him in at three and a half. It achieved this sleight of hand by banishing love and other emotions, explaining that the "emotional appeal" of holding the Reichardts to their word was less important than legal rules mandating that all families look basically the same.[10]

The General Rule Masks Continued Ties to Birth Families

Seven decades later, when Conni interviewed me about the possibility of adopting Taynan, Utah was still following the rule that allowed the Reichardts to break their promise. Any PACA Conni and I negotiated, even signed and notarized, would have been a mere deal, not legally binding.

One New Jersey birth mom, Jeanne, was in a situation a lot like Conni's. Having left school in ninth grade, she too was living with her dad because she couldn't support herself and the toddler she already had. Her dad, like Conni's, said she'd have to move out if she kept the baby.[11] Donna and Steve, an infertile couple, sought Jeanne out and convinced her that the baby would have a better life with them. They promised visits at least twice a month, that Jeanne would be "a big part of the baby's life" and have a special name like "Aunt Jeannie" or "nannie," and that the baby could meet his brother.[12] Donna and Steve broke their promises. The New Jersey Supreme Court saw the PACA Jeanne and the adoptive parents made as just an "informal arrangement," which Donna and Steve could honor or break as they wished.[13] That gives adoptive parents like the Reichardts, like Donna and Steve—and like me, had I not gotten pregnant—too much power. Neither legal principles nor society's interests justify tipping the scales so drastically in favor of adoptive parents, especially since the very economic and social resources that enable people like us to adopt in the first place also arm us to out-lawyer the almost invariably less resourced birth mother.

While New Jersey still refuses to recognize PACAs as contracts, in 2013, Utah opened the door to visitation and sharing of information through pictures and letters but only for kids adopted out of foster care.[14] If Conni and I had agreed to a PACA, it would have been just a deal if she surrendered the child directly to me or through an agency, but it would have been a legally binding contract if we had arranged it through the Utah Division of Child and Family Services. That kind of technicality keeps the game rigged in favor of people who can hire lawyers to explain and exploit the distinction.

States that refuse to recognize PACAs as contracts ignore half of what happens in an adoption. While adoption creates a legal relationship where none existed before, the new family does not and cannot entirely erase the first one. Infants who get adopted can retain emotional and cultural as well as genetic ties with birth relatives, and older children carry still more from their first families. Law can't stifle adoptive children's questions about their origins, nor birth parents' desire to know that their children are safe and sound. Nor should it try.

Today, fully half of US states treat PACAs as legally binding within limits. In all states, contracts relating to kids must be consistent with a child's best interests. A court can set aside a PACA if a birth parent is drunk, disorderly, or abusive. Some states impose additional limits, like Indiana's provision that PACAs are binding only for children over two years old, adopted out of foster care, who have a "significant emotional attachment" to the birth parents.[15] Most important, states that enforce PACAs do not allow a broken visitation agreement to undo the adoption. Instead, courts remedy the breach by ordering the adoptive parents to allow visitation, just as they would when divorced parents squabble over custody.

Meet the Stepparents

The early open adoption cases grew out of no-fault divorce. Before the 1970s, divorcing spouses had to prove that one of them was at "fault" by proving adultery, for example, or abuse. Many divorcing couples perjured themselves to establish fault, creating a whole industry of private investigators who could trump up evidence of infidelity or domestic violence that would let people exit bad marriages. Starting with California, lawmakers, unhappy spouses, and lawyers quickly welcomed no-fault divorce, which required only a bare claim of what California dubbed "irreconcilable differences" to justify ending a marriage.

Though divorce rates peaked in the late 1970s and have decreased since, divorce still shapes the social and legal landscape. As of 1990, just half of marriages—54 percent—were the first for both spouses. Consequently, as of 1994, nearly 7 million American kids, or about 15 percent of all children living with two-parent families, were living in step-families.[16] While stepparents have no rights or duties in relation to the children who they're often deeply involved in raising, the newly formed family can make the stepparent a full legal parent through adoption.[17] That requires terminating one of the genetic parent's rights and duties, because family law generally allows only two people to be legal parents, even when, as in Paul Stickles's case, there are three functional parents.

PACAs can bridge the gap between the two-parent limit and a three-parent reality. Before the 1980s, those PACAs were mere deals, only as strong as the adoptive parents' desire to keep their word. In 1994, the Uniform Adoption Act—a model statute, like the Uniform

Parentage Act explored in chapter 3 on repro tech—proposed treating stepparent PACAs as binding contracts to "give more children the advantage of living in a household with two legal parents . . . while not depriving these children of access to their noncustodial parent's family."[18]

Treating stepparents' PACAs as binding contracts makes particular sense, since another deal often underlies the PACA. Say a father is faced with a daunting bill for past-due child support. When his ex-wife asks him to consent to her new husband adopting their kid, the dad will often say "Okay, as long as you forgive that child support debt." This pay-off is a deal, because courts won't enforce agreements that deprive children of financial support. Nevertheless, it drives many stepparent adoptions.[19]

Case #2: Stepparent Exception: *Weinschel v. Strople* (1983)

Bruno and Sally Ann Weinschel, a well-off couple with homes in Florida and Vail, made their PACA at the same time they resolved their drawn-out custody battle. They were no strangers to family contracting, having entered two reconciliation agreements en route to divorce. When the dust settled, Bruno had custody of their children Lisa and Dana, then nine and six years old. Sally had generous alimony (around $775,000, paid over three years) and visitation (a month in the summer and weeks at Christmas and spring break, in addition to letters and phone calls). But the alimony was contingent on Sally consenting to Bruno's new wife, Shirley, adopting the kids. That meant a court terminating Sally's legal rights and duties regarding her daughters, save for post-adoption contact.

They all did their part for two years, until Lisa's tutoring conflicted with Sally's visitation time. If Sally, Bruno, and Shirley had gotten along well enough to find a new time to visit, we'd never know about the case. But Bruno and Shirley had an agenda to cut Sally off from the children by denying phone contact, returning mail, offering the children rewards to cut visits short, and refusing to let the children call Sally "Mommy." They justified their conduct by claiming that it was confusing for the children to have two moms.

The lower court took the extreme step of undoing the adoption, reasoning that adoption, by definition, severs all aspects of a biological parent's relationship with her kids—including visitation—making adoption with a PACA a contradiction in terms. The Maryland Court of Special Appeals disagreed, allowing the PACA to stand despite the "unusual" nature of the arrangement because, it explained, "[b]eing unusual, however, does not make it illegal, against public policy, or contrary to the best interests of the child."[20]

The message of this book could be expressed in a bumper sticker as "UNUSUAL ≠ ILLEGAL." But unpacking the Maryland court's declaration requires more explanation of what lawyers mean by "illegal," "public policy," and "best interests."

Illegal

Most people think of illegality as designating something as forbidden—like drunk driving—but it has a different meaning in the argot of lawyers. Drunk driving is illegal in that a state statute forbids it and punishes violations with fines and jail time. Agreeing to buy or sell a baby is likewise a crime. But law can also take a neutral position, especially toward controversial agreements. Take gambling debts. Most states don't allow gambling, so casinos generally can't get courts to enforce gamblers' IOUs. Those gambling debts, in lawyer speak, are "unlawful," meaning that the law does not recognize them as legally binding contracts.

Maryland law didn't forbid PACAs, so illegality was not a bar to enforcing Bruno and Sally's agreement. But before the court could enforce the agreement, it had to decide whether the agreement unlawfully violated public policy or undermined the children's best interests.

Public Policy

Some agreements are deals because they violate a public policy like protecting public health, as we saw with the agreement for anonymity between Donor 276 and the California Cryobank in chapter 3. In that case—*Johnson v. Superior Court*—the California courts didn't enforce that promise because it undercut the public policy of protecting Brittany Johnson's need to get information about her kidney disease. The court in *Weinschel* didn't say precisely why Bruno and Sally's PACA didn't run afoul of public policy, but the opinion contains to clues as to the court's reasoning.

Lawyers use the phrase *sub silentio* (Latin for "in silence") to describe how courts can implicitly support ideas. Reading between the lines, we find the court quietly addressing the growing diversity of families wrought by more women joining the work force and increasing numbers of single parents and step-families. The novelty of those changes, even to a judge willing to honor them, is reflected in the court's statement that the divorce court "allowed" Sally to resume using her maiden name.[21] Instead of finding that PACAs violate public policy, the court in *Weinschel* seems to have concluded that PACAs can further the public policy of supporting a blended family. But the court did not express blanket support for PACAs, instead limiting its holding to when the biological and adoptive parents know each other and a PACA can solidify a blended family.

Weinschel was among the first cases of its kind. Even after *Weinschel*, most states still reasoned that PACAs undermine the public policy of lumping all sticks of parenthood into one bundle and calling it a status. *Weinschel* matters for all of us, as well as Lisa and Dana Weinschel and their parents, because it conveys the message that parenthood has contractual elements. Biological and adoptive parents can agree to leave the visitation stick of the "parent" bundle with birth parents like Sally. Shirley, for her part, can retain all the other sticks about raising Lisa and Dana, from deciding where they go to school to whether they celebrate Christmas, Hanukah, or both.

Best Interests of the Child

A final potential bar to enforcing a PACA—the best interests of the child—runs throughout adoption law. Since the first modern adoption statutes in the 1850s, it's become the paramount concern in adoption. But "best interests" is a flexible concept that can produce different outcomes from different judges and changes as childrearing ideas change.[22]

Until the mid-nineteenth century, fathers, as heads of household, were entitled to child custody when marriages ended, while the mothers were entitled to only "reverence and respect," as jurist William Blackstone put it.[23] After the Civil War, Americans' growing tendency to valorize purportedly feminine domestic virtues, which historians call the "Cult of True Womanhood," led courts to start placing children with mothers, at least during their "tender years" when it was thought that only a mother could properly nurture them.[24] Fast forward to the 1970s, when another shift in social mores led family law to adopt a posture of gender neutrality, placing children with both mothers and fathers.[25]

By 1983 the court in *Weinschel* could go one step further. Instead of treating parenthood as an all-or-nothing status and kids as all needing the same thing, it allowed some room for tailoring. Lisa and Dana's best interests could be served by a PACA, even if the best interests of other kids would not. The PACA between birth mom Debbie Groves and Lon and Loralee Clark exemplifies that tailoring. In the 1990s, Lutheran Social Services in Montana helped Debbie and the Clarks negotiate an open adoption that included phone contact with three-year-old Laci, visitation as long as Debbie gave the Clarks two days' notice, and permission for Debbie to take Laci out of school if Debbie had to "go to Butte for some emergency."[26] But the Clarks didn't keep their promise. Because times were changing and Debbie and Laci had a strong and stable bond from their three years of living together, the Montana Supreme Court held that the PACA furthered Laci's best interests, and fine-tuned its terms to give Debbie monthly weekend visits and weekly phone calls. Though the court enforced the PACA, it likely would have refused if, say, Debbie was drinking, using drugs, or otherwise threatening Laci or her adoptive family.[27]

Status and Contract

If "UNUSUAL ≠ ILLEGAL" is a bumper-sticker-length description of this book's core message, a less pithy, but equally accurate, bumper sticker would quote English scholar Sir Henry Maine's 1861 declaration that "the movement of the progressive societies has hitherto been a movement from *Status to Contract*."[28] As if to prove Maine right, the remainder of the nineteenth century saw African Americans shed the status of slaves—mere property instead of people—and acquire rights to contract into marriage as well as employment. Wives of any race gradually emerged from "coverture" (woman's subordinate legal status during marriage) to obtain rights like keeping their wages.

Birth moms, once derided as fallen women, can now make a contractual argument to undo an adoption because their consent to the adoption was the product of force, fraud, or misrepresentation. These defenses, which apply to all kinds of contracts, play a particularly important role in states that treat PACAs as mere deals.

Case #3: The Misrepresentation Exception to Permanence: *Vela v. Marywood* (2000)

Corina Vela found herself pregnant at the outset of her sophomore year at Austin Community College. Worried about burdening her parents and jeopardizing her education, she turned to a Catholic agency called Marywood, which promised her a "sharing plan" in which she would select adoptive parents—Corina wanted Catholic Mexican Americans with no other kids—and get post-adoption visits, letters, and pictures. Although adoptive parents at Marywood all signed a document agreeing to cooperate with the sharing plan, birth mothers like Corina did not. Four days after giving birth, a tearful Corina signed papers to surrender her son but only after Marywood reassured her that "she would have an opportunity to be in that child's life forever," that the baby would have "two mothers, both of whom would have input into his life," and that "the birth family would be like the child's extended family."[29] The counselor testified in court that the sharing plan was an "empty promise," which adoptive parents could honor or break as they liked, but she didn't share that back when Corina asked whether visitation rights were guaranteed. Instead, she assured Corina that Marywood's people would encourage the adoptive parents to respect Corina's wishes.[30]

The very next day Corina asked to visit her son. Two days later, the agency let her, for an hour. That afternoon, Corina told Marywood that she'd changed her mind about the adoption, but the agency said it was too late. In less than two weeks, Marywood got a judge to recommend terminating Corina's rights and placed the baby with adoptive parents, a quickie process that took two years for Corina to undo. She finally got her son back, because any contract can be set aside if one person was tricked into consenting.

The Texas courts found that Marywood had misled Corina into thinking that the PACA was a binding contract. The agency had promised that she'd be part of the child's life, and when Corina asked whether the PACA was legally binding, Marywood doled out "half-truths that would lead a reasonable person in Corina's circumstance to believe she had a continuing right to see her child."[31] The court said that Marywood owed more to this young woman who, "faced with a life-changing situation . . . found comfort in and placed reliance on Marywood's counseling."[32] That child paid a high price for Marywood's misrepresentations and the slow progress of a legal claim through the court system. He lost his first two years with his mom, only to lose, at two, the people he thought of as family. A dozen years later, Marywood closed, due to the steep decline of babies available for adoption. Perhaps that very shortage led the agency to promise Corina a contract when all they really had was a deal.

Technical Difficulties

Contract law generally requires big agreements to be in writing, like selling land or a two-year employment contract, so it's hardly surprising that family law generally requires PACAs to be in writing and signed by everyone involved. Another technicality—incorporation into the decree—would surprise anybody but repeat players like lawyers and adoption agencies.

In California, for example, a PACA must be filed in court and made part of the adoption decree to be legally binding. Carla Moquin's case is illustrative. When she gave birth to Peri, she couldn't see her way to keeping the baby as well as her year-old daughter, especially with her husband unemployed and her marriage crumbling. So she picked a couple whose adoption agency profile promised, "You will . . . become part of our lives forever." They got along so well that they appeared on a Discovery Health Channel show on adoption, and

Carla sent breast milk during the baby's first months. Before the baby was born, they signed an agreement promising photos twice a year, telephone calls, and at least one visit a year. A lawyer should have warned Carla that it was titled "Preliminary Open Adoption Agreement," and that it wasn't legally binding unless filed in court.[33] But birth parents considering adoption generally don't have funds to hire independent counsel.

The adoptive parents never filed the PACA, and less than a week after the adoption was finalized, the adoptive mom told Carla to stop sending parenting-related e-mails. Carla, like Corina Vela, sought to undo the adoption. Unlike Corina, Carla lost her case. The California courts kept the adoption in place and refused to order more contact.[34]

A Nevada birth mom was also taken in by a carefully negotiated and signed agreement for phone calls when the adoptive parents first got home and once a month for the next three months, periodic letters and pictures, a visit near the baby's first three birthdays, and a videotape as the child started walking. The Nevada Supreme Court allowed the adoptive parents to walk away from those promises because the PACA wasn't incorporated into the adoption decree, even though, the court said, many birth parents "fail to realize . . . that, if the agreement is not incorporated in the adoption decree . . . any contact with the child may be had only upon the adoptive parents' permission, regardless of the agreement."[35]

In foster-care adoptions, more birth parents have legal counsel to tell them these things because terminations for abuse and neglect are criminal proceedings. But a birth parent who's trying to hold on to all the sticks in the parenthood bundle often won't bargain for post-adoption phone calls and visits. Foster mother Cris Beam's book *To the End of June* chronicles how this tension, on top of background conditions like trauma, class, race, gender, sexuality, addiction, and youth, all contribute to the often-unhappy endings of foster-care stories.[36]

Case #4: Foster Care Exception: *Adoption of Vito* (2000)

Fortune had dealt eight-year-old Vito a bad hand: he was born to a cocaine-addicted mother whose three older children were already in foster care. But his luck turned a month later, when a Latino foster family took him home from the hospital, treated him as their own, and later sought to adopt him. The odds were against that outcome. Kids in foster care may wait two years for adoption and get shuttled between ten or twenty homes during those long years.[37] Many of the placements add difficulties like an unfamiliar language or religion or cruelty and neglect. Only around 10 percent get adopted into permanent homes each year. Plus, Vito was African American, and black kids can wait twice as long as white kids to get adopted out of foster care.[38]

Vito also benefited from his foster family's willingness to cultivate ties with his birth mom, once she resurfaced in his third year. But by then Spanish had become his mother tongue, imposing language barriers between mother and son during those visits to the Framingham, Massachusetts, prison where she was incarcerated for shoplifting. Even when his English improved, their time together lacked "emotional sharing," the court said, and he easily separated from her at the end of each visit. That's hardly surprising, since the foster family was the only family he'd ever known. He called his foster parents Mom and Dad and saw his foster siblings as his brothers and sisters. Like them, he identified as Latino. He even looked a bit like them.[39]

Agreements vs. Orders

Adoption cuts birth ties to make room for a new relationship with the adoptive family, and in most private adoptions, the birth parents consent to it—albeit with hands forced by circumstances.[40] A principle that lawyers call *parens patriae* (Latin for "parent of the country") justifies the statutes that allow the state to take children whose parents abuse, neglect, or abandon them. As a nineteenth-century jurist put it, courts exercising their *parens patriae* powers are motivated by "all the anxious care and vigilance of a parent" to protect those who have no other lawful protector.[41]

The state stepping into the shoes of Vito's birth mom profoundly changed the situation. The judge was the one making choices in Vito's case, so lawyers call it an "order," an imperious word that captures the non-consensual nature of what was happening. *Vito* presents the rare case of a court-ordered visitation, which I'll call a PACO, or Post-Adoption Contact *Order*, to signal its non-consensual quality.

The government, as we've seen in the chapters on reproductive technologies, generally tries not to intrude into private family life, though poor people are often treated as exceptions to that rule. Here, the foster parents demonstrated their willingness to maintain ties between Vito and his mom by taking him to visit her in prison. But their PACA negotiations with the birth mom went nowhere. Ordinarily, the lack of a PACA would lead a court to apply the general rule and completely sever ties with the birth family. In Vito's case, the trial court extended itself into the family, exercising its *parens patriae* power by ordering eight yearly visits.[42] It had the power to reach out and order those visits, the highest court in Massachusetts held, because "the best interests of a child should not be held hostage to the negotiating skills of adults."[43]

PACO as an Exception to the PACA Exception

Exceptions are usually narrowly defined, lest they swallow the general rule. The court in *Vito* held that a PACO is appropriate only in "compelling circumstances" that further a child's best interests. In the trial judge's view, Vito's best interest, as an African American boy being raised Latino, was to maintain connections to his birth family to help him solidify his racial and ethnic identity during his teen years. But the appellate court disagreed, finding the racial reasons too speculative. Instead, the legal question was whether Vito and his birth mom shared a "significant, existing bond." Finding no evidence of a bond, the court held that a PACO was inappropriate for Vito. His adoptive parents, the court said, would be the ones to exercise "wise guidance" to help him navigate his transracial adoption.[44]

The Massachusetts courts' back-and-forth over transracial adoption mirrored splits between adoption professionals. We saw in chapter 4 that agencies and white adoptive parents commonly deemed black children "unsuitable" for adoption until the 1950s and 1960s. Then, in 1972, when most adoption professionals had rejected that view, the National Association of Black Social Workers opposed transracial adoption to help African American kids form a "total sense" of themselves "physically, psychologically, and culturally."[45] Vito's need for close ties within his race seems to have influenced the first judge who heard Vito's adoption case, as it has with some scholars, though it has never gained widespread legal traction.[46]

Divisions of class and sexuality posed additional challenges for another foster-care adoption—of Cardel, Raine, and Ravyn, black siblings ranging from two to six years old when they were adopted by Kelly Vielmo and Jack Montgomery, a white gay couple in Washington, DC. The children's birth mom knew she couldn't raise them, yet didn't want to give them up. Finally, a judge placed them with Kelly and Jack. The couple set up a personal blog for the mom so she could follow their progress through photos, drawings, and stories from the kids' lives. The birth dad, however, balked when faced with the prospect of white gay strangers raising his children. That changed on the third day of trial, when the birth dad spent a little time with the new dads and Cardel, the four guys playing paper airplanes outside the courthouse. Back in the courtroom, the birth dad took the stand to tearfully announce that Cardel "would do well with them, that he was in the right place." After the adoption was finalized, he said, "Cardel will have opportunities I never had."[47]

As in most adoptions, everyone would have chosen a more common parenthood experience. Birth parents would keep their children, and most adoptive parents tried to conceive through either sex or repro tech before turning to adoption. Since college, I've wished that two eggs could make a baby, so that my lady love and I could have a child genetically linked to both of us. But once you're in Plan B, you start to appreciate the beauty of its landscape. Indeed, many adoptive parents say they wish they'd just started there instead of wasting years banging their heads against barriers to Plan A.

LAW AS IT SHOULD BE RE PACAS

According to adoption scholar Joan Hollinger, "'Openness' has become the mantra of contemporary adoption."[48] Benefits include remedying some of biological parents'—especially birth moms'—sense of loss, giving adopted kids "a piece of themselves missing from their otherwise secure adoptive family relationships," and giving adoptive parents information vital to meeting child's medical, developmental, and emotional needs.[49] Since some birth moms voluntarily relinquish their children only if they get post-adoption contact, a PACA might also save a child from years of dislocation in foster homes.

Hollinger notes that many adoptive parents prefer to limit that contact to annual letters and photos, fearing, she says, "entanglements that raise the specter of shared parenting."[50] Family law also proceeded with caution. California gradually recognized PACAs as legally binding, first for relative adoptions, then for adoption by non-relatives (but allowing visitation only if the child had an "existing relationship" with the birth parent), and finally to all adopted children, as long as it's in the child's best interest.[51]

Open adoption is relatively new, and enforceable PACAs are of even more recent vintage, so researchers are still charting their impact on kids. Adoption researchers Harold Grotevant and Ruth McRoy's 1998 study of open adoption arrangements suggests that they often involve "more pain up front" but in three to four years, the kids and both adoptive and birth parents are "much more settled" than in closed adoptions.[52] They also report that open adoption works best when the families choose the type of contact, prepare for it, and put their agreement into writing. It helps if the birth mom has had more education and the child hasn't been mistreated.[53] Because not everyone fits this profile, the researchers conclude that "a variety of adoption arrangements should be available by practice and by law."[54]

Joan Hollinger remains cautious about treating PACAs as contracts, noting that the Grotevant study involved only children adopted as infants, adoptive parents who were mostly white and upper-middle-class, and PACAs that were mere deals. It could be, Hollinger suggests, that binding PACAs are more problematic for kids who are older or have special needs.[55] It's possible to accommodate Hollinger's concerns and also recognize PACAs. On the law side, family law could allow for variety with clear, simple rules that allow PACA enforcement as well as an unambiguous way to designate a particular

PACA as a mere deal. As a matter of policy, adoption professionals could recommend binding PACAs only when the people choose it, prepare for it, and commit their agreement to writing.

The Massachusetts Model

In 1851, Massachusetts passed the first modern adoption statute, and today its open adoption statute could provide a model for enforcing PACAs. In the *Vito* case, we saw that Massachusetts courts recognize a judge's power to order post-adoption visitation when it's in the child's best interest, and the Massachusetts legislature has likewise enacted a PACA rule that balances the interests of everyone in the adoption triad.

PACAs are binding contracts in Massachusetts if

- The birth and adoptive parents agree to contact before the adoption.
- The court approves the PACA's terms, making sure that it
  - Protects the child's best interests
  - Has fair terms
  - Was not entered into under coercion or duress
  - Is notarized and
  - Is signed by the child if he or she is over age twelve

Massachusetts PACAs must also contain two clauses that should help prevent misunderstandings. The first states that breaching the PACA won't undo the adoption and that a court will instead hold the adoptive parents to their promises, a remedy lawyers call "specific performance." The second clause states that no one has relied on promises outside the written agreement, preventing adoptive or birth parents from arguing that the "real" agreement was for something other than what they agreed to on paper. The PACA is then filed in court and made part of the adoption decree. If circumstances change, courts can modify it, though only to reduce, not increase, contact.

If Paul Stickles had made his PACA with the Reichardts in Massachusetts instead of Wisconsin, and in 2014 instead of 1929, he could have continued visiting his son on Sundays as long as the PACA was in writing, was made part of the adoption decree, a court ensured that its terms were in the child's best interests and fair, that Paul didn't sign under duress, and that Paul signed knowing that the Reichardts' breach would not undo the adoption. That court couldn't increase the visits, though it could reduce or even stop them if it found that they harmed Paul Jr.

These contractual protections don't prevent the losses that are part and parcel of adoption, but they can reduce them. Most important, the states like Massachusetts that treat PACAs as binding contracts have made the adoption process incorporate the experiences of both the birth parents and adoptees. Take Jacqueline Michaud's 1983 PACA with James and Cynthia Wawruck. Alongside provisions about the frequency and location of visitation—"twice a month for three (3) hours each visit at the Wawrucks' home"—it required the adults to take into account the girl's "tender years," and her "high sensitivity to her . . . state of uncertainty." Like the parenting agreements Victor, Karen, and I signed, Jacqueline and the Wawrucks' PACA included promises not to bad-talk each other, using the very same terms we did: "good faith" and "respect and affection."[56] When the Wawrucks broke those carefully negotiated promises, a judge acknowledged the love underlying the PACA as well as the different forms that families take:

> Traditional models of the nuclear family have come, in recent years, to be replaced by various configurations of parents, stepparents, adoptive parents, and grandparents. We are not prepared to assume that the welfare of children is best served by a narrow definition of those whom we permit to continue to manifest their deep concern for a child's growth and development . . . [I]n the present case the "Open Adoption and Visitation Agreement" was openly and lovingly negotiated, in good faith, in order to promote the best interest of the child.[57]

The word "lovingly" too seldom appears in adoption cases, but the even more striking language of the *Wawruck* case comes from the nine-year-old daughter. Speaking to her attorney, she said that an agreement between her birth mom and adoptive mom would be "the best world that she could imagine."[58]

She's right. Plan B parenthood is an imaginative enterprise. So is Plan B romance, which I turn to in the coming chapters.

PART II

Plan B Partnership

The next four chapters address agreements between adult partners who make emotional and financial contracts and deals, looking first to cohabitation and then to marriage. Coupled with stories of uncommon parenthood covered in earlier chapters, these different arrangements show that there's no such thing as "the" traditional American family. Though marriage remains the most common model, people form families in different ways when law, finances, personal preferences, or plain inertia lead them to cohabit instead.

First, I'll map law's approach to cohabitation agreements, then to premarital agreements. As with repro tech and adoption, the rules have changed over time and today some states are friendlier to these arrangements than others. Overall, the trend mirrors Plan B parenthood, with states increasingly recognizing that love comes in different packages, and that uncommon is not a synonym for unnatural.

In addition, these adult-only agreements introduce a second big theme of this book. In both cohabitation and marriage, it's common for one partner to focus on keeping house while the other keeps up the family bank account. But family law tends to devalue the homemaking side of this exchange. The law, the next four chapters show, could and should remedy that legal myopia and value caregiving as highly as wage labor, and also honor other nonmonetary contributions to family life, like fidelity. The stories of Plan B partnership in this section show that all kinds of American families have been making a wide variety of contracts and deals since the country's founding.

SIX

Basics of Cohabitation Agreements

CONTINGENCIES

"An offer without contingencies? Are you sure that's a good idea?" I ask Karen.

Buying this little brick colonial is our first big contract, a starter contract to see if marriage might work. It's early 2008, the tip top of an already in-flated housing market in Washington, DC, so buying is probably not smart, and the realtor's insistence that we make a non-contingent offer above ask-ing price seems like one lunacy too many. At least Karen and I are both lawyers who have bought and sold a couple of houses before, so we know that a contingency would let us out of this contract if we can't get a bank to lend us money.

Assuring us that we won't have any trouble finding a lender, the realtor reminds us that we got outbid by a family from California on that house around the corner two weeks ago. After more back-and-forth, Karen and I finally sign the non-contingent offer. If this deal falls through because we can't get a loan, we're out half of the down payment for the whole house.

We still don't have a mortgage a week later when the investment bank Bear Stearns collapses nor when rumors start flying that the two huge national banks holding our savings accounts might collapse. Then, when we finally find a bank willing to lend to us, my blood pressure spikes even higher when the loan officer insists we sign a loan agreement containing a huge error.

"I'm not going to sign an agreement that puts us in default the moment we sign," I tell him for the third time. Again, he insists that it's just a technicality and he can't correct the error. Karen and I go back and forth about whether to sign.

Finally, a magic word from contract law offers a way out. When I tell the loan officer that I'll happily sign if the bank "indemnifies" us against loss due to any misstatements in the paperwork, the loan officer knows that I'm saying they'd bear the risk for any mistakes. Within hours, the bank makes the change that he said was impossible.

That mortgage is the only formal contract Karen and I make when we move in together. Like many live-in couples, we make sure we're both on the title of the house but don't write out a formal living-together agreement setting out who owns everything else. I do pull power of attorney forms off of the web so that we can make financial and medical decisions for one another if disability strikes, but there are no wills or any explicit promises about Karen's relationship to Walter. Partly that's because I'm the one who would push for a signed document, and I'm worried that a formal cohabitation agreement might make marriage seem unnecessary. We may not be an "us" yet in relation to Walter—legally, Karen would be a stranger to him if we broke up—but making sure that we're both on the house title and working out when to take contractual risks like that non-contingent offer make Karen and me an "us" in other ways.

It would be different if one of us was home full-time, or if Walter and I were moving into Karen's townhouse. If Karen and my positions were switched, I'd have wanted an explicit agreement about my role in Walter's life. But Karen's temperature runs lower than mine, letting her trust that if things unfold in a non-family direction, I wouldn't cut her off from the boy who calls her Gaty.

————————

FIVE STORIES OF COHABITATION

Love in the Time of the Colonies

Unmarried couples have lived together from the very founding of our country. Consider Charles Carrollton, who signed the Declaration of Independence and served as Maryland's first US senator. His rich and influential parents, Lord Carrollton and Elizabeth Brooke, didn't marry until Charles was twenty years old. All through his childhood, they lived together as an unmarried couple in Annapolis.[1] They were hardly the only ones. According to historian Nancy Cott, colonists often got married only when the woman got pregnant. Although rich people might host elaborate weddings to show off their wealth for friends and neighbors, many others, especially in the south and rural areas, entered what Cott calls "informal marriages" because clergy and government magistrates were so scarce. Instead of having a wedding, these couples became "married" by following three steps: (1) consenting to marry; (2) moving in together; and (3) exchanging the husband's support for the wife's domestic services.[2] According to Cott, this conduct plus community approval for the union mattered as much or more than legal formalities.[3]

This history is important because it shows that American family law has been willing to let actions speak as loudly as formal agreements on paper, at least when social norms recognize the relationship. Today, the social acceptability of cohabitation may well justify law following suit to honor the often implicit promises made within cohabiting couples.

Bargaining in the Shadow of Slavery

Law has respected some arrangements more than others. Consistent with documentarian Ken Burns's assertion that "race is at the center of all American history,"[4] legal rules governing cohabitation have had a racial cast. Until Reconstruction, family law deprived slaves of the right to marry, rendering their intimate relationships less respectable and making them seem more like animals than civilized human beings. Consequently, enslaved people had no choice but to enter informal unions known as "taking up" or "sweethearting."[5] While masters might allow or even encourage slaves to create more formal families through makeshift ceremonies that could involve jumping a broomstick, those unions remained outside legal protection. A master could and often did disregard the union by selling off one member of the family or sexually imposing himself on the "wife."[6]

The conduct that produced Thomas Jefferson and Sally Hemings's six children was nominally unlawful in many places under statutes banning interracial sex as well as marriage between whites and "Negroes."[7] However, the masters were seldom punished, because these laws were meant to protect white supremacy, not black women. Prosecuting white men would have disturbed their ability to increase their slaveholdings by siring baby slaves and also undermined slavery by honoring enslaved women's humanity. Accordingly, more states nullified interracial marriage than criminalized interracial sex or living together (then known by the exotic term "concubinage").[8] Fornication—non-marital sex—was also a crime, handily making an interracial couple's intimacies unlawful even where the law forbade only interracial marriage.

Many African American men paid with their lives for having sex with white women, or even being suspected of it. In 1934, a group of three hundred white supremacists from the Florida panhandle took action against a twenty-three-year-old black farmhand named Claude Neal because of his relationship with a white woman, Lola Cannidy. They abducted him, castrated him in the woods, hanged him to the point of choking, then lowered him to continue cutting off body parts. Not one of these assailants was ever charged or spent a day in jail for Claude's death.[9]

White men who engaged in interracial intimacy themselves often escaped criminal punishment and lynching, and some even dared to openly flout the ban. Richard Mentor Johnson's relationship with his "octoroon" slave Julia Chinn didn't keep him from being elected Martin Van Buren's vice president in 1836. Richard lived with Julia in the early decades of the nineteenth century, treating her with the dignity due a wife even though Kentucky would not let them marry.

He also educated their daughters Adaline and Imogene and gave them property after they married. But when Richard died, his brothers inherited his estate, because Kentucky law refused to recognize Julia as his legal wife or the girls as his legitimate children.[10]

Richard Johnson might have contracted around this outcome by making a will. In 1887 the Georgia Supreme Court allowed one of the richest planters in Georgia, David Dickson, to bequeath the bulk of an estate worth half a million dollars—the equivalent of $12 million in 2013—to Amanda Dickson, the daughter he had by his teenage slave, also named Julia, before the Civil War.[11] Although David would not have been able to marry Julia in Georgia, the court said that he could use a will to provide for Amanda, reasoning that "a testator, by his will, may make any disposition of his property, not inconsistent with the laws or contrary to the policy of the State," even to benefit "a bastard" or "a colored woman and her children."[12] Today many states apply the same rule to same-sex couples, allowing them to provide for one another through wills and other agreements but refusing to fully recognize them as family.

Do-It-Yourself Marriage

Family law has treated some cohabitants as family through common law marriage. But common law marriage rules are so complex and varied that couples can easily stumble into the cohabitation version of Plan B while believing that they are married. Although many people think that common law marriage requires a period of living together, it actually only requires consent and holding out as husband and wife. Much of the country used to recognize common law marriage, but as of 2009 only ten states and the District of Columbia recognized it.[13] That change has led couples like Victoria and Robert Hewitt to mistakenly believe that they are common law spouses. When Victoria got pregnant in 1960, she and Robert were college students in Grinnell, Iowa. They entered what Iowa would have recognized as a common law marriage when Robert told Victoria that they didn't need a ceremony to be husband and wife and that he'd "share his life, his future, his earning and his property" with her.[14] She took his name, and they told their parents they were married. They moved to Illinois, where he went to dental school while she took care of their home and three children. Later, she worked in his office. But when they separated after fifteen years together, Mrs. Hewitt found out that Illinois saw her relationship as "illicit" and "meretricious," a fancy word for prostitution.[15] Although Illinois would have treated their marriage as legal a century earlier, it had abolished common law marriage in 1905.

Unfortunately for people like Victoria, Illinois is among the few states that have not replaced common law marriage with new rules that honor living-together contracts. It reaffirmed its disdain for cohabitation exchanges as mere deals in 2006, when Eugene Costa made claims based on living with Catherine Oliven for twenty-four years, playing the role of stay-at-home dad and homeschooling their daughter, Elsa, while Catherine built up her business. Catherine put all the property in her name, so when they separated, Eugene had no right to anything.[16]

Homemakers, male and female, deserve better. A California case led the way, giving lawyers a shorthand for living-together exchanges: "Marvin agreements."

Marvin Agreements

The original Marvin agreement came into being because Lee Marvin's sixteen-year marriage kept him from marrying Michelle Triola, an aspiring singer. They moved in together in 1965, and Michelle took his name, as many cohabiting women do. Lee promised to support her for life and in exchange, she would give up her singing career to become his full-time "companion, homemaker, housekeeper, and cook."[17] Seven years later, they broke up, and in 1976—exactly two hundred years after Charles Carrollton, the son of non-married parents, signed the Declaration of Independence—the California Supreme Court resolved their dispute in the landmark case *Marvin v. Marvin*, which allowed Michelle to sue for breach of this contract to exchange homemaking for financial support. That decision brought the term "palimony" into popular speech. A cross between "pal" and "alimony," it reflects cohabitants' existence in the borderland between friends and family. Having a new word to describe Michelle's claim helped family law and the public recognize the new view of cohabitation, just as this book's new terminology—Plan A and Plan B families—seeks to make room for other uncommon family connections.

While most states followed California's lead, in the actual *Marvin* case, Michelle won the battle but lost on appeal. Lee never paid any of the $104,000 the trial court awarded her.[18] When Michelle moved in with actor Dick Van Dyke in the late 1970s, she got their cohabitation agreement in writing.[19] That their partnership lasted until she died three decades later may evidence the benefits of signing on the dotted line.

There's a Limit

Living-together agreements are limited by the same factors that keep courts from enforcing some ordinary business agreements. In families as well as business, courts will not enforce agreements if someone signs under duress or the terms are grossly one-sided. With cohabitation agreements, family law also refuses to enforce an agreement that's basically money for sex, slapping it with the label "meretricious." Consequently some living-together agreements are just deals, like Catholic Archbishop Eugene Marino's promise to Vicki Long that he'd financially support her in exchange for living together and sexual intimacy.[20] Nor will courts enforce agreements between people who are dating, like the promise of sixty-five-year-old former Lockheed president Duane Wood to support German actress Birgit Bergen if she would be his "companion, his confidante, homemaker, and . . . social hostess."[21] Because Duane and Birgit never lived together in their seven years as a couple, the court said that she never provided the "domestic services which . . . amount to lawful consideration for a [palimony] contract."[22]

COHABITATION 101

Given that many unmarried couples have lived together without marrying throughout American history and that more couples cohabit every year, it seems strange that family law has pretended that marriage is the only way to form a family. Invidious discrimination provides part of the explanation, particularly when you consider the historical bar against interracial marriage and today's just-now-receding ban on same-sex marriage. But there are also good reasons to treat marriage as Plan A and give spouses more rights and duties than live-in couples. Most cohabitants strike different contracts and deals with each other than spouses do. A few vital statistics and a brief survey of what experts in economics, sociology, anthropology, and psychology say about family exchanges show how family agreements work and why it makes sense for law and society to recognize cohabitation as a kind of marriage à la carte.

Vital Statistics

Family law needed to honor Marvin agreements because millions of Americans were openly living together. Between 1960 and 2000, cohabitation rates increased 1000 percent. In that period, the number of cohabiting couple households in America went from less than half a million to nearly five million.[23] The numbers continue to rise, with a 39 percent increase over the first eight years of the twenty-first century, an average of more than 237,000 households a year.[24]

But even with this increase, five times more households are made up of married couples. Every decade of the twentieth century, around 90 percent of Americans had married at some point in their lives.[25] As of the 2010 Census, married couples comprised nearly half (48 percent) of US households, a statistic revealing that marriage remains Plan A for most people even as divorce rates hover around 40 percent.[26] That same year, the next most common household after marriage consisted of a person living alone (27 percent), followed by cohabiting couples (10 percent).[27] Though the continued prevalence of marriage is partly due to remarriage, that fact only confirms the gravitational pull of marriage for most people.

Marriage and cohabitation, in short, are alternative ways of forming adult partnerships. Before I consider how law ought to treat people like Eugene Costa and Michelle Marvin, it's worth noting what experts outside the law have to say about common exchanges that couples make.

Expert Views of the Care and Feeding of Families

Economists, sociologists, anthropologists, and psychologists all offer insights about the importance of exchange in couples' lives. The key here is recognizing the continuing relevance of the common swap of financial support for homemaking that I call the "pair-bond exchange."

No Such Thing as a Free Lunch

A whole branch of economics known as "home economics" explores reciprocal exchange in families.[28] While many people resist this frame, arguing that few of us experience the back-and-forth of family life as a quid pro quo exchange, these economists argue that underneath the seeming gifts of family life are exchanges hidden in plain sight. Consider Barack and Michelle Obama. Barack tells a story of Michelle's exasperation as his political star rose, pulling him away from family activities well before his memoir made them financially secure: "You're gone all the time and we're broke?" she asked him. "How's that a good deal?"[29] Those expectations are common. A husband's probably in the doghouse if his wife throws him a birthday bash and he never even gets her a card. He may get a pass during an unusually hectic time, as Barack probably got to speak to the Democratic National Convention, as long as he shows up in other ways. Even as president, Barack makes time for regular date nights with Michelle, and just about all of us reasonably expect some back-and-forth in making dinner, paying for groceries, cleaning up, paying the rent, doing the laundry, mowing the lawn, and making the bed.

Nobel laureate economist Gary Becker views marriage as "a written, oral, or customary long-term contract between a man and a woman to produce children, food and other commodities in a common household," with one partner specializing in homemaking and the other in wage labor.[30] In this view, the slacker spouse is a free rider—like a commuter jumping the turnstile—for taking your time, money, and attention without "paying" by reciprocating.[31] Unsurprisingly, the discipline known as the dismal science generally ignores the role of love. Becker's even been known to bracket the word in scare quotes ("love"),[32] though another leading economic theorist, Judge Richard Posner, adds evolutionary biology to economic analysis in his book *Sex and Reason*, to better explain what he calls the "emotional character of the love bond."[33]

Economic Lives

Viviana Zelizer, the economic sociologist whose work was mentioned in the adoption chapters, critiques that view as reductionist. But she doesn't embrace the other extreme, which treats love and exchange as opposites. Instead, Zelizer sees markets as both shaping and being shaped by social ties, dubbing this view "Economic Lives." She also coined terms for the other approaches, "Nothing But" and "Hostile Worlds."[34]

Zelizer sees Chicago-school law and economics scholars like Becker and Posner as mistakenly committing the analytical error of Nothing But. This approach sees the world as transacting business of all sorts in a single currency, from sex to Slurpees. Through that lens, an interaction is all economic exchange or all something else like coercion.

Hostile Worlds approaches, in contrast, see sharp, impermeable boundaries between money and contested commodities like love, babies, and body parts and claim that any overlap between markets and intimacy will contaminate one or both. The very opposite of Nothing But views, Hostile Worlds analysis treats love and contracts as realms so far away from each other that the currency of one has no meaning or value in the other. For example, the court in the *Baby M* surrogacy case discussed in chapter 2 refused to enforce a surrogacy contract between Mary Beth Whitehead and William Stern, declaring: "There are, in a civilized society, some things that money cannot buy."[35] The $3 billion a year market in reproductive technologies could not exist if this were true.

Courts have also taken a Hostile Worlds approach when examining pair-bond exchanges. Back in 1889 the Iowa Supreme Court treated Nancy Miller's homemaking labor as a pure gift when it refused to enforce her husband Robert's formal, written promise to pay her $200 a year to "keep her home and family in a comfortable and reasonably good condition" in exchange for him providing "the necessary expenses of the family."[36] The Millers were trying to patch things up after Robert ran around with other women. Alongside promises to pay for homemaking, they agreed that "past subjects and causes of dispute, disagreement and complaint" would be "absolutely ignored and buried."[37] But rather than enforce the Millers' carefully worded reconciliation agreement, the court demoted it to a mere deal because, it reasoned, Nancy did only what "the law already required her to do."[38]

According to Zelizer, both views distort the reality of family life. Seeing a dinner date as Nothing But a market exchange of a meal for sexual favors afterward ignores crucial aspects of social life, just as a Hostile Worlds view of that same dinner fails to explain why a woman not wanting sexual intimacy might insist on splitting the bill. Nothing But views bleach out love and other emotions, while Hostile Worlds approaches bleach out exchange elements of intimacy.

Reciprocal Gift Exchanges

Anthropologist Marcel Mauss provides another model that accommodates both exchange and emotion. According to Mauss, a gift usually comes with an obligation to reciprocate—a back-and-forth that creates a social and even spiritual bond. The slacker husband in this view dishonors himself by failing to reciprocate all of his wife's "gifts." She'd be better off finding someone more adept at holding up his end of what Mauss calls "gift exchanges."[39]

Expectations of reciprocity also hold sway outside the family. Tithing 10 percent of your income is part of many religious communities, and some people say it helps pave the way to eternal life. Carpoolers take turns behind the wheel. Colleagues swap information to get ahead at work. It's hard to imagine any kind of genuine, lasting relationship that doesn't include both giving and getting: not a tit-for-tat with precise accounting but instead something more along the lines of a tit for two or three tats.

Pair-Bond Exchanges

Evolutionary biologists take a different route to the same conclusion. Viewing life through the lens of natural selection, they see exchange as a cornerstone to family and indeed, the human family. [40] According to sociobiologists, our proto-human ancestors started an exchange that changed everything, providing the building blocks for both family and social organization.

Anthropologist Helen Fisher tells a vivid story of our hairy foremothers spending much of their days collecting roots and other vegetables while their male counterparts ranged over wider territory, hunting. Although their ancestors had mated freely, these protohumans gradually formed what Fisher dubs "the most fundamental exchange the human race would ever make."[41] A female would focus her sexual and grooming attention on a male and share her foraged vegetables with him; he, in turn, would share his proceeds from the hunt. Whether these relationships lasted a few months, a year, or a lifetime, they were reciprocal. The female expected a share of the meat the male hunted, and he expected sexual access and a share of "her" vegetables. Gradually, Fisher contends, males also began to protect females from dangers, and over thousands of years, also began to help feed and protect the young. That exchange slowly transformed those children from "hers" into "theirs." This account, if true, provides a genealogy of the pair-bond exchange.

E. O. Wilson, the father of sociobiology, contends that these male-female pair-bonds helped greatly in caring for completely helpless human babies and raising kids through the ten-plus years it takes humans to become self-sufficient. Pooling their resources was absolutely essential to get expensive-to-rear children to reproductive age so they could start the cycle again.[42]

Wilson also suggests that pair-bonding brought us society itself. Over millennia, he asserts, our distant ancestors extended these reciprocal exchange networks, first between families, then eventually—unlike other species—even between strangers.[43] This last stage defines human society for Wilson:

Reciprocation among distantly related or unrelated individuals is the key to human society. The perfection of the social contract has broken the ancient vertebrate constraints imposed by rigid kin selection. Through the convention of reciprocation . . . human beings fashion long-remembered agreements upon which cultures and civilizations can be built.[44]

In sum, a wide range of scholars echo the central claim of this book, that love and contracts are not opposites. To the contrary, economists, sociologists, anthropologists, and evolutionary scientists have concluded that it's entirely natural to speak of families and exchange in the same breath. If they're right, families can't be undermined by talking about family-based exchanges because families are already chock-filled with them.

Family law, we'll see, easily acknowledges half of that truth by recognizing the provider side of pair-bond exchange agreements. But when it comes to valuing the caretaking half, it's a different story. Before I examine the legal rules' tendency to undervalue the homemaking half of pair-bond exchanges, let's pause to examine what those lawmakers are missing.

Tending

While the studies we've discussed have looked at both ends of the pair-bond exchange, UCLA psychologist Shelley Taylor zooms in on the caregiving half, which falls within the larger category known as "social affiliation." She argues that social connections are so important that we come out of the box programmed to connect, a drive so strong that she dubs it the "tending instinct."[45]

Taylor didn't set out to study tending but stumbled on its impact in her laboratory studies about how stress affects health. In study after study, she found that good tending reduces stress and its emotional, physical, and social toll.[46] Bad tending, in turn, increases stress and its consequences. People who are abused or neglected as children have more health and emotional problems as adults, including depression, drug and alcohol abuse, heart disease, diabetes, and cancer.[47]

Conversely, people with close, supportive ties to family and friends are less likely to get sick—from cancer or colds—and when they do, the disease is often less severe.[48] In one study, terminally ill cancer patients who shared their feelings in a support group lived nearly a year and a half longer on average than members of a control group who suffered on their own.[49] Having just one good friend at work translates to fewer sick days.[50] No wonder divorce and a spouse's death are among the most stressful events that a person ever experiences.[51]

Taylor sums up her findings about the deep-seated drive to take care of others with the phrase "tend and befriend" and argues that this instinct complements the better-known "fight or flight" response to stress.[52] According to Taylor, tend-and-befriend behavior catalyzed human evolution:

> Calming the young and getting them out of harm's way can ensure that their lives will continue. But protecting both yourself and your offspring is a formidable task, and so women who drew effectively on the social group for help may have more successfully dealt with threats than those who did not—hence the befriending response.[53]

That "formidable" tending work deserves respect and protection. According to Taylor, we would not be human without it. Yet, as she puts it, "social support is often at its best when it's invisible, present only as a protective but unused resource."[54] This very invisibility has too long kept families and family law from fully acknowledging the credit that caregivers deserve for bestowing the benefits of all that tending.

Tending and Cohabitation

Having canvassed scholarly views of family exchanges, we now turn back to the subject of this chapter, cohabitation. Living together as a couple—married or unmarried—provides some of the deepest social connections of our lives. That kind of social connection, Taylor argues, is "as natural, as biologically based, as searching for food or sleeping."[55] Her insight echoes another core theme of this book—that love comes in different packages. Because, as Taylor puts it, "nature does not leave vital tasks to chance," we have backups to ensure that essential functions like social connection will be performed.[56]

Everyday experience confirms that observation. Architects design skyscrapers with both elevators and stairs, treating elevators as Plan A—the common route—and stairs as Plan B for more unusual circumstances like emergencies and when people want a workout.

The building metaphor illustrates a related point. We've seen in each chapter that family law rules change over time as technology and social mores push and pull them in various directions. A century ago, for example, family law let men abandon their non-marital children by freeing the men of paternal duties like support. Today changing views of family and gender roles have led law to require men to support all their children, whether born in or out of marriage. Along the same lines, early nineteenth-century architects designed buildings assuming that people would take the stairs, but the advent of elevators and escalators made them the main mode of moving from floor to floor, relegating stairs to a Plan B route. A greening twenty-first century may well place stairs more centrally to encourage their use, and elevators in locations suited for wheelchairs and ascent to the heights of skyscrapers.

Family law can do the same. If social connection ranks right up there with food and sleep, people, given a choice, will generally prefer a reliable source of that connection. Marriage, in this view, is Plan A for most people—and therefore for family law—because it represents the longest-lasting reliable form of chosen family connection. Despite growing rates of cohabitation and living alone, Americans continue to see marriage as the optimal arrangement.[57]

Even so, marriage is not for everyone. Law forbids people to marry if they're already married to someone else, and also in much of the country if they have a same-sex partner. Often one or both partners are unwilling to marry as a matter of ideology or ambivalence, or the couple simply gives in to inertia. The fact that as of 2010, married households still outnumbered cohabiting ones by five to one need not translate to a legal erasure of cohabitants from the landscape of legitimate relationships any more than the fact that five times more people take the elevator in a building should lead to destruction of the stairs. Law can simultaneously encourage stable connections and acknowledge other forms that connection takes.

Gender Roles in Pair-Bonding

In all kinds of relationships, women continue to do much of the tending for the men, children, and other women in their lives. The rise of so-called helicopter parenting—from supervised playdates to parents' presence at every soccer practice—has only increased the time and effort tending entails.[58] Today's American fathers change more diapers than their fathers did, but they still do much less of the work it takes to maintain a household and care for kids, leaving women holding the grocery bags most of the time.[59] On an average day in 2012, only 20 percent of men did housework like cleaning or laundry, compared with 48 percent of women. Moms of young children spent 1.1 hours bathing or feeding them each day, two and a half times more than dads, who spent just twenty-six minutes on these tasks.[60] Not surprisingly, men enjoy on average thirty minutes more leisure time a day than women do.[61]

All that care—for children and whole families—means that many women scale back on wage labor. A 2004 study showed that over their prime earning years American women earn 38 percent of men's wages.[62] True, women represent half of the American workforce, bringing home more of the family income than they used to. A 2005 study found that about a quarter of married women make more than their husbands.[63] But that pattern lasted more than three years for only 60 percent of those couples, and on average women still work fewer hours for lower wages, only bringing home 37 percent of the average family's income as of 2009.[64] Though it may seem unfair at first glance, this updated version of the ancient pair-bond exchange continues to be a good deal for many men and women.

Marriage, which often entails the most pronounced version of the pair-bond exchange, illustrates its benefits. Generally speaking, marriage improves health, happiness, and economic stability more than just about anything else. Husbands and children especially seem to benefit. Men who marry and stay married have an almost 90 percent chance of living past sixty-five, while women's life expectancy is not affected by marriage. As Shelley Taylor explains:

Married men typically get many perks that single men and married women do not usually enjoy. For example, depending on the marriage, husbands may be fed, clothed, and picked up after, at least more so than is true for single men or for women. Someone else very often shops, cooks, cleans the house, does the laundry, and may even buy their clothes and do their errands.[65]

Married men also, Taylor explains, eat more nutritious meals and are less likely to smoke, drink heavily, or abuse illegal drugs than single men.[66] Children with married parents similarly enjoy more financial stability, do better in school, and when they grow up are more likely to have good jobs and get married themselves.[67]

Though tending is largely gendered, gender itself is flexible, as indicated by the many men who are the primary caregivers in their families for periods of time. That flexibility, writes Taylor, is part of being human:

> We are the most flexible species on earth, and we have the ability to play almost any role we choose. Women can take on roles that traditionally fell to men, as surely as men can take on what traditionally have been thought of as women's roles. Both genders have the capacity for tending.[68]

A sign of that flexibility is the fact that human fathers are way more caring and attentive than our primate relatives.[69] In addition to dutifully providing for their kids, dads give love, emotional support, and help with learning. Even so, Eugene Costa (the home-schooling dad we met at the beginning of the chapter) did more than many men. While some fathers, like the foraging Aka in Central Africa, keep their kids in sight a whopping 88 percent of the time, the typical American father has direct contact with his baby just under an hour a day.[70] Women like Victoria Hewitt do the bulk of caregiving.

In Taylor's view, our neurochemistry predisposes women toward caretaking but also primes the pump of men like Eugene Costa who do take on caretaking to do more of it. Living with a pregnant woman and caring for a young child decreases a man's aggressive hormones (like testosterone) and ups levels of prolactin, a hormone associated with pregnancy and lactation.[71] One study showed that just fifteen minutes of holding a baby can produce a measureable elevation in a man's prolactin level.[72] Enough men who are about to become dads experience symptoms of pregnancy like weight gain and morning sickness that the phenomenon has a name—"couvade." Not surprisingly, the men who experience couvade show particularly high prolactin levels and decreased testosterone.[73]

But the hormonal changes fathers experience are so much more modest than mothers' that researchers have to use a different scale to measure them.[74] Today, only a third of fathers who don't live with their kids pay the full amount of court-ordered child support, though 80 percent of them have no apparent financial reason for not paying.[75] Fathers are more likely than mothers to abandon children.[76] Development agencies have learned to channel money through women because they tend to spend money on family items like medicine and school fees, while fathers may well squander it on cigarettes, alcohol, and other women.[77]

Though these patterns reflect the continued confluence of gender and housework, many people manage to depart from those traditional roles. Men can and often do change diapers, just as women are often the primary breadwinners for their families. Same-sex couples are particularly adept at equitably dividing housework, perhaps because there's supposedly no natural way to assign tasks from preparing dinner to preparing tax returns. Same-sex couples also report valuing equality more than heterosexual couples, so heterosexual wives are more likely than their lesbian counterparts to shoulder primary responsibility for cooking, cleaning, and so-called "kin maintenance" work like showing affection and writing holiday cards. Heterosexual husbands, likewise, are more likely than their gay counterparts to pay the bills.[78] As more gay couples marry, they may start to divide these tasks less equitably, and having kids can also change things.[79] One in three gay male couples raising kids have one parent at home full-time, the same rate as straight couples with kids. Lesbians lag behind, with one in four having one parent engaged in full-time homemaking, perhaps because of their greater commitment to equality or the lower earnings of women on average, which make it harder for one woman to support a whole household.[80]

A Caveat on Tending

A caveat on the applicability of Taylor's research on tending bears mention. We don't all get the care and friendship we both want and need. Too many relationships are marred by abuse, not to mention neglect and abandonment. Lots of books address these problems and make proposals for how law can do better.[81] This book looks at a sunnier side of family life, asking how family law should treat the caregivers who faithfully tend to people in their household.

The question is how to value that work. In the coming chapter we'll see that lawyers and judges too often support property hoarding by recognizing only half of the pair-bond exchange. They're more willing to put a dollar amount on tasks that are commonly done for wages—chauffeur, landscaper—than on the domestic ones like taking a partner to chemo.

SEVEN

Legal Rules of Cohabitation Agreements

PARTNERSHIP

"Is it okay with you if I go to Kyrgyzstan next month?" Karen asks one night over dinner.

Six months we've lived together, and still I can't read whether she expects me to say "yes" or "no." I do quickly find out that Kyrgyzstan is a country in Central Asia and that a law school there has invited her to spend a week working on a start-up legal clinic. How her eyes shone that night in the vodka bar a year ago, telling me how liberating she found her first overseas social justice project in a tiny, poor country she'd never heard of. That's our deal: I support her work, and she supports me with late-afternoon calls to see if I need her to pick up Walter from daycare. I held up my end by cheerfully giving the green light for her to go to Ukraine, a trip that was scheduled to happen two weeks after this Kyrgyzstan trip. The question is whether my end of the deal requires saying that it's fine with me if she stays over there for the ten days between those jobs to travel around.

It's not our first negotiation. When Karen and I moved in together, we'd already developed a pattern: I cook, and she cleans up while I give Walter a bath and tuck him into bed. Her embrace of technology has landed calls to Comcast on her to-do list; mine includes adding her people's names to my tattered address and birthday books. It took more time to come to an agreement that she'll join Walter and me for dinner every night. One day, maybe a month into living together, she said that she hadn't been expected home for dinner every night at six thirty since high school. Ultimately we agreed that all three of us sit down to dinner just about every night she's in town, and I don't squawk about her work trips.

This time it's harder. I have the teaching schedule from hell and have just weathered a commute stretched to ninety minutes thanks to an overturned truck on the Beltway, topped off with a tongue-lashing from the executive director of Walter's new daycare, reminding me that their dollar-a-minute late policy lets hardworking staff get home to their families.

Still, by dessert, wanting to hold up my end of the deal swapping my flexibility with her travel for her presence at dinner when she's in town, I say yes.

Come October, Karen's in Kyrgyzstan on the first job, and I'm on some side street trying to skirt another Beltway pileup. I've already called daycare twice to report that I'll be a little late, and I can't read the map without reading glasses, which I don't have in the car. Finally, I get to daycare and fork over $20 as penance for the late pickup along with a side of profuse apologies. Once home, rushing to whip up Walter's mac and cheese, Karen calls in the thin envelope of time we can talk between her work tasks and mine. The pasta boils over as I listen to how impressed she was by a law student's bravery of writing a paper on same-sex marriage. Picking up the pot—one from Karen's house and still unfamiliar to me—I scorch my hand.

"It's okay, Martha," she tells me, trying to quiet my sobs across an ocean.

"It's okay, Mommy," Walter says, stroking my arm.

My tears dissolve Karen's plans, bringing her home for the week between gigs. That change of plans, that first October we live together, marks the modification of Karen's deal with herself to accept every international gig she's offered, replacing it with another: the commitment to a mothering role in this family.

LAW AS IT IS RE COHABITATION AGREEMENTS

Moving in together made Karen and me feel more like an "us," but acts of caring for one another and Walter sealed the deal. Family law would ignore these homemaking tasks unless we jumped through another hoop. In the District of Columbia, we could have "held ourselves out" as married—filing joint tax returns, sharing a last name—if we were a straight couple. The District did allow couples to register as domestic partners, but that provided fairly discrete rights like hospital visitation. For more robust "us-ness," our only option was to contractually agree to take on rights and duties like property sharing.

Both law and society act as if marriage is the sole form of legitimate family. This chapter reveals the facts that lie beneath superficial equations of marriage and family by mapping the exceptions to that general rule. As with reproductive technologies and adoption, contract operates as a dividing line between the live-in couples whom law treats as family, more or less, and those it treats as legal strangers. Like parenthood agreements, these living-together agreements get treated as legally binding contracts or mere deals, depending on their terms and the state in which the couple lives.

An outline illustrates the way family law treats marriage as the general rule and cohabitation as exceptional:

> *General Rule:* Marriage creates full rights and obligations, like property sharing upon divorce and Social Security benefits.
> *Exception:* Unmarried couples can formally contract into property-sharing rights vis à vis one another but not for public benefits like Social Security.

Low-income Americans are particularly affected by this rule because they are more likely to live together than those with a college education and middle-class incomes. They're also less likely to enter those contracts or even have a lot of property to share. Some legal scholars would correct this problem by making cohabitation a recognized family status, either by treating live-in couples as if they were married or by abolishing the legal significance of marriage. I propose a third approach. It retains marriage as the family type conveying the most rights and obligations while also having family law recognize many cohabitants' reasonable expectations about what's shared and what's not.

The biggest pattern to keep in mind—which we'll also see in prenup cases in chapters 8 and 9—is that family law often fails to properly value the contributions of caregivers. That myopia hurts cohabiting couples more than spouses. By marrying, spouses generally contract into property-sharing rules that mitigate the injuries of family law's insistence that homemaking labor is a pure gift, done without expectation of return, ever. Live-ins, in contrast, usually don't have a moment of formal contracting in to being an "us." People who are dating may just stay overnight more often, move clothes and other things in bit by bit, and eventually give up one of their apartments. They often enter a pair-bond exchange with similar informality, making oral agreements to pool finances and provide caregiving and then acting on those promises. The question is whether law can and should recognize those promises.

Case #1: Skirting the Ban on Same-Sex Marriage: *Posik v. Layton* (1997)

The treatment of same-sex couples shows how law changes, setting the stage for future changes like the one I propose. Just over a decade ago, no state recognized same-sex marriage, so living together was the only option on the menu for gay couples. Consequently, around 10 percent of live-in couples are same sex, though gay people constitute only about 3.5 percent of the general population.[1] Even in late 2014, a year and a half after the federal government began to recognize same-sex marriages, about a third of the states still have laws known as Defense of Marriage Acts that fence same-sex couples out of marriage.[2] If a Texas couple gets married in Massachusetts and then heads home to Texas, they're married for federal purposes like immigration or federal taxes but still single for issues governed by Texas law like state taxes and child custody. Both before and after the watershed same-sex marriage cases of 2013, same-sex and other unmarried couples in Texas, Florida, and many other states could contract around a good measure of DOMA's insults and injuries by creating a living-together contract.

In the 1990s, Emma Posik and Nancy Layton did just that. The couple got around the Florida law by creating, through contract, a do-it-yourself arrangement that's something like marriage à la carte.

Like many couples, they met at work. Emma was a well-established nurse in her fifties and Nancy an up-and-coming thirty-something anesthesiologist. When Nancy was moving her practice, she asked Emma to sell her home, leave her job, and become a full-time homemaker. Emma's ability to lend Nancy $20,000 may have given Emma bargaining power, because Nancy signed an agreement giving Emma many of the rights a spouse would have in exchange for Emma's taking on housewifely duties. Contract, in short, gave Emma much of what Florida law would have if it had extended marriage equality to same-sex couples (which it still does not). Most important, the contract provided that if they broke up, Nancy would pay Emma $2,500 a month for the rest of Emma's life.[3]

Four years later, Nancy wanted to move another woman into the house. Emma objected, so Nancy left. Emma sued to enforce the contract, and lost at trial, since the judge found that any loss she suffered from quitting her job, selling her house, and moving to be Nancy's full-time homemaker was offset by benefits she enjoyed while she was "permitted" to live with Nancy.[4]

But Emma won big on appeal. The Appellate Court enforced the contract, concluding that same-sex couples could contract into some of the rights and obligations of marriage, like the $2,500 a month palimony provision. Even though Florida banned same-sex couples from marrying, the court explained, it did not take away their freedom of contract, allowing Nancy and Emma to "privately commit by contract to spend their money as they see fit."[5] The court quickly clarified that it was not "condoning the lifestyles of homosexual or unmarried live-ins," but merely "recognizing their constitutional private property and contract rights."[6]

Recall that *Posik* was decided in 1997, six years before the US Supreme Court would strike down sodomy laws as unconstitutional in *Lawrence v. Texas*. Even the states that made sodomy a crime allowed courts to enforce living-together contracts of same-sex couples.[7] Courts examining *Marvin* agreements relegate them to mere deals if they are "meretricious," a swap of sex for money, and the Florida court in *Posik v. Layton* viewed Emma and Nancy's palimony agreement as separate from their sexual relationship, noting that their lawyer-written contract carefully avoided mentioning sex at all.

The Importance of a Piece of Paper

While Florida law recognized cohabitants' right to make contracts, it also imposed a hurdle to exercising that right by requiring that the contracts be in writing. Contract law calls this writing requirement a "statute of frauds," because it's intended to prevent people from fraudulently claiming a contract when none ever existed. But contract law also recognizes that conduct can substitute for writing. Emma and Nancy are unusual in putting their agreement down on paper. Most cohabiting couples make their agreements orally or implicitly through their actions over time. According to one study, only 20 percent of cohabiting couples have written agreements about property, leaving the remaining 80 percent without any legal recourse in states like Florida.[8]

Law already allows businesses to create binding contracts through actions as well as words on the page. When two people operate a business for profit, but don't bother to incorporate or execute other documents that formally create the business, business law treats them as a partnership and applies partnership law rules to determine who owns what. Couples living together also should be legally treated as an "us" to the extent that they operate a household for their personal and financial benefit.[9] As we'll see later in this chapter, the American Law Institute, an eminent group of judges, professors, and lawyers, has proposed such a rule, giving live-ins a name—"domestic partners"—that reflects their legal kinship to business partners.[10]

Even with the writing requirement, *Posik v. Layton* represents an important development in the law of family contracts because it allows people like Emma to protect their investments (financial as well as emotional) in an intimate relationship. In a way, law and social norms give same-sex couples an edge over straight live-ins. Straight couples can contract into property-sharing rights by marrying, but that option is novel for same-sex couples. Emma, Nancy, and others like them may be more likely than straight couples to put agreements in writing, since a formal contract has been, for many of us, for most of our lives, the closest we could get to a wedding.[11] Two years into tennis great Martina Navratilova's relationship with Texas beauty queen Judy Nelson, they signed an agreement to share everything 50/50 and even treated the signing a bit like a wedding by videotaping it.[12] Martina's stature, and Judy's tell-all memoir *Love Match*, ensured that many queer people knew that living-together contracts could make their relationships legally recognized, at least to some extent.[13]

Straight or gay, a couple in a long relationship might make both oral and written agreements. When celebrity lawyer Johnnie Cochran's twenty-seven-year relationship with Patty Sikora Cochran foundered—just as he was getting O. J. Simpson acquitted of murder charges—part of their agreement was in writing and part of it was oral. The written part made Patty full owner of their North Hollywood house and provided that Johnnie would financially support their son, as well as pay for a new car and swimming pool for Patty, while the oral part covered Johnnie's promise to support Patty "financially, emotionally, and legally" for the rest of her life.[14] Johnnie litigated hard to defeat Patty's palimony claim. He argued that their agreement was merely a deal—not legally binding—because they never lived together full-time (he was married to one woman, then another, for much of their relationship). Nevertheless, the court decided in Patty's favor, concluding that living together two to four days a week and jointly raising their son was sufficient to show a "long-term, stable, and significant relationship."[15] It reached this conclusion to protect what it called Patty's "reasonable expectations" arising out of their long-term exchange of financial support for homemaking labor.[16]

Case #2: Gratuitous Insults in *Featherston v. Steinhoff* (1998)

Unfortunately, other states, such as Michigan, have failed to honor that pair-bond exchange, instead mistaking the caretaking half of the exchange as a pure gift unless the caregiver can muster proof that intimates living together intended to pay for services as if they were strangers.

When Karen Featherston and Lee Steinhoff met, she was working as a housecleaner to support her two daughters and barely making ends meet through a combination of public assistance and odd jobs.[17] Shortly after their son, Kyle, was born, Karen started college and moved into Lee's house, making them part of the 40 percent of cohabiting households with kids. Three years later she dropped out to work for Lee, with his encouragement but not with any pay for a good while. Lee and Karen had a traditional pair-bond exchange, with Lee providing most of the financial support while Karen mostly cared for their home and the children, sometimes attending school or working at Lee's business. Lee orally promised to provide Karen with "a roof over [her] head" and also that he wouldn't "throw her out on the street" if they broke up, but they didn't share a bank account and the house remained in Lee's name.[18]

When they separated after eight years, the Michigan courts refused to enforce Lee's promise, erasing the value of Karen's caregiving and sacrifices for the family by masking them as pure gifts. The court noted that Michigan, like most states, had abolished common law marriage decades earlier, and that family law presumes that homemakers in live-in couples "gratuitously performed services" unless they prove that they expected pay for them. By putting this burden on Karen, it refused to recognize how Lee and the rest of the family benefited from work that the trial court described as Karen's "cooking and cleaning, laundry, shopping and caring for children and ferrying children hither and yon, [and] also at [Lee's] office."[19]

The presumption that caregiving is a pure gift is particularly hard on children like Kyle. As of 2008, more than 4.2 million children were living with cohabiting parents—around 6 percent of the kids in the United States.[20] About half of those kids were born to the cohabiting couple.[21] Children increase the chance of a starker pair-bond exchange because the amount of time spent tending them often requires someone to cut back on wage labor. Yet the law too often treats all that work as a pure gift unless the caregiver can prove an explicit agreement like the one Emma Posik got from Nancy Layton.

Case #3: Give Back, Loretta: *McLane v. Musick* (2001)

The gift presumption can hurt male as well as female caregivers. Howard McLane and Loretta Monroe began dating in 1990, down in the Florida Keys, where he fished and she kept books for local businesses.[22] He moved in with Loretta and her parents. Then a hurricane led them all to move upstate to live in a double-wide trailer on ten acres. Both trailer and land were titled in Loretta's name, bought with money from mortgaging her house in the Keys.[23] They lived together as if they were husband and wife, pooling their finances in a joint bank account for everyday bills as well as big expenses like a bulldozer and road-grader for him to start an excavating business. While they intended to get married and make wills, Howard said they "just never got around to it," but, he went on, "I think we done everything except the vows."[24]

They never even made explicit oral promises like the promise in *Featherston v. Steinhoff* that Lee would keep a roof over Karen and the children's heads. Howard and Loretta didn't have kids, but they did raise a pot-bellied pig named Charlie, who grew to several hundred pounds and lived in the house. Perhaps because Charlie required less attention than a child, they—like many cohabitants—had a more muted version of the pair-bond exchange, with both contributing financial support. Howard deposited a $70,000 inheritance into the joint account, and also improved the land by putting in a road, a garden, and a pond, while Loretta bought their trailer and the land. Loretta also did household tasks like grocery shopping.[25]

But then Loretta got sick. Lacking insurance, she delayed going to the doctor. When she finally did, he said her breast cancer was the worst he'd ever seen. Howard's inheritance went to pay for Loretta's doctors, drugs, and hospital stays, as well as their living expenses.

He also made other financial sacrifices by cutting way back on his excavating work to take her to chemo and radiation treatments. Plus, he wanted to stay close to home in case she needed him.[26]

After Loretta died, Howard faced an additional loss, having mistakenly thought, he said, that "everything was ours."[27] Had they been married, he could have held onto a good part of their property. But he was left with nothing because her relatives took their home and land, leaving him to sue for reimbursement of around $40,000 for medical bills and time spent nursing Loretta and $70,000 for work he did to improve their land and home.

Howard explained that "we were trying to build something"[28]— a joint enterprise—but the court only recognized half of their partnership. It might have been otherwise. Recall that partnership law imposes duties to share property just by operating a business together for profit. Contract law also allows actions to speak as loudly as words on the page through rules recognizing oral agreements, ones made through actions, and sometimes even by silence or failure to act.[29] Howard and Loretta's actions—pooling their finances (including his $70,000 inheritance), him working on the house and land where they lived, her providing their home and doing housework, and him taking care of her financially, emotionally, and physically through her cancer treatments—all seemed to create a partnership that the law should recognize. But the Florida court recognized only half of Howard and Loretta's pair-bond exchange, his "provider" actions of excavating the land.

A California court was blunter about the value of Donnis Whorton's pair-bond exchange with Benjamin Dillingham III, a Harvard MBA then working as the San Diego mayor's chief of staff. In the late 1970s, Donnis had agreed to drop out of college to move in with Benjamin and serve as his full-time "chauffeur, bodyguard, social and business secretary, partner and counselor in real estate investments," as well as "constant companion, confidant, traveling and social companion, and lover."[30] In exchange, Donnis claimed, Ben was to share his considerable wealth with Donnis and support him for life. But when they broke up seven years later, the court enforced

only the promises to be a "chauffeur, bodyguard, secretary, and partner and counselor in business investments," reasoning that those services had "monetary value" and thus are done by people expecting to
be compensated. In contrast, being a companion and confidant, the
court said, was not "usually monetarily compensated nor considered
to have a 'value' for purposes of contract consideration."[31] The court
said that it couldn't value Donnis's domestic contributions to their
household because being "intertwined" with Donnis and Benjamin's
sexual relationship made them meretricious.[32]

Most courts don't say outright that wage labor is more valuable
than caregiving work. Instead, they mask the value of caregiving—
and only that half of the exchange—as a gift.[33] Had these couples
been married, the gift rhetoric would not cause as much harm, because the general rule makes both spouses owners of property acquired during the marriage. But Howard didn't marry Loretta, and
Donnis couldn't have married Benjamin back in the 1980s, so neither
couple was "family" with the right—or duty—to share property. At
the end of the day, Howard walked away with $30,000 for land-
scaping the property but nothing for driving Loretta to chemo and
radiation appointments or spending his inheritance on her medical
bills, while Donnis settled his claims against Benjamin for a more
comfortable sum.[34]

This double standard shows the wrong-headedness of the *Featherston* presumption that caregiving is a mere gift. It's outrageous to
treat road excavation as more valuable than driving a partner to
chemo and paying for those treatments. Since Howard and Loretta
were, the judge said, in a "close family-like relationship," which triggered the gift presumption, then the court should have honored what
it called the "reciprocity of services, benefits and duties, which characterize normal family life."[35] In short, family law should stop masking caregiving as a pure gift, and instead recognize both sides of the
pair-bond exchange.

Tending generally improves the health, happiness, and welfare of
family members, in both everyday life and crises like Loretta's illness.
Instead of holding all cohabitants to the standard that Emma Posik

and Nancy Layton managed to meet—a formal signed agreement for property sharing and palimony—family law should recognize that couples often enter agreements they intend to be binding by actions instead of words.

In Howard and Loretta's case, the years of swapping financial support for caregiving—taking turns being the main provider—should furnish sufficient evidence of the pair-bond exchange. Family law judges already exercise great discretion to decide what is an "equitable" distribution of spouses' property at divorce, or what custody arrangement is in a child's best interest, so they can determine that a relationship walks like a pair-bond exchange and talks like a pair-bond exchange probably is a pair-bond exchange.

The next case shows how family law can do that.

Case #4: Going with Skip and Flo in *Byrne v. Laura* (1997)

Inertia prevented Skip Lavazzo and Flo Byrne from putting their agreement into writing, just as it did with Howard and Loretta, but finances kept them from tying the knot.[36] The California courts resolved these difficulties better than the courts in *Featherston* or *McLean* by letting Skip and Flo's actions and spoken words provide the evidence needed to demonstrate a devoted couple's pair-bond exchange.[37]

It took decades for Skip and Flo to hook up permanently. In the 1980s, the recently widowed Flo reunited with Skip, her high school sweetheart, picking up where they'd left off forty years before when she, at eighteen, broke off their engagement. Skip, too, had married someone else, though his marriage had ended in divorce in the 1970s. Once they were reunited, Skip still wanted to marry Flo, and proposed again and again. But she turned him down every time, explaining that she couldn't remarry without losing insurance for her disabled daughters.

Their story demonstrates how both law and society have changed. When Skip and Flo were first dating back in the 1940s, moving in together would have invited scorn and maybe even arrest, a history that partly explains why older people are less likely to live together than young couples. But by 1988, Flo simply moved her things out of her rented San Mateo house and into Skip's place in San Francisco. Like many couples, they did for each other. She deposited paychecks from her part-time job in a school cafeteria into their joint account, and also cleared out the refuse of Skip's fourteen years of bachelorhood by getting new carpets, curtains, and appliances into the house. Day to day, Flo did all of the couple's cooking, shopping, cleaning, and laundry, as well as taking care of Skip when he got sick. Skip, for his part, not only promised that he'd always take care of her, often telling her she'd always "have a roof over [her] head," but made good on his word by using his income as a plumber to pay nearly all their living expenses, giving her money whenever she needed it, making her the beneficiary on his retirement accounts, and setting up a conservatorship for her children.[38]

Skip died unexpectedly in 1993—two weeks before a Hawaii cruise during which he planned to surprise Flo with a marriage ceremony—leaving her in a state of shock. All at once, she lost Skip, their home, and all their belongings. Although Skip had promised to put everything in Flo's name, he never got around to making a will because he was, Flo testified, "a procrastinator" who "didn't move too quickly on things."[39] Consequently, Skip's estate, worth over $1.2 million, was slated to go to heirs who came out of the woodwork. But the California Court of Appeal didn't let the heirs take what Flo was entitled to.

Following *Marvin v. Marvin*, the court in Skip and Flo's case concluded that Skip's property should go to Flo to honor their pair-bond exchange, finding that Skip contracted to transform his property into theirs. The judge even used the language of exchange when it said that "Skip promised Flo when she moved in, and many times thereafter, that he would take care of her for the rest of her life in exchange for her services as a homemaker."[40] It also noted that Skip acted on his promise by giving "Flo money to buy anything she needed and [seeking] to provide her with a comfortable life," and she, in turn, "fully performed the role of a loving spouse during all the time they lived together."[41] Skip's heirs tried to get the court to calculate the amount due to Flo as if Skip had hired her as a cook and house-cleaner, but the court refused. Instead of pretending that Skip and Flo were arm's-length commercial actors, the court honored the love that motivated their exchange. In the court's words, "Skip agreed out of love and concern to care for Flo for the rest of her life," which entitled her to much more than compensation for the value of her services "as if she had been his maid."[42]

Couples living together can be rich like Johnnie Cochran or living in a trailer like Howard and Loretta. They may make formal, written agreements like Emma Posik and Nancy Layton, or orally agree to swap financial support for homemaking, as Skip and Flo did. Providers maybe even use the same words: both Lee Steinhoff and Skip Lavazzo promised to keep a roof over their partners' heads. They may be pushed by law, finances, or simple inertia into living together instead of marrying. But all of them deserve legal recognition for the reasonable expectations they developed during their lives together as a couple.

LAW AS IT SHOULD BE RE COHABITATION AGREEMENTS

Scholars have proposed different reforms to protect people like Emma Posik, Karen Featherston, Howard McLane, and Flo Byrne. I offer a third, more contractual, approach based on what I see as cohabiting couples' reasonable expectations.[43] Which proposal you prefer depends on whether you think that marriage's importance to individuals and society justifies assigning spouses greater rights and duties than cohabitants.

Progressive scholars of the family rightly note marriage's long history of exclusion and hierarchy, and seek to demote marriage from its most-favored-relationship status. Some say we ought to focus instead on mother/child bonds, or all kinds of caregiving unions.[44]

At least regarding same-sex couples, objections about inequality carry less weight as more and more of the country allows same-sex couples to marry. Yet marriage still grants extra privileges to the already privileged. The likelihood of divorcing before their fifth anniversary is 34 percent for high school dropouts, significantly higher than the 23 percent rate for high school graduates and the 13 percent rate for college grads.[45] Since 1980, Americans have tended to marry someone with a similar income, compounding the economic advantages of marriage. Racial and gender disparities also exist. While the likelihood of marriage goes up along with income, black men earning more than $100,000 a year are less likely to marry than black men who earn $75,000. White women are twice as likely to marry as black women, rates that also hold true for college graduates. A 2010 study found that half of black couples divorce within the first decade of marriage, compared with less than a third of white couples.[46]

What can law do to remedy this uneven distribution of the many social, emotional, health, and economic benefits of marriage?

One Option: Greatly Expand Marriage

Cornell law professor Cynthia Bowman contends that cohabitants should be treated as if they are married if they live together for two years or have a child together.[47] Her proposal also preserves contractual freedom by allowing cohabitants to explicitly contract out of property-sharing and other aspects of being a family. Essentially, she flips the default by treating live-in couples as family unless they contract out of it, whereas the current rule recognizes "us-ness" only to the extent that they say so in a contract.

Another Option: Abolish Civil Marriage

The more radical solution, put forward by American University law professor Nancy Polikoff, would abolish the legal relevance of marriage and extend familial rights and duties to non-couples like adult sisters or close friends as well as couples. Polikoff, whose scholarly and law-making work has played a key role in expanding social and legal definitions of family to include queer families in their many forms, calls her proposal "valuing all families."[48] Instead of treating spouses as the most significant relationship, Polikoff's proposal would take a case-by-case approach, tailoring the definition of family to the function of rent control, family medical leave, inheritance, and other situations that trigger rights and duties of family members.[49]

Pros and Cons of Each Option

The Bowman and Polikoff proposals each have strengths and draw-backs. Bowman's proposal would help people like Karen Featherston, Howard McLane, and Flo Byrne, and would be easy to implement, since it essentially reinstates common law marriage (without the requirement that the couple consider themselves married). However, its omission of non-couple arrangements leaves out some family arrangements that are common in communities of color. African American women, for example, are three times more likely than white women never to live with an intimate partner and more likely than white women to center their lives around extended kin.[50] Moreover, it may make less sense to treat cohabitants as if they were married than it once did. Back in 1968, Barnard College expelled Linda LeClaire for living with her boyfriend. Cohabitation was so unusual that the *New York Times* published a series of articles about the "affaire LeClaire" with titles like "Father Despairs of Barnard Daughter."[51] Today more than seven million American couples live together and four out of ten babies are born to unmarried parents.[52] If cohabitants deliberately choose not to marry, applying all the rights and duties of marriage to them may well impose a higher level of "us-ness" than they have opted for themselves.

The major upside of Polikoff's proposal is its capacious vision of "family," extending legally recognized "us-ness" well beyond marriage and romantic couples. Pushing both law and society to recognize that love comes in different packages is a central purpose of this book. But replacing the general rule that "marriage = family" with new rules tailored to thousands of different legal rights and remedies could produce great uncertainty. Family law differs from state to state, so substantive rules likely would vary across state lines even more than they do now. Moreover, an elderly mother and her adult daughter might be "family" for some purposes, like testimonial privilege; but not for others, like splitting property when one moves out. Law is complicated enough already. People in families ought to be able to signal in a simple, universally understood way that they are a family and to anticipate the consequences of that election. Marriage provides that signal.

An upside of both Bowman's and Polikoff's proposals is that they would remedy the current maldistribution of wealth by getting more people covered by public benefits like Social Security. My proposal does nothing for Social Security coverage but does combine other elements of Bowman and Polikoff's proposals, while also going further than theirs to improve the value that law assigns to homemaking labor.

Like Bowman, I believe that family law ought to recognize the reasonable expectation of property sharing that comes with sharing a life together as a couple. Like Polikoff, I believe that one size does not fit all when it comes to matching people's intent to the rules that govern their relationship. However, unlike both of them, I believe that marriage vows make for a different relationship than living together without those formal promises. Therefore, we ought to keep marriage as the legal threshold to being treated as an "us" when it comes to institutions outside the relationship, like the IRS and the Social Security Administration. But cohabitants could and should be recognized as an "us" in relation to one another through property-sharing rules.

Proposal: Cohabitation as Marriage à la Carte

Marriage brings the full panoply of rights and duties, from soup to nuts. Because cohabitation covers a wider range of circumstances, it's more like ordering à la carte. Living together for a short time offers a taste of commitment, while longer relationships commit people more fully socially, emotionally, and financially. It's not a stretch to compare late-life couples who seek to shield assets for their adult children from prior relationships to a late-evening coffee and dessert. It makes sense for different legal rules to apply to relationships entered with such different intent, which have different financial, social, and emotional valences.

In emotional terms—a register this book takes as central to family life—my own experience is that cohabitation feels quite different from marriage, a difference that law and society should recognize. Structural differences between cohabitation and marriage likely shape those emotions. You can't marry by happenstance, as basically occurs when a couple drifts into sharing an apartment because it's cheaper. It's also harder to exit a marriage, which is one reason that marriages last considerably longer on average than cohabiting relationships.[53] Consequently, live-in couples and spouses make different kinds of long-term financial commitments to one another. While many couples agree that one person will provide more money and the other will provide more household support, spouses are more likely to have one person working full-time while the other tends to the household full-time.[54] These contracts and deals provide a framework for understanding how family law can tailor its rules to match the reasonable expectations of both spouses and cohabiting couples.

ALI Domestic Partnership

The American Law Institute (ALI) has proposed that family law recognize cohabitants as "domestic partners" and accord them the type of property-sharing rights and duties sought by Emma Posik, Karen Featherston, Howard McLane, and Flo Byrne.[55] The ALI rule would apply to couples who have lived together for a period of time—perhaps two or three years—as a legislature or court sees fit. If they have a child together, property-sharing rules could kick in earlier. Should a couple live together for a short period, they could still qualify as domestic partners if they engage in family-like behaviors, like making explicit promises to each other about their relationship, intermingling their finances, becoming economically interdependent through a pair-bond exchange, acknowledging their "us-ness" by naming each other beneficiaries on insurance policies or wills, and parenting a child together. Notice that many of these actions involve contracts like life insurance policies and deals like swapping homemaking for financial support.

For couples who qualify as domestic partners under the ALI proposal, breaking up would mean that their property would be divided as if they were married and also that a provider like Lee Steinhoff would make what the ALI proposal calls "compensatory payments" that reimburse losses a primary caretaker sustained due to the relationship, like Karen Featherston's dropping out of school, working for Lee's business without pay, and caring for their home and child. Just as the rules we encountered earlier in this chapter allow cohabitants like Emma Posik and Nancy Layton to contract into property-sharing arrangements, the ALI domestic partnership proposal allows people to avoid those financial obligations by making an explicit agreement or even taking actions like keeping separate finances.

Concrete differences between cohabitation and marriage as well as family law's growing tendency to recognize that families come in a variety of configurations all argue in favor of the ALI's domestic partner approach.

Marriage Lasts Longer

The cohabiting relationships in the four cases we've discussed lasted between five and eight years, around as long as the average live-in arrangement. At the five-year point, only half of cohabiting couples are still together, while five years into a marriage, nearly 75 percent of spouses are still together.[56] The longer you live together, the more that relationship is likely to affect your wallet, your heart, and your world views. If psychologist Shelley Taylor is right that most of us are hardwired to find and cultivate reliable social connections, family law and society ought to provide special support to especially durable relationships.

The relative longevity of marriages may explain why marriage remains the family form that most people choose when they have that option, and therefore why family law uses marriage as a defining feature of family. Even the people least likely to marry—poor people—hold up marriage as the gold standard, a goal to strive for later in life.[57] If cohabitation replaces marriage as the most common choice, law and society may flip the default. In any case, I agree with Yale law professor William Eskridge that society will continue to encourage people to form lasting, reliable connections that sustain our health and welfare, individually and as part of communities.[58]

Spouses Adopt a Starker Pair-Bond Exchange

Perhaps because live-in relationships don't last as long as marriages, cohabitants often strike a more muted version of the pair-bond exchange than spouses do. While women who live with men—whether married or not—do more housework than their partners, wives do more cooking, shopping, and cleaning than cohabiting women, even when they're not raising children.[59] Live-in couples are less likely than spouses to have a sole breadwinner, and fewer cohabitants pool their finances.[60] Consequently, cohabiting women are generally less financially dependent on their partners than wives are on husbands. According to a 1999 study, cohabiting women make 90 percent as much as their male partners, compared with wives, who make just 60 percent as much as their husbands.[61] Along the same lines, a 2012 study found that married women participate less in the labor force than cohabiting women, and those rates get lower the longer the marriage lasts.[62]

Still, most cohabitants do commingle their finances, and many swap full-time homemaking for financial support, as Emma Posik and Karen Featherston did. Family law should recognize these co-habitants' reasonable expectations. Instead of an all-or-nothing approach that treats a couple as "family" if they're married, and as mere pals if they're cohabiting (unless they have a formal written agreement like the one in *Posik v. Layton*), family law can and should take a sliding-scale approach.

Trending Toward Choice

Both law and society have increased family choice. When my parents got married in the 1950s, law and society treated marriage as a pair-bond exchange struck to raise the next generation. Over the 1960s, however, many Americans came to see marriage more as a vehicle for self-actualization, a partnership between best friends and lifelong lovers.[63] Starting with California's no-fault divorce law in 1969, family law embraced this new view by greatly expanding the grounds for divorce.

Collectively, these revolutionary changes (and others, like treating domestic violence as a crime) are part of the long-term transition of how we view marriage. Bit by bit law and society have moved away from seeing it as a permanent institution—a status dictated by Nature or God with assigned roles for men and women—and toward the view that marriage is a human creation that partners can tailor to their needs. Different partnerships merit different rules.

Actions Can Speak as Loudly as Words

Some tailoring is done by actions instead of words on the page. Accordingly, a rule that is based on live-in couples' reasonable expectations would allow oral promises and behavior to show that they entered a pair-bond exchange. Once family law acknowledges the prevalence of pair-bond exchanges in cohabiting relationships, and the variety of ways that couples evidence their exchange, it can discard the legal fiction that caregiving is a pure gift.

Family promises seem as important as commercial agreements, and contract law generally enforces oral agreements, requiring signed writings only for big transactions like the sale of land.[64]

Family law could require repetition of pair-bonding behavior over time before enforcing cohabitants' oral or implicit agreements. While the ALI proposal would require judges to exercise discretion in deciding how long to award palimony and precisely how to divide property that either person acquired during their relationship, judges make these calls every day in divorces. It would increase courts' caseloads, but that burden seems less onerous than the current rule's burden on caregiving cohabitants like Howard McLane and Karen Featherston. Judges' workloads are hardly more important than the interests of millions of caregivers and kids who are born to cohabiting couples, who currently suffer economically, socially, and emotionally from the current rule's refusal to recognize the "us-ness" that cohabitants themselves adopt through pair-bond exchanges.

While homemaking spouses fare better, the final chapters on family law show that there's room for improvement there, too.

EIGHT

Basics of Marital Agreements

CONTRACTUAL MUSH

"'Gaty's Day?' What's that? Why would you want to put that in front of a judge?" the lawyer asks.

A month before our wedding, Karen and I are here in this lawyer's office to make sure that we've made Karen as much of a parent as the law will allow. But that's edgy enough for the attorney without all the language she's dubbed "extraneous." I explain to her that all that mushy stuff is in the contract so that a judge doesn't see it. Like the Utah lawyer who reviewed Victor and my initial coparenting agreement, this lawyer would rather fold Karen in as Walter's third parent with as little flowery language as possible. She has circled my suggestion that we start off by proclaiming the "spirit of love, hope, cooperation and mutual respect" we bring to the agreement, and also the part about Karen reading Walter *Curious George* the first night she came over for dinner. But Gaty's Day bugs her the most.

To defend this infusion of love into otherwise lawyerly language, I tell the lawyer that Gaty is Walter's name for Karen, that he gave it to her when he could barely talk. Gaty's Day was Victor's idea, a Sunday between Mother's Day and Father's Day, to honor her in-between situation. Walter was just four years old then and made a card with me for her. When I asked Walter to tell me special things about his Gaty, he dictated, "She reads to me" and "Gaties make Mommies happy."

"It's true, Gaties do make Mommies happy, and even Walter knows that if Mamma ain't happy, ain't nobody happy," I finish, relieved to hear Karen's chuckle. The lawyer still looks puzzled, so I explain that I put the story in our contract to function like a levee. If any one of us gets awful or stupid or mean, I hope that it could hold us back from getting even more awful. The idea is that reminding us of the full hearts with which we started out could decrease the likelihood of an acrimonious, expensive legal fight that would hurt Walter most of all.

Knowing that I've slipped into law professor mode, I glance over to Karen and see her wipe away a tear. That feeling is precisely what I'd like to cue up if one of us became a drug addict or went orthodox and shaved her head, either of which could land us in some other lawyer's office to negotiate a separation agreement. The point of committing these emotions to paper is to evoke them later, if need be, to trigger memories of the full hearts and big hopes on the front end of our marriage.

To make Karen a legal parent, we each give and take. Victor and I give Karen the right to visitation with Walter if she and I break up, and Karen takes on the duty of paying child support. We also build in the possibilities of change, amping up her visitation and child support after we've been married for a while. Fortunately, DC has just enacted a law recognizing a status like Karen's, calling it "de facto parenthood."

It takes two more trips to the lawyer's office to hammer out terms that satisfy Karen, Victor, the attorney, and me, from lawyerly technicalities to the emotional terms we all call "mush." What started out as an addendum to Victor's and my coparenting agreement has blossomed into a bouquet of wills and powers of attorney, alongside the amended parenting agreement. As we sign the lawyer says that she's never had clients think through everything so carefully, then adds, "in a good way." On the way downstairs, clutching documents still warm from the copying machine, Karen squeezes my hand, as if she too feels that signing on all those dotted lines brought a family into being every bit as much as the vows of forever that we plan to recite, all dressed up and surrounded by a hundred dear ones summoned to celebrate with us.

————————

SEVEN STORIES ABOUT MARRIAGE

That agreement used a contract to bestow on Karen the status of parent. Marriage has long been a patchwork of status and contract, a little more of one or the other in different times and places.[1] The status part is most obvious but if you scratch the surface of marriage—straight or gay—you'll find contracts there, too.

Some courts have said that marriage should be reserved for straight couples, reasoning that only couples who can get pregnant by mistake really need the bonds of matrimony, a claim so illogical that it must cover up some other reason that the judges are not willing to support openly.[2] Maybe they believe that marriage needs one man and one woman because husbands are born to be the man of the house while wives live out their destiny as the little woman. These status-based views of marriage are giving way to a more contractual view that largely replaces divine mandate with human choice and the variety that choice produces.[3]

As of mid-2014, much of the country allows people to freely choose whom to marry, within limits like the ban on incest. That seems to move same-sex relationships from a contract regime to one based on status, since the ban on same-sex marriages made living-together agreements, wills, and powers of attorney the sole route to legal recognition for gay or lesbian unions.

But spouses have long begun their marriage with voluntary, reciprocal promises of support, care, and fidelity.[4] Likewise, divorce usually involves a legally binding agreement, because the vast majority of divorcing couples privately decide how to divide property and determine child custody and support instead of having a judge make all those decisions.[5] Additional exchanges shape the years of family life between these bookends. When they're legally binding they're contracts; otherwise, they're mere deals.

The First Family

Martha Custis, a wealthy twenty-seven-year-old widow with two kids, married George Washington in 1759 on her plantation, aptly named White House. Each got and gave something valuable. Martha got her kids a father—who'd later become the father of our country—and George got enough money, land, and slaves to triple the size of his Mt. Vernon plantation. Day-to-day during their long marriage, they cut other deals. She managed their immense holdings so he could leave the plantation to fight the American Revolution. Though Martha was unhappy about George becoming president and didn't attend his first inauguration, she came around to supporting his political career by acting as hostess at affairs of state.[6] Fast-forward more than two centuries to the First Couple in 2014, Michelle and Barack Obama. They forged their own deals, including Michelle extracting promises from Barack and his campaign staff that he'd spend time with their daughters in exchange for her active engagement in his first presidential bid.[7]

Something New

Any surface similarities between the Washington and Obama marriages coexist with monumental changes in marriage contracts and deals over the last two centuries. Consider the different experiences of Martha Washington and Michelle Obama, which reflect the huge upgrades of African American men and women of all races from their eighteenth-century status as property and/or subordinates to full citizens. An ancient common-law rule called "coverture" transferred Martha Washington's property, including land and 285 enslaved children, men, and women, to George and took away her power to own property or enter contracts, all under the rationale that marriage "covered" Martha's legal identity with his. The slaves had still less power. Historian Henry Weincke has documented the story of one of them, Ann Dandridge, who was Martha's half-sister.[8] Unlike Martha, Ann couldn't get married because antebellum law didn't let slaves marry. Legally recognizing slaves' kinship would honor their humanity, which would undermine slave-law's treatment of them as mere things.

In contrast to her enslaved ancestors, Michelle Obama is free to contract a marriage and also, unlike married women in the past, to enter contracts with landlords and banks. This economic citizenship mirrors her political citizenship, which she exercised by voting for her husband, an act all but unthinkable for the first First Lady.[9]

Barack Obama, too, illustrates expansions in who could marry. When he was born in 1961, over a third of the states still treated the marriage of his African father to Ann Dunham, a white woman, as a crime.[10] The US Supreme Court didn't give interracial marriage a constitutional seal of approval until 1967, when Richard and Mildred Loving successfully petitioned to overturn miscegenation laws.[11] In 2013, the federal government began to recognize same-sex marriage, but as of late 2014, about a third of the states still ban it.[12] On the fortieth anniversary of *Loving v. Virginia*, Mildred Loving emerged from her quiet life focused on family and church to speak up for same-sex marriage, declaring: "I am still not a political person, but I am proud that Richard's and my name is on a court case that can help reinforce the love, the commitment, the fairness, and the family that so many people, black or white, young or old, gay or straight seek in life. I support the freedom to marry for all. That's what *Loving*, and loving, are all about."[13]

Broken Engagements

While the landmark *Loving* case upgraded interracial unions from mere deals to legally binding marriage contracts, sometimes law moves in the opposite direction, demoting family contracts to mere deals. Engagements, for example, used to be legally binding. The exchange, "I'll marry you if you sleep with me" and its breach were so common in the nineteenth century that breach of promise to marry cases clogged court dockets.[14] Often, plaintiffs like Alice Hattin were pregnant, which sharply limited their chances of ever marrying. An 1879 court ordered Enoch Chapman to pay $6,000—around $140,000 in 2013 dollars—for injuring Alice by, in the judge's words, using his promise of marriage to "ruin" her, "destroying her character and blighting all her prospects in life."[15] By the 1930s, many states, alarmed by the number of breach of promise cases and sizeable judgments, passed so-called "heart balm" legislation that left jilted fiancées to bear their own losses, so that today, engagement is more of a deal than a contract. However, women can still sue for breach of promise to marry in some states, with limitations like Maryland's requirement that they're pregnant and have corroborating evidence.[16] Even where heart balm legislation bars recovery for noneconomic damages like humiliation, jilted fiancées can sue to get back engagement rings and wedding gifts.[17]

To Have and to Hold

Where engagement today is less contractual than it used to be, marriage retains many elements of a legally binding exchange. The marriage vows "to have and to hold" sound romantic, but they reference property rights, as in both owning ("having") and possessing ("holding") real estate. Marriage has long had financial implications. When Richard Loving was killed by a drunk driver in 1975, the legal recognition of their marriage meant that Mildred could collect his Social Security benefits, inherit from him, and make decisions about burial.[18]

If they'd divorced, a court would have divided their property and possibly awarded alimony. Celebrity divorces make the news in part because there's lots more money at stake. When Michael Douglas divorced Diandra, his wife of twenty-two years, she reportedly got $45 million, and Ivana Trump is said to have left her marriage with the Donald with over $20 million.[19]

Contractual reasoning undergirds this property sharing. The idea is that one spouse can contribute to the family welfare mostly through earnings and the other mostly through cooking, cleaning, homework help, and other tasks that sustain family life. Consequently, the reasoning goes, the primary homemaker owns a share of the property bought with the breadwinner's paycheck because it's the fruit of an exchange of financial support for caregiving.

Wedding Alterations

Deciding whether to divorce also became more contractual over the twentieth century. Before the 1970s, unhappy spouses in most states could only dissolve a marriage for "fault," meaning one person's adultery, say, or extreme abuse. After that, no-fault quickly became the majority rule because divorce for what California called "irreconcilable differences" reflected society's growing view of marriage as a vehicle for individual fulfillment, allowing unhappy spouses to part ways. That spirit of freedom also paved the way for letting spouses contract around the general rule of property sharing by entering a prenuptial agreement, or "prenup," to tailor financial arrangements.

That move toward contract can be a mixed bag. When Catherine Simeone, an unemployed nurse, got divorced from her neurosurgeon husband, Frederick, in 1990, the Pennsylvania Supreme Court enforced their prenup, explaining that "women are no longer regarded as the 'weaker' party in marriage, or in society generally," so that family law no longer presumes "that women are uninformed, uneducated, and readily subjected to unfair advantage in marital agreements."[20] That sounds empowering until you consider that Catherine was twenty-three when she married thirty-nine-year-old Frederick, who had $300,000 in assets and earned $90,000 a year. Their prenup provided her $200 of alimony a week and maxed out at $25,000. Their pair-bond exchange ended up being a raw deal for her, since she'd spent seven years becoming a specialist in running their household, only to find herself out of a job while he continued his medical practice.

Some people entering prenups are savvier because they've been married before. Take Michael Douglas's second marriage, to Catherine Zeta-Jones, who, unlike Catherine Simeone, has won Academy and Tony awards. Their prenup reportedly provides that if they divorce, she'll get $3.2 million for every year they're married, plus a $5 million "bonus" if he's caught cheating. Similarly, when rap master and entrepreneur Jay-Z married singer Beyoncé in 2008—joining his $300 million and her $100 million—the prenup is said to have bound him to pay her $10 million if their marriage failed within two years, $1 million for every year they stay together, and $5 million for each of their children. Since contracts are all about tailoring, some prenups have a "sunset clause," which contracts out of property sharing, then back into it if the marriage lasts, say, a decade. The prenup of General Electric CEO Jack Welch with his second wife had a ten-year sunset clause, which meant that she got around $180 million when Jack left her after fourteen years for the woman who became his third wife.[21]

As in any business arrangement, couples can modify their contract when circumstances change. In the case of golf virtuoso Tiger Woods, his widely publicized infidelities altered the bargaining power between him and his wife, Elin. Press reports said that Tiger and Elin renegotiated their prenup in an effort to stay together, upping the $20 million they initially agreed she'd get in a divorce.[22]

Lesser mortals also exercise their freedom to contractually alter property-sharing family law rules. When schoolteacher Betty Johnson got pregnant by her on-again, off-again boyfriend James Dawley, he reluctantly agreed to marry her if they entered a prenup that limited her rights to his earnings as an engineer and included his promise to support her and her daughter for at least fourteen months. When they split up in 1976, the California Supreme Court enforced their prenup, even though it seemed to encourage divorce, explaining, "Spouses who enter into an antenuptial agreement cannot forecast the future; they must, as a realistic matter, take into account both the possibility of lifelong marriage and the possibility of dissolution."[23]

Four decades later, a good number of newlyweds agree, especially in midlife marriages. When forty-something lawyer Lisa Padilla married fifty-something businesswoman Allison Klein in 2011, they signed a prenup to protect the retirement funds each had built up during successful careers,[24] just as the wealthy forty-six-year-old widow Gloria Perkinson entered a prenup in 1986 with retired pipefitter Franklin to give him $150,000 if they divorced (shielding $4.8 million in stock from her late husband's bottling company).[25]

Sex, Drugs, and Religion

Money is the main focus of most prenups. But couples also make written, formal agreements about other big things like fidelity and drug use,[26] as well as narrower issues like arbitration,[27] taking turns supporting each other through graduate school,[28] sharing the value of a spouse's medical degree,[29] agreeing who gets frozen embryos stored at a fertility clinic,[30] and determining who pays attorney's fees in child support or custody proceedings.[31] Family law generally treats these agreements as mere deals during the marriage. But at divorce it elevates some of them to contracts. Some religious agreements are just deals, like raising kids Jewish or Lutheran,[32] while others can be legally binding contracts, like a Jewish ketubah, which promises to obtain a religious divorce known as a "get,"[33] or the Muslim marriage contract provision called a *mahr*, which promises to pay the wife a set amount if the marriage ends.[34] Any attempt to limit child support is always a deal, as we saw in the *Kesler v. Weniger* sperm-donor case discussed in chapter 3.[35]

Real Deals

Even though deals don't fly in court, they can carry tremendous emotional and social weight in the wide world beyond the reach of law. A friend told me that her deal with her husband is that neither one gets fat, because, as she explained, "He's already hairy; can you imagine if he was fat *and* hairy?" Family law won't enforce their agreement, any more than it will enforce an agreement to have sex twice a week. Indeed, family law won't even enforce the basic wedding vow of financial support in an ongoing marriage, as Lydia McGuire discovered to her chagrin.

In 1953 Charles McGuire, a rich Nebraska farmer, refused his wife Lydia's requests for indoor plumbing, a working furnace, and a car with heat. The court told her that she could get these basic necessities only if she divorced him, but as long as they were married, their living conditions were entirely up to Charles.[36] That rule still holds true.[37]

Other exchanges that make families run smoothly, despite everyone's understanding that they'll never be legally binding, include

- A couple's wedding vow to support each other's careers
- One cooks in exchange for the other cleaning up
- One mows the lawn in exchange for the other vacuuming
- A Chinese American mom agrees with her Jewish husband that they'll raise the kids as Jewish in exchange for having them learn to speak Mandarin

- A wife looks the other way about a husband's affairs in exchange for reliable social and financial support[38]

These reciprocal promises pile up to help shape each family. Alongside love, legally binding contracts, and other shared commitments, they help make a family an "us."

MARRIAGE 101: "GIFT" EXCHANGES IN PLAN A FAMILIES

Conventional wisdom instructs that love is a gift, the very opposite of a bargained-for exchange. But it also says that marriage is a two-way street. We saw in chapter 6 how anthropologist Marcel Mauss captures both truths with the phrase "gift exchange," which connotes both altruism and expectation of a return gift down the road. This complexity—melding gift and exchange—is hardly surprising, since marriage is so old and so widespread, serving so many social, economic, and emotional functions to individuals, communities, and the state. Though the magnitude of marriage already fills volumes, it's worth noting here a few factors that shape marital contracting.

Marriage as Plan A

This book calls marriage Plan A and cohabitation Plan B. While some people may bristle at any implication that marriage deserves the highest grade, I use the Plan A/Plan B distinction to convey a much less controversial point. Marriage is the most common family form, and law and society grease the tracks in that direction. Calling it Plan A simply reflects its role as the default approach, just as caffeinated coffee is the default unless you specifically order decaf. If most people start choosing cohabitation over marriage, then the default should change.

Marriage rates are declining. A 2012 study found that 73 percent of Americans over fifteen years old had gotten married.[39] But that may be because people marry later than they used to. The study reported that in 2009 the median age for the first marriage was twenty-eight for men and twenty-six for women, a five- to six-year increase from the 1950 averages of twenty-three for men and twenty for women.[40] Taking a longer view, nine out of ten adults have gotten married since 1800, when records started to be kept.[41] That's rational. Marriage confers enormous benefits, and not just through the thousands of legal rules that treat married people differently from unmarried ones. As the discussion of Shelley Taylor's work on social affiliation in chapter 6 makes clear, married women, on average, are better off financially than single women, as are their children. Married men, for their part, enjoy better health and live longer, and suffer less from addiction and other illness than single men. Granted, many marriages are marred by abuse and inequality, but overall, marriage furthers health, wealth—and perhaps even wisdom, if a couple grows emotionally in their union.

Divorce requires an accounting of a couple's wealth and debts, as well as allocating the emotional losses that come when a child shuttles between two households. While fewer wives devote themselves full-time to homemaking than did in the 1960s, divorce still extracts a higher price from many primary homemakers than their husbands. As in chapter 7, which examines family law's devaluation of caregiving in cohabitation, this chapter focuses on how family law could do a better job of valuing the contributions of primary homemaking spouses. The solution offered in chapter 9 happens to benefit relatively privileged women, because more educated, affluent people are most likely to marry. Moreover, it may apply to fewer couples over time due to declining marriage rates and changes in married life. Economists Betsey Stevenson and Justin Wolfers contend that couples increasingly are held together by shared interests instead of the pair-bond exchange, since they have replaced that bargain with contracts with restaurants, house cleaners, and nannies.[42] Nevertheless, recognizing the value of caregiving in marriage could ripple outward to benefit cohabitants as well as those housecleaners, nannies, home health aides, and others who tend for a living.

Spiritual and Menial Housework

The low value accorded tending work correlates with larger hierarchies of race, class, and nationality. University of Pennsylvania law professor Dorothy Roberts has dubbed paid domestic labor "menial housework," in contrast to what she calls "spiritual housework." Menial housework, according to Roberts, includes strenuous, unpleasant tasks—like cleaning bathrooms—that are thought to require little intellectual or moral skill and accordingly garner trifling respect and remuneration. It's so devalued that as of early 2014, only three states protect domestic workers with rules about minimum wages, maximum hours, or freedom from harassment.[43] Spiritual housework, in contrast, includes "quality time" spent in bedtime rituals like bathing and story time or coaching manners over the dinner table. Practitioners of spiritual housework—more likely to be white and at least middle-class—get praise as good mothers, while those who perform menial housework—largely women of color, often poor, often immigrants—get tarred as bad mothers for leaving their own children untended while they care for other families.[44]

The distinction between spiritual and menial housework plays out in different feminists' view of homemaking labor. Some, following Betty Friedan, have championed the rights of women to escape the kitchen in search of economic self-sufficiency in wage labor. Generally, that means paying other women to do that menial housework. Sociologist Patricia Hill Collins focuses on these paid domestics, contending that many of them would "remove themselves from the exploited labor force in order to return the value of their labor to their families."[45] Along the same lines, welfare activists have argued that the state should support women staying at home as "a radical challenge to the socially defined gender roles of poor Black women, who had never been seen primarily as homemakers or mothers."[46]

Marriage Equality

An equally radical challenge took the form of same-sex couples' fight for marriage equality. The emotional and political intensity of that movement shows that marriage remains synonymous with "family" in many respects, fueling both same-sex couples' fervent desire to marry and the equally passionate desire of anti-gay folks to keep them from forming families deemed real by law and the wider culture.[47]

Just over a decade ago, a discussion of same-sex couples would have been in the cohabitation chapters of this book, because they could legalize their relationships only through contracts like living-together agreements and jointly held mortgages.[48] Until 2003 they were criminals in a good number of states, a status that changed after the US Supreme Court declared in *Lawrence v. Texas* that Texas couldn't "demean" gay people by "making their private sexual conduct a crime."[49] That same year, Massachusetts became the first state to recognize same-sex marriage. Over the next decade, other states followed suit, so that by 2012 over 114,000 same-sex couples were married in the United States, and another 108,000 were in civil unions or registered domestic partnerships.[50] But many more states declared that they'd never recognize same-sex marriage, as did the federal government. As of late 2014 about a third of the states still refuse to extend marriage equality to same-sex couples (though, in 2013, the Supreme Court struck down the clause of the federal law that defined marriage as a relationship between one man and one woman for federal purposes, and eighteen months later it allowed lower courts to recognize same-sex marriage in nearly a dozen more states).[51] In short, same-sex couples remain on the borderland of Plan A and Plan B as a good number of couples, judges, and talented lawyers work to nudge the United States as a whole to adopt a position already embraced by countries like Argentina, France, and South Africa.[52]

Marriage equality is granted or denied through substantive legal rules. Law also includes procedural rules that dictate how people get a court to give them the benefit of those substantive rules. The final section of this chapter examines one element of procedure: Plan A and Plan B methods of resolving disputes.

Contracting Out of the Courtroom

Throughout this book, we have seen that since the 1970s family law has become increasingly friendly to family agreements. The grounds for divorce have also changed. It used to be that divorcing couples had to convince a judge that either husband or wife was morally culpable ("at fault") and the wrongdoer paid for his or her bad actions by giving up property, alimony, or child custody. Today, family law has abandoned much of that moral judgment. All states recognize no-fault divorce, meaning that one spouse doesn't have to show that the other was to blame for the marriage's demise, though some states still give a divorcing spouse the option to claim fault. Because no-fault is now the general rule, courts rarely dig into salacious, shameful stories of adultery and abuse, making divorce a more matter-of-fact distribution of assets, debts, and parental rights and duties. No-fault divorce is so businesslike that drafters of the new divorce laws renamed it "dissolution," a term borrowed from the law of business partnerships.

The Power of Partnership

That partnership metaphor also underlies the gender neutrality that has come to dominate divorce law. In the mid-twentieth century, only ex-husbands paid alimony and moms generally got child custody. Today, thanks to advocacy by both feminists and men's rights groups, family law treats spouses as equal partners instead of assigning rights and duties according to gender. An ex-wife might pay alimony, and the kids might live with their dad. Both law and society have come to see a marriage with kids as a parenting and romantic partnership, with divorce ending only the romance part. Legal scholars use the term "private ordering" as shorthand for the freedom to determine the contours of your family relationships—essentially in private—instead of deferring to the rules laid down in state houses and courtrooms. One important method of private ordering in family law involves couples contracting out of courtroom divorce through alternative dispute resolution.

Plan A—courtroom divorce—is a highly formal, stylized battle between adversarial litigants, fought through ritualized motions and arguments that are structured by statutes and case law, all on a timeline set by the court and further constrained by ornate rules of evidence that determine what sorts of things a court can and should consider. Mediation, the increasingly popular Plan B alternative, is much more informal. Instead of making arguments to a judge, a couple sits at a conference room table with a mediator who's well versed in family law and dispute resolution. Unlike judges, mediators help couples reach agreement but do not make decisions themselves. Lawyers can prepare people by informing them of legal rights and duties, but they're generally not present at the mediation. Ideally, a mediated solution balances everyone's interests. In many cases, mediation can be cheaper and quicker and can help a divorcing couple lay the groundwork for more amicable communication over the years as they finish raising their kids.[53]

Sold on these benefits, I wrote the parenting agreements that I entered into first with Victor, then with Karen, to keep us out of court. First, we promised to resolve disputes through family therapy, and if that doesn't work, through mediation. LGBT organizations like Gay & Lesbian Advocates & Defenders (GLAD), the National Center for Lesbian Rights, and Lambda Legal have long urged same-sex couples to mediate end-of-relationship disputes instead of taking them to court, both to protect everyone—especially children—from the conflict, expense, and disruption of a drawn-out court battle and to prevent the people breaking up from inadvertently hurting the rest of the LGBT community by creating bad law with the help of homophobic or clueless judges.[54]

I took that idea one step further by adding in another clause, which I call "jerk insurance," as extra protection against a court battle. Behavioral economists refer to this type of clause as a "Ulysses contract," after the wily hero of Homer's *Odyssey.* While sailing across the wine-dark seas, Ulysses comes across the sirens, famous for their beautiful songs that enchant sailors to dive into the sea and to their deaths. Ulysses has his men tie him to the mast, instructing them not to untie him no matter how desperately he begs, and also to plug their own ears so they could steer the ship past the deadly mermaids. Along those same lines, a Ulysses contract strikes a deal between your present self and your future self, binding your future self not to do something stupid or self-destructive.[55] Yale legal economist Ian Ayres established a website, stickK, that puts this idea into action by helping people make deals with themselves to stick to their resolutions to lose weight, stop smoking, or achieve other personal goals.[56]

My Ulysses contract took the form a provision that lawyers call a choice of law and forum selection clause:

> Should one or both of us seek to legally enforce this agreement, we agree that this agreement should be construed under the laws of Massachusetts in a court of competent jurisdiction in Massachusetts.

In plain English, this means that if one of us turns into such a jerk that neither therapy nor mediation can resolve the conflict, we'll be stuck litigating in Massachusetts courts, applying Massachusetts law. When we signed the agreement I lived in Utah and Victor lived in Texas, so that little clause erected a huge logistical and financial barrier to the winner-takes-all forum of courtroom battle. Even hiring a lawyer in our home states to challenge or defend the jerk insurance clause would be difficult, because that Texas or Utah attorney would have had to come up to speed on Massachusetts rules regarding its enforceability.

We're not the only ones who want to decide for ourselves how to resolve disputes in our most precious relationships. University of Maryland law professor Jana Singer sees a "velvet revolution" in family conflict resolution that has largely replaced public courtroom disputes with private mechanisms like mediation and a newer process called "collaborative law."[57] Each uses contracts and deals to help divorcing families resolve disputes about money, property, and the care and feeding of children.

Mediation

Chapter 5 explored mediation's role in post-adoption contact agreements: some states require birth and adoptive parents to mediate a dispute before bringing it before a judge. The informality of mediation may provide people more space to voice the fears, hopes, and other emotions that get crowded out of courtroom discourse. On the other hand, having a lawyer vigorously advocate for you can be a huge help if you're especially vulnerable—as a young, single high school graduate might feel in relation to the doctor/lawyer couple who adopted her child—and also level out other power disparities that occur when one person is particularly aggressive or persuasive, or has the upper hand socially, economically, or physically.

Collaborative Lawyering

In the 1990s, the process of collaborative lawyering sought to combine the best elements of mediation and legal representation, and also took one giant step further by having people formally agree to collaboratively reach a durable and mutually agreeable settlement. Clients get the benefit of having a lawyer by their side throughout the process and also maintain privacy, informality, and a streamlined timeline. It's consistent with two central messages of this book. First, it honors the role of emotions in disputes by including mental health professionals as necessary to help divorcing spouses work through any fear, anger, or other fiery emotions that get in the way of resolving the financial and legal disputes. Second, collaborative divorce treats divorce as a rite of passage that many, if not most, people in American society experience instead of as a moral failing.[58] That moral neutrality echoes this book's treatment of different family forms as morally neutral alternatives.

Collaborative lawyers observe that the vast majority of divorces get settled on the courthouse steps—or earlier—leaving only 3–5 percent of cases to be decided by a judge. It's silly, expensive, and needlessly combative, they argue, to prepare for a formal, adversarial contest that probably won't happen and that too often wreaks irreparable collateral damage from claims about poor parenting or financial mismanagement.

Instead of pretending that the emotions of divorce can be set aside for rational conversations about finances and child custody, the process addresses emotional and communication challenges. By including mental health professionals trained to be divorce coaches, collaborative lawyering further honors emotional experience by requiring honesty and cooperation from everyone involved. Proponents of collaborative divorce contend that the "us-ness" of that process facilitates creative problem-solving and sets the stage for calmer interactions over the post-divorce years as parents continue coming together over a lifetime of births, graduations, marriages, and deaths.

Attorney Pauline Tesler and psychologist Peggy Thompson wrote the book *Collaborative Divorce*, which provides examples of couples who have benefited from collaborative lawyering. For example:

- Ronald and Maxine, who'd married in their sixties, avoided a winner-takes-all outcome through the collaborative process. Although Maxine had Ronald sign a prenup right before the wedding to protect the wealth she'd inherited from her parents, by divorce time, she was embarrassed to leave him with just Social Security payments to live on after he'd left his job to live near her ranch. Moreover, the last-minute prenup may not have held up in court, so they negotiated a solution with the help of lawyers and a financial advisor. Ronald left the marriage with an apartment to live in and sufficient funds to support himself. After signing the paperwork, they shook hands, "politely, though sadly" and thanked each other for being so considerate during the collaborative process.
- Adam and Sue relied on the collaborative process to break a log-jam about their house. Adam, a supermarket executive, wanted to sell it and buy two condos near each other so that he could remain close to the kids. Sue, a homemaker who did not choose the divorce, wanted to stay put. By working through her emotions, Sue came to see that the whole family could be better off in the condos because Adam could stay in the children's lives, and Adam realized how the house provided Sue needed peace and security during the upheaval of divorce. Their negotiated solution was to sell the house eighteen months after the divorce, when one of the kids finished middle school.[59]

Those financial terms are legally binding contracts. Collaborative divorce can also involve deals that a court might not enforce, like setting ground rules for a teenage son's driving privileges and pledging not to bad-mouth one another. Many final resolutions combine contracts and deals, as when a couple negotiated how to continue as co-owners of a winery business.[60]

These contracts and deals are made possible by another contract. At the beginning of the process lawyers, clients, and any financial or mental health professionals involved all sign a Collaborative Divorce Team Participation Agreement. It provides that everyone agrees to proceed with "honesty, cooperation, integrity, and professionalism geared toward the future well-being of the parties and their children" and also "to comply with and to promote the spirit and written word" of the agreement.[61] The clients hire one financial consultant and a child specialist, if one is necessary, avoiding the cost and acrimony of a battle of the experts. The lawyers agree to withdraw from the process if they find out that a client is lying or otherwise taking advantage of the collaborative process. Perhaps most powerfully, everyone agrees that if the collaborative process fails and the couple reverts back to the general rule of courtroom divorce, the lawyers, divorce coaches, financial consultants, and child specialists are all disqualified from assisting either client in a future proceeding. That Ulysses contract is even more expensive than the jerk insurance clause I wrote into my parenting agreement with Victor, because it requires everyone to start from scratch, paying a whole new set of professionals to help work out the dispute.[62] According to collaborative lawyers, removing the threat of litigation and pointing everyone toward settlement can help people find creative solutions that are harder to see in a storm of litigious motions and arguments.

Limits on Private Ordering

Privately ordered dispute resolution is not for everyone. Its critics worry about losing the safeguards built into courtroom procedures: an open record, appeal, the requirement that unbiased judges apply the law to the facts in front of them. Privacy could cover up injustices wrought by biased or untrained mediators, allowing more injustice than might occur with publicly vetted judges.[63] Even the staunchest proponents of collaborative divorce admit that it's inappropriate for people with serious mental illness, when one or both people are unwilling or unable to work collaboratively, and in domestic violence situations. Its harshest critics see fatal flaws in the collaborative process that make it wrong for anyone by undermining lawyers' professional obligations to maintain client confidentiality and zealously represent their clients' interests. Some also claim that collaborative divorce can be much more expensive and drawn-out than its supporters claim, partly because the pressure of court deadlines forces a divorcing couple to make hard decisions.

Most disturbing for present purposes—because it could undermine two of the proposals in this book—is that private ordering could further disempower someone already in a one-down position socially, emotionally, or economically. If a sperm donor doesn't have the bargaining power or sophistication to insist on a dad contract instead of a donor contract, he and the child may end up disserved by deference to private ordering. The same goes for birth moms who settle for less post-adoption contact than they really want, or adoptive parents who settle for more of it. The question is whether these dangers are sufficiently dire to cause us to revert to old rules that made a genetic dad a legal dad no matter what or papered over the relationship between adopted children and their birth families.

In contrast, this book's proposals about cohabitation agreements stand to help cohabitants who don't have much bargaining power. Inertia is such a powerful force that most live-in couples never explicitly agree who owns what or whether one owes the other palimony after a breakup. The proposal in chapter 7 recognizes pair-bond exchanges made through conduct, not just words on a page, and thus protects those who feel they are unable to demand respect and recognition for their contributions to the household.

In all the Plan B situations addressed thus far—repro tech, adoption, and cohabitation—people have to opt into these uncommon forms of family. Accordingly, contracts and deals play a prominent role in determining who is family and who is not. The final chapter examines agreements that might alter the terms of the state-supplied marriage contract. We'll see that even common forms of family like marriage have hidden contractual elements and accord more freedom of contract than most people think.

NINE

Legal Rules of Marital Agreements

MARRIAGE CONTRACT

"Shall we fudge the time on the ketubah?" I ask Karen, thinking that I know her answer.

A month before the wedding, I little guess that marrying into a Jewish family will make its rituals so much a part of my life that in a year I'll be the one making sure to pick up challah by dinnertime on Fridays. For now, I defer entirely to Karen on the question posed by the San Francisco artist creating the Jewish wedding contract. She wants to know whether we want to pretend that we're getting married after sundown to avoid running afoul of the Jewish prohibition of marrying on the Sabbath.

"Sure," Karen replies, surprising me. Karen's Judaism is largely cultural. I didn't expect her to bend to the laws of Moses and Israel, laws which were hardly written with us in mind and which wouldn't recognize this interfaith, same-sex marriage. The text acknowledges as much by omitting the traditional provision that the promises are made under "the laws of Moses and Israel."

While it lacks that choice of law clause, otherwise it reads a lot like other contracts. It begins with a preamble ("We enter into this mutual covenant as equal partners and loving, supportive companions in life"), followed by promises (love, respect for "each other and our combined cultures," and creating a home "filled with loving kindness and faith"), and ends with our signatures.

But Karen doesn't see the point of flouting a Jewish tradition at the very moment we are following the part of it that we do embrace. So I tell the artist to pen in 8:00 p.m., safely after sundown on an East Coast August evening.

In Judaism, the ketubah is the real marriage contract, and the wedding ceremony largely window-dressing, so we sign it a few minutes before the ceremony. Our families are clustered around a table set up in a side room graced by portraits of the well-heeled Bostonians who once lived in this house. For my mom, this is the performance, since I'm the first in our family to have a Jewish wedding. Right after it's done, she enthuses, "Oh, Martha, it's like a movie!"

A month later, hanging up the ketubah in our dining room—right next to our marriage license—I realize that the design we picked for its vibrant colors and simple, square images is also a patchwork. Like our family.

––––––––––

LAW AS IT IS RE MARITAL PAIR-BONDING EXCHANGES

Family law has long treated marriage as both a contract and a status, though today these two aspects of marriage are quite different from those in force in ancient Israel or at America's founding. Instead of rendering wives legally invisible, law now gives husbands and wives the same rights to child custody, property ownership, and entering contracts. It also generally requires divorcing spouses to share the property acquired during the marriage. Yet the work that many wives do caring for their families remains largely invisible to modern family law.[1]

This chapter largely focuses on how contractual thinking can remedy that problem but also touches on marital agreements about fidelity and religion. This format differs from the cohabitation cases, which discussed only the monetary issues of palimony and property sharing. Because marriage generally lasts longer and involves more social, emotional, and financial meshing, it makes sense that reported cases on marital contracting touch on a wider range of things that shape family life. As a whole, these agreements reveal once again the lie behind claims that family and contract are opposites.

Marital Agreements about Money

The first set of cases shows that family law decides who owns marital property—and owes alimony—based on an assumption that spouses enter a pair-bond exchange. Given that the exchange is essentially a contract, family law logically gives spouses the freedom to contract around those property-sharing rules. However, that freedom is only partial, leaving too many homemaking spouses with next to nothing for their contributions to family health and welfare.

An outline explains the general rule of property sharing, the prenup exception, and the way that both legal rules mask the value of homemaking:

General Rule: Divorcing spouses split property acquired during the marriage because family law presumes that both wage-earning and homemaking contribute to families[2]

Mask: Gift rhetoric often covers up both sides of the pair-bond exchange

Exception: Spouses can enter into prenups that limit property sharing and alimony upon divorce[3]

Mask: Gift rhetoric covers up the provider's free ride of taking valuable homemaking labor without giving anything in return

Before the 1970s, most courts treated any attempt to contract out of property sharing as merely a deal because, they reasoned, the government set the terms of the marriage contract, not the spouses themselves.[4] Some scholars argue family law should correct the problem of devalued caregiving by returning to the old rule that treated marital contracts as mere deals.[5] But I think that the long history of family exchanges argues for spouses holding onto their contractual freedom. Instead, courts could recognize that property-hoarding prenups fundamentally alter a couple's pair-bond exchange. The solution is to compensate the homemakers for their time and trouble.

A property-hoarding prenup transforms the relationship into a one-way exchange, called an "illusory promise" in legalese. Illusory promises are mere deals because they're not reciprocal.[6] Therefore, in prenup cases, courts could give up the legal fiction that all those trips to the grocery store and hours folding laundry were pure gifts, with no expectation of any return, because the provider didn't hold up his or her half of the "gift" exchange. Otherwise, homemakers are like menial servants, toiling day and night without remuneration other than room and board.

The following three cases illustrate the contractual core of the general rule and the injustice served up when courts recognize only the provider side of pair-bond exchanges in prenup cases.

Case #1: Marriage as Partnership: *Flechas v. Flechas* (2001)

The divorce case of businessman Miguel ("Mike") and Eunice Flechas shows a typical pair-bond exchange and how family law's general rule recognizes homemaking as a valuable part of that exchange.[7] Mike and Eunice married in 1991, when they were both fifty-four. Like many midlife newlyweds, they wanted to protect some property for their children from prior marriages. Eunice had around $500,000 from selling her house in Georgia to move to Mississippi as well as an inheritance from her mother, about one-twelfth of Mike's net worth of $6.4 million. Consequently, they made an oral agreement to keep the property they brought into the marriage separate. But they didn't say anything about Mike's income, which ranged from $217,000 to $379,000 a year while they were married.

The divorce court had to decide whether to divide the $1.6 million that Mike made while Eunice refurbished their home, kept house, cooked meals, and took care of his younger son. The question was whether to recognize what she did as well as all she'd given up to marry Mike: quitting her job as a teacher, selling her house, moving into Mike's house, and not getting re-licensed to teach in Mississippi because they agreed she'd manage their household full-time.[8]

The Mississippi Court of Appeals decided in Eunice's favor. As a matter of contract law, it said that their prenup applied only to the property they brought into the marriage, leaving Mike's income earned during their marriage to be divided under the general rule requiring property sharing. The court could have stopped there, and just awarded Eunice the $300,000 she sought. But it expanded the case's significance by explaining the rationale behind the property-sharing rule. The court said:

> Marriage is considered a partnership with both spouses contributing to the marital estate in the manner in which they have chosen. Eunice . . . made a significant indirect economic contribution to the marriage through quitting her job in Georgia, ending her career, selling her home to move to Pascagoula to become Mike's wife, acting as custodian of the marital home and surrogate mother to Mike's younger son, and contributing to the stability and harmony of the marital relationship while sacrificing her own career during her best earning years.[9]

Consistent with the traditional exchange of swapping homemaking for financial support, the court insisted that both sides of the pair-bond exchange contribute to family wealth:

> Although contributions of domestic services are not made directly to a retirement fund, they are nonetheless valid material contributions which indirectly contribute to any number of marital assets, thereby making such assets jointly acquired.[10]

Since Eunice was, the court said, "chief cook and bottle washer," she was entitled to much more than the $36,000 awarded by the trial court. If the lower court's disregard for the value of Eunice's sacrifices and contributions to the family had stood, Eunice would have gotten only around $6,000 a year—plus room and board—in return for her years of labor and sacrifices for the marriage. A live-in maid would do better.

A number of family law scholars agree that courts should honor the contributions—different and equally valuable—that both partners make to family life.[11] Unfortunately, as the next case shows, most courts retain the fiction that the caregiving side of pair-bonding is a mere gift even when the provider opts out of his property-sharing obligations.

Case #2: Barry Bonds Hits a Home Run for Prenups: *In re Marriage of Bonds* (1999)

Baseball superstar Barry Bonds took full advantage of family law's willingness to enforce prenups.[12] Bonds's money and fame make the case unusual—the trial judge recused himself after word got out that he'd requested Barry's autograph[13]—but the part that matters for our discussion is the way it illustrates the exception to property sharing. Though most couples share property acquired during the marriage, some couples contract out of the pair-bond exchange by signing an agreement saying that the one making the money gets to keep that money (as well as the houses, cars, furniture, and everything else bought with it).

Historically, as we've seen, couples could not contractually adjust the terms of their marriage. But today courts treat women as competent adults who can order their own affairs. Of course, as courts began to enforce prenups like other contracts, they also applied rules that protect vulnerable parties in all contracts, like requiring genuine consent (which is absent when, for example, one person pressures the other to sign right away).[14]

In 2000, Barry Bonds wanted out of his six-year marriage to Susann (known as Sun). He had a $43 million, six-year contract to play for the San Francisco Giants, but when Barry and Sun met in Montreal in 1987, he was not yet an All-Star. Both were twenty-three, and Barry was playing for the Pittsburgh Pirates. Neither one could have known that he would play for twenty-two years, set a record for most Major League Baseball home runs (762), and be named MVP seven times. Sun was newly emigrated from Sweden, working in a sports bar and harboring ambitions of doing makeup for the stars. Within months, they were living together, engaged, and planning to fly to Las

Vegas for a small wedding. The day before the wedding, en route to the airport, Barry took Sun to his attorney's office.[15] There they signed an agreement that would change their pair-bond exchange into a one-sided agreement:

> We agree that all the earnings and accumulations resulting from the other's personal services, skill, efforts and work, together with all property acquired with funds and income derived therefrom, shall be the separate property of that spouse.[16]

In plain English, as Barry testified at trial, this meant "What's mine is mine, what's yours is yours."[17] At the time, Sun had no property or income, and Barry took care of all her expenses. Her job was being the baseball player's wife, providing emotional and social support to him and, later, their two children. Without asking whether Sun performed her side of the pair-bond exchange, the California Supreme Court let Barry evade his half.

The court focused on voluntariness, ruling that Sun signed the agreement of her free will. Unlike the lower court, the Supreme Court refused to see Sun as a timid victim bullied into signing the prenup, instead describing her as an "intrepid" woman who "emigrated from her homeland at a young age, found employment and friends in a new country using two languages other than her native tongue, and in two years moved to yet another country, expressing the desire to take up a career and declaring to Barry that she 'didn't want his money.'"[18]

That focus on voluntariness overshadowed another important consideration. The court didn't mention domestic details like how much time Sun spent grocery shopping, preparing meals, and caring for their children and the household. Given the Bonds' income, they may have hired a lot of help, and Sun's job may have been to supervise the staff, spend time at the gym to look good, and to accompany Barry on the road. But with two kids and Barry's training, travel, and game schedule, it seems likely that she spent many hours each week managing the household. We'll never know, because the family law rules on prenups see all that time, and perhaps the work itself, as essentially irrelevant.

Many observers thought Sun should have won. After the case came down, the California legislature passed a law to protect spouses in Sun's situation. It required the person signing to have at least a week to review the prenup and either have a lawyer or waive the right to counsel in a separate agreement.[19] In 2012, NCCUSL—the group that proposed the model legislation on repro tech discussed in chapter 3—published the Uniform Premarital and Marital Agreements Act, which similarly beefs up procedural road blocks to a winner-takes-all prenup.[20]

Case #3: Caring about Care Work: *Borelli v. Brusseau* (1993)

But extra time and an attorney's advice do not address the core issue of valuing the homemaking side of pair-bond exchanges.

Seventy-something San Francisco businessman Michael Borelli married Hildegard in 1980, when she was thirty-nine. The day before their wedding, they signed a premarital agreement that reserved most of his property—worth around $1.5 million—for his daughter from a prior marriage.[21] Unlike Sun Bonds, Hildegard didn't challenge the prenup's validity. Instead, she sought to enforce an oral agreement they made later to modify it.[22] That oral agreement brought their arrangement back toward the pair-bond exchange and California's general rule that spouses share property acquired during the marriage. Yet the California courts refused to allow Hildegard to enforce that modification.

Within a few years of getting married, Michael suffered heart problems and a stroke. By 1988, his doctors recommended that he live in a nursing home because he needed constant care. Understandably, he preferred to live at home, even though he and Hildegard would have to modify their house. Maybe he realized that his reduced marital obligations under their prenup would justify Hildegard in feeling less obliged under the caretaking half of the pair-bond exchange. In any case, Michael offered to alter the prenup by changing his will to give Hildegard some of his property—around $500,000, including money for her daughter's education—if she'd disregard the doctors' advice and provide the nursing care herself at their home.

Hildegard accepted and performed her part of their agreement, personally providing round-the-clock nursing care for Michael until his death a year later. But Michael never changed his will. Hildegard sued and lost because family law clung to the fiction that her caretaking was a pure gift even when Michael didn't keep up his end of the gift exchange.

To apply this double standard, the court had to ignore that Michael himself had slipped out of his obligations. Instead of attacking Michael's property-hoarding prenup, it chastised Hildegard for trying to do what Michael actually did—tailor the terms of the marriage contract—declaring that Hildegard couldn't adjust those terms because "a wife is obligated by the marriage contract to provide nursing type care to an ill husband."[23] Citing pre–World War II cases, the court in *Borelli* said that a husband's agreement to compensate a wife undermines the public policy of wives caring for husbands. Hildegard, as the spouse whose contributions came in the form of care, feeding, and cleaning, had no right to contractually adjust her side of the deal. The court waxed sentimental to justify depriving her of that contractual freedom:

> [T]he marital duty of support [under California law] includes caring for a spouse who is ill. . . . [It] means more than the physical care someone could be hired to provide. Such support also encompasses sympathy[,] love[,] comfort[,] companionship and affection. Thus, the duty of support can no more be "delegated" to a third party than the statutory duties of fidelity and mutual respect.[24]

The court's contempt for Hildegard's conduct as "sickbed bargaining" and "unseemly" is unfair, given Michael's earlier bargaining to get out of his support obligations. By concluding that "even if few things are left that cannot command a price, marital support remains one of them,"[25] the court simply ignored the fact that family law allowed Michael, as a financial provider, to contract out of his side of the pair-bond exchange. This double standard undermines the very foundation of families and family law.

Under *Borelli*, family law sees agreements to put a monetary value on homemaking as contrary to public policy and therefore demotes them to mere deals. But it should be contrary to public policy to let Michael Borelli contract out of his provider obligations while holding Hildegard to her caregiving end of the pair-bond exchange.[26] It makes no sense that family law gives so much contractual freedom to a more propertied person like Michael to help him hoard his wealth but so little to dutiful, caregiving spouses like Hildegard. Family law can do better, and contracts offer a means to that end.

LAW AS IT SHOULD BE RE PAIR-BOND EXCHANGES IN PRENUP CASES

Much as some might like to return to an imagined golden age untainted by exchange, the better approach corrects the errors of *Borelli* without returning to the old rule that deprived spouses of freedom of contract. Recall that the *Flechas* case treated marriage as a partnership, using that commercial template for the most personal of relationships. The proposal I make for correcting the problem of devaluing Sun Bonds's and Hildegard Borelli's caregiving builds on the partnership metaphor by adding a rule to prevent a property-hoarding spouse from having his cake and eating it too.

The Three-Step Solution: Unmasking the Myth of the Gift

If marriage is a partnership, both partners are entitled to a return on the time and resources they've invested in their joint enterprise. If one person contracts out of that partnership—by hoarding partnership property to him- or herself—it's no longer a joint enterprise. The promise to share is now illusory. Accordingly, the property hoarder should be treated as having contracted out of the privilege of treating "housewifely duties" as mere gifts.

The first two steps of the three-step solution should look familiar because family law already follows them:

> *Step 1:* Apply the general rule that recognizes the pair-bond exchange through property-sharing unless the couple has entered a property-hoarding prenup.

Step 2: Ask whether the prenup is involuntary, one-sided, unfair, or contrary to public policy.

If it is, revert to step 1 and apply the general rule.

If it's not, then the prenup is a contract. Go to step 3.

Step 3: Since the prenup transformed the pair-bond exchange into an illusory promise, abandon legal fiction that home-making is a pure gift.

Calculate the market value of cooking, cleaning, home health care, etc.

Adding step 3 would correct the current double standard that allows providers but not caregivers to contractually adjust the terms of the pair-bond exchange. It's fine—and may facilitate generosity in families—to pretend that homemaking labor is a gift as long as the homemaker is protected by the property-sharing rules of divorce law. But if richer spouses insist on property-hoarding prenups, then courts should abandon the myth of the gift and award the homemaking spouses the value of all that work.

Here's how it would work:

Step 1: When a couple divorces, the court assumes that marriage is a pair-bond exchange and consequently divides the family's property and may award alimony. If there's a prenup limiting property sharing or alimony, the court proceeds to step 2 to determine whether it's legally binding.

Step 2: The court figures out whether the prenup is a contract or a mere deal by asking how long the person from whom property is hoarded had to read it; whether he or she had counsel; whether a non-marital pregnancy, domestic violence, or the threat of deportation exerted undue pressure to sign; and whether it's in writing.[27] If one of these defenses demotes the prenup to a deal, the court reverts to step 1 (the general rule) and divides the property. But if the prenup is a binding contract, I propose that family law add step 3 to the analysis.

Step 3: The court figures out whether the prenup contract frees the provider from holding up his or her side of the pair-bond exchange. If so, the court should recognize that the prenup changed the pair-bond exchange to an illusory promise. Since illusory promises are not legally binding, a property-hoarding prenup should lead the courts to discard the myth of the gift. Freed of the homemaking-as-a-gift fiction, the court could calculate an amount to fairly compensate care-givers like Sun Bonds, Eunice Flechas, and Hildegard Borelli for the months and years of cooking, cleaning, and caring for sick family members. Barry might argue that Sun didn't do much, but it's clear that both Hildegard and Eunice would be entitled to compensation for what their husbands would have had to pay a cook, housekeeper, and caregiver.

That amount ought not to be decreased by the value that the caregiver received during the marriage. The point is to prevent the provider from free riding, so the remedy falls within the category of relief that lawyers call "restitution." In restitution cases, the goal is to disgorge a wrongdoer's ill-gotten gains. Therefore, property hoard-ers ought to pay for the tending they took without fully providing in return. The caregivers' gains were not ill-gotten, because they are not taking advantage of their partners.

Accounting for Prenup Modification

In *Borelli*, the court would go through these steps first for the prenup that the Borellis signed right before the wedding, and then for the modification they made after Michael got sick. If the initial agree-ment was binding at step 2, the court would then examine the modi-fication under step 2 for voluntariness and other requirements for legal enforceability. If the court concluded that the modification was legally binding at step 2, it wouldn't have to calculate the value of Hildegard's caregiving at step 3 because Michael and Hildegard had already agreed that it was worth around a third of his estate. But if the modification was not legally binding, perhaps because it was oral instead of in writing, or if Michael didn't have a lawyer review it, then the initial prenup would still render the pair-bond exchange an illusory promise. Accordingly, the court would drop the pretense that Hildegard's bed-pan emptying and other care were pure gifts and calculate what Michael would pay to get the tending that Hildegard did for him over their entire marriage, including that last year of round-the-clock, in-home medical care.

The dissenting judge in *Borelli* wrote a separate opinion suggesting that he might be open to this approach. Judge Poché criticized the majority for applying a double standard by allowing Michael but not Hildegard to alter family law obligations, pointing out that the pre–World War II cases on which the majority relied no longer held sway because, he said, "Modern attitudes toward marriage have changed," with many wives working outside the home and many husbands doing "domestic chores that make a house a home."[28] Since California allows spouses to contract with each other and gender roles are changing, Judge Poché reasoned, spouses' duties to provide medical care for one another shouldn't be taken as imposing a state-mandated duty to *personally* provide that nursing care. Judge Poché wrote when Bill Clinton was president and worried that the majority's ruling, applied to the Clintons, meant that "if Mrs. Clinton becomes ill, President Clinton must drop everything and personally care for her."[29] In 2012, when Hillary Clinton was serving as the secretary of state, the *Borelli* decision would have required her to drop everything to care for Bill personally if he became ill, jeopardizing diplomatic relations and other issues of national importance.

Difficulties in making exact calculations shouldn't make courts retain the fiction that homemaking is a pure gift. Sure, you can buy Cadillac care or Hyundai homemaking, and rates vary around the country. But the courts could rely on averages. Hourly rates for a home health aide in 2012 ran around $21, a housecleaner about $20, and nannies around $15, while the average cab ride costs around $13.[30] In breach of contract cases, courts don't require mathematical precision in calculating losses, just reasonable certainty of damages. Since homemaking is one of the tasks that is invisible if done well—from help with homework to laundry—lots of tasks would inevitably go unaccounted for despite the most precise calculations. At the end of the day, the goal should be to provide economic and social support for homemaking labor to correct the current rule's policy of ignoring it.

In sum, the problem in prenup cases isn't too much contract but too little. Ignoring the exchange can harm families as much or more than recognizing the value of both sides of the pair-bond exchange.

LAW AS IT IS RE SEXUAL AGREEMENTS

Family law has fumbled just as badly when asked to value fidelity in reconciliation agreements. While the vast majority of reported cases on prenups focus on money, a strand of cases addresses topics like sex and religion. If it's surprising that courts get involved with that, the results of the cases are more surprising still. I'll start with sex.

For centuries, family law interpreted a woman's "yes" in her wedding vows to imply a blanket consent to sex any time her husband wanted it. Accordingly, the traditional definition of rape was forcible intercourse with a woman not the defendant's wife. Marital rape was not a crime until the 1970s, when feminists fomented rebellion and won significant reforms. Today, spouses might make a number of deals about sex: agreeing to frequency, say, or techniques. The law won't get involved with any of them unless the sex is nonconsensual or other interests are triggered, like bans on public sex. The type of sexual agreement that shows up in case reporters is a reconciliation agreement entered to induce a cheated-upon spouse to take the cheater back.

Case #4: Investing in Fidelity: *Diosdado v. Diosdado* (2002)

After Manuel Diosdado had an affair in 1993, he and his wife, Donna, separated. However, they managed to reconnect and used a signed writing to formalize Manuel's promise never to cheat again if Donna would take him back. That agreement, they hoped, was an alternative to divorce. Manuel's attorney wrote its "Obligation of Fidelity" clause, which provided that the couple intended to be in an exclusive relationship premised on emotional and sexual fidelity and mutual trust. It also precisely defined breach as "any act of kissing on the mouth or touching in any sexual manner" anyone outside the relationship and set out the consequences of breach: the cheater would immediately move out of the house and also have to pay the other spouse $50,000 off the top of any property settlement if they divorced.[31]

The Diosdados signed the agreement, moved back in together, and things were fine for five more years. Unfortunately, Manuel had another affair, a breach that landed the Diosdados in divorce court.

Equally unfortunate, to my mind, is the court's demotion of Donna and Manuel's formal written reconciliation agreement to a mere deal. It reasoned that because spouses could get divorced without showing fault like adultery, courts couldn't enforce a reconciliation agreement including a fidelity term. Holding Manuel to his formal written promise, the court said, ran contrary to public policy by undermining the no-fault provisions of California's divorce laws through testimony about the emotional angst that no-fault divorce meant to banish from the courtroom.

But the court misread the agreement. Donna and Manuel's agreement didn't reinstate fault-based divorce. It didn't say that they could divorce only for adultery or other kinds of fault. All their Ulysses contract did was try to preserve their marriage by creating a clear and immediate consequence—moving out and giving up $50,000 in property—to help Manuel keep his promise. It clearly defined that promise by specifying what counted as infidelity. Donna even had an eyewitness to prove that he breached the agreement. California's refusal to honor to what amounted to a formal restatement of Donna and Manuel's wedding vows protects neither marriage nor no-fault divorce. Instead, it encourages the cheaters of the world to continue making this kind of empty promise and punishes the innocent spouses who rely on them.

Indeed, the court in *Diosdado* explicitly said that California law values Barry Bonds's right to hoard his property more than Manuel's promise of fidelity. Quoting from the *Bonds* case, the court explained that it had the power to displace Donna and Manuel's judgment of what could save their marriage with what it called the law's "social policy with respect to marriage:" "Marriage itself is a highly regulated institution of undisputed social value, and there are many limitations on the ability of persons to contract with respect to it."[32] By enforcing Barry's property-hoarding prenup but refusing to enforce Manuel's promise to forsake all others, the California courts announced that property-hoarding has a higher social value than fidelity.

Another California couple, Monica Mehren and Christopher Dargan, similarly found that Christopher's written promise to give up some property if he relapsed into cocaine use was merely a deal.[33] Christopher, an attorney, was not bound by the agreement he wrote up himself. I have yet to figure out why family law gives so much contractual freedom to a rich person like Barry Bonds to help him hoard his wealth but so little to spouses like Donna and Monica who try to reconcile after affairs or drug addiction. Family law can do better.

LAW AS IT SHOULD BE RE FIDELITY AGREEMENTS

The current rule allows cheaters to prosper at their spouses' expense. Courts should enforce reconciliation agreements like Donna and Manuel Diosdado's fidelity agreement as well as other so-called "bad boy" clauses like Christopher Dargan's promise not to slide back into cocaine use. Those clauses don't reinstate fault-based divorce because they have no effect on the grounds for divorce, only the consequences of conduct that leads to divorce. Even no-fault states sometimes account for fault like adultery in deciding issues like alimony and property distribution on divorce.[34]

The North Carolina Court of Appeals enforced a reconciliation agreement between Linda and Henry Dawbarn. But in that case, Linda got Henry to transfer their three houses to her, the furniture in them, and the couple's cars shortly after she confronted him about his affair. The marriage lasted nine more years but they ultimately divorced.[35] The court allowed the agreement to stand, reasoning that it didn't create an incentive for Linda to leave the marriage—which would have violated public policy—since the property transfer had already happened. That kind of technicality helps someone aggressive or furious enough to get that property at the moment of signing, but it would surprise many, and perhaps most, people.

The flip side of the *Dawbarn* court's concern is that enforcing a reconciliation agreement would force a couple to stay married. According to Henry Dawbarn, he stayed married to Linda for those nine long years after their reconciliation because the agreement's terms left him with so little.[36] Contract law rules police against vagueness and coercion—and indeed might police the arguably unconscionable terms of Henry Dawbarn giving up virtually all of the marital property—and require signed writings as proof of particular kinds of agreements. Those rules should prevent injustices in reconciliation agreement cases. Moreover, since contract law won't impose a penalty, instead just compensating a victim of breach for actual losses, a court wouldn't enforce an agreed-upon consequence for infidelity if it seemed wildly out of proportion to the losses suffered because of men or women behaving badly.

LAW AS IT IS RE RELIGION AGREEMENTS

Infidelity originally referred to a straying away from religious doctrine, but today it denotes a breach of the marriage vow. Just as family law treats that promise to forsake all others as a mere deal, it refuses to enforce promises that spouses make to raise their kids a particular religion, reasoning that doing so would violate constitutional principles requiring the separation of church and state. However, some courts are willing to enforce two formal, written religious promises relating to marriage, one Jewish and the other Islamic.

Case #5: Getting a "Get": *In re Marriage of Goldman* (1990)

When Kenneth and Annette Goldman dissolved their decade-long marriage in 1989, the Illinois courts faced the daunting task of determining whether their Jewish marriage contract known as a ketubah was a binding contract or just a deal. Like many Orthodox Jewish divorcées, Annette sought to enforce the provision that required Kenneth to ask a rabbinical tribunal for a divorce under Jewish law, commonly called a "get."[37]

While Kenneth and Annette's ketubah included Kenneth's promise to "honor and cherish," as well as "protect and support Annette," and Annette's promise to fulfill "all the duties incumbent upon a Jewish wife," the ketubah was silent on the issue of getting a *get*.[38] The court nevertheless found this promise embedded within a choice of law clause. In a business contract, a choice of law clause provides that any dispute will be governed by a particular state's law. In a ketubah, however, that clause took the form of Kenneth's statement to Annette, "Be thou my wife according to the law of Moses and Israel," and language right before their signatures that read: "This Covenant of Marriage was duly executed and witnessed this day according to the usage of Israel."[39] The court found that bringing the agreement within the laws of Moses and Israel imported Jewish traditions and customs, including the rules about Kenneth seeking a *get* in the event that he and Annette got divorced under civil law.

Deciding that the laws of Moses and Israel applied didn't resolve the whole problem, however. Jewish law requires that the husband voluntarily approach the rabbis, and Kenneth refused. (The wife cannot request a *get*.) Though he was Orthodox before marrying Annette—and had granted his first wife a *get*—he had abandoned Orthodoxy for the more liberal strand of Judaism known as Reconstructionism by the time he and Annette were married. Yet Annette became Orthodox during their marriage. By the time they divorced, Kenneth viewed Orthodoxy as hostile to women, "antimodern" and "repulsive."[40]

Kenneth knew a lot about hostility to women. Without a *get*, Jewish law would treat Annette as "agunah"—meaning "chained" in Hebrew—neither married nor unmarried, and thus unable to remarry under Jewish law. Were she to remarry civilly, Jewish law would treat the children of that marriage as the progeny of a forbidden relationship, and thus unable to marry Jews themselves. Initially, Kenneth said he'd give Annette a *get* if she'd share custody of the kids with him, but he later refused on the ground that she was a "liar" and a "cheat" and that she was "'going to pay' for what she'd done to him by being married to him for the rest of her life."[41] The Illinois courts got around this conundrum by applying another principle of

Jewish law that made an exception for abandonment. Since Kenneth had abandoned Annette, it found, Jewish law compelled him to at least grant her a *get*.

Those customs may seem different from the practices that courts imply in business contracts. The dissenting judge in *Goldman* thought that the Constitution's religious freedom protections make the ketubah a promise different from ordinary promises. The majority opinion justified its decision to enforce the ketubah against Kenneth—ordering him to request a *get* from the Rabbis—by recognizing a civil side of Jewish law, one that deals only with people's relationship with one another instead of their relationship with God. Under Jewish law, it found, marriage and divorce are secular, contractual undertakings. "Kenneth need not engage in any act of worship nor profess any religious belief," the court explained, so that the court order compelling him to approach the rabbinical tribunal was not an "excessive entanglement" with religion.[42]

Courts in New York have reached the same conclusion, mostly to require a husband to seek a *get*, though in a 1926 case the court interpreted the ketubah as giving a widow rights under Jewish law to the house in which she and her husband had lived.[43] Reasonable minds, however, can differ. An Arizona court saw the phrase in the ketubah invoking the laws of Moses and Israel as too vague, violating the rule that enforceable contracts must have reasonably certain terms, and others see enforcing ketubahs as breaching the barrier between church and state.[44]

Case #6: Muslim Marriage Contracts: *Odatalla v. Odatalla* (2002)

While fewer Muslim marriage contracts have reached the courts, those agreements, like ketubahs, have been treated as binding agreements. The cases, however, enforce a different contract term. While Jewish wives want to compel their husbands to give them a *get*, Muslim women getting divorced have asked courts to enforce the "mahr," a financial provision in their wedding contracts.

Shortly before an imam performed the 1996 wedding of Houida and Zuhair Odatalla at the home of Houida's parents in New Jersey, her family and Zuhair negotiated the terms of the *mahr*.[45] Bride and groom both read the agreement, then signed it voluntarily before witnesses, as required by Islamic law. The *mahr* required the husband to pay the bride a sum certain—"one golden pound coin"—at the time of the wedding and an additional $10,000 "postponed" to another time.

The groom performed part of the agreement by handing Houida one golden pound coin during the wedding ceremony. When Houida filed for divorce in 2002 on the grounds of extreme cruelty, she asked the court to order Zuhair to pay the $10,000 promised in the *mahr*. Like the ketubah's silence on the issue of the husband seeking a *get*, the Islamic marriage contract says nothing about when the bride can demand that her husband fulfill the financial promise he made. Customarily, the wife enforces the promise only at divorce or widowhood, when she's likely to need money to live on her own.

Courts follow precedent—the rules laid down in prior similar cases. In *Odatalla*, the New Jersey court followed earlier cases enforcing ketubahs, overcoming the husband's arguments regarding the First Amendment, vagueness, and public policy. As to religious freedom, the court answered the husband's contentions with a query asking why a contract promising to pay money should be less of a contract just because it was entered into at the time of an Islamic marriage ceremony. In the court's view, "[t]oday's diverse community," brought into being through immigration of people of various religious beliefs, requires constitutional principles to "keep abreast of these changes in the fabric of our community."[46]

The New Jersey court's reasoning on the issue of vagueness segues with material covered in earlier chapters on cohabitation and marriage in that contracts' terms can come from custom and behavior as well as words on the page. Courts routinely consider evidence outside of a written document—calling it "parol," meaning "spoken"—as long as it doesn't contradict the terms of a written agreement. In *Odatalla*, the court found that the custom of the wife demanding payment of the *mahr* at the time of divorce or death was consistent with the word "postponed" in the writing that they signed at their wedding. Similarly, courts have considered oral or implicit agreements between cohabitants and spouses in cases like *Byrne v. Laura* (chapter 7's story about Skip and Flo) and *Goldman*, especially when there are actions that back up this off-the-page evidence.

The court in *Odatalla* also rejected Zuhair's arguments that the *mahr* violated public policy, just as the court in the *Weinschel v. Strople* adoption case we saw in chapter 5 rejected Bruno Weinschel's public policy objection to the open stepparent adoption he'd agreed to in his divorce. Far from being against public policy, the court in *Odatalla* concluded that treating the *mahr* as a legally binding contract furthered the important public policy of honoring "a custom and tradition that is unique to a certain segment of our current society."[47]

LAW AS IT SHOULD BE RE RELIGION AGREEMENTS

The Jewish and Muslim marriage contract cases are rightly decided. Like the intimate agreements for parenthood—through repro tech or adoption—or between cohabitants, these agreements deserve to be honored. That means that a *mahr* might not be enforceable if its particular terms or interpretation undermined public policies, as would be the case if Houida Odatalla got only the $10,000, and lost her civil law rights to property sharing and alimony.[48] Similarly, a contract forcing Donna Diosdado to have sex with Manuel any time he wanted would undermine public policy by allowing him to commit a crime by raping her. Law can recognize contracts while still policing these extreme situations. That recognition encourages spouses like the Odatallas and Diosdados, not to mention the Fleschases, Bonds, and Borellis, to invest in their relationships by making binding exchanges that help them become and stay a family, and also, when necessary, sever that relationship.

CONCLUSION

Ending this book with a discussion about religion bookends its beginning with memoir, appropriate packaging given its arguments showing the role of love and other emotional considerations in family law. As economic sociologist Viviana Zelizer argues, intimate life and exchange are not opposites. To the contrary, family exchanges shape the law just as the law in turn shapes both families and the exchanges they make. Treating love and contracts as Hostile Worlds demotes both to a two-dimensionality that ignores their rich and complex relationship. More important, recognizing those contracts and deals makes it easier for families to decide for themselves, more or less, how to live in the sacred social circle we call family.

Epilogue

LEGAL ADVICE: SALT LAKE CITY 2013

"How's that working out?" the Utah lawyer asks.

We're at a Salt Lake City memorial service for the friend who hooked me up with this lawyer. It's been a decade since she explained to me how gay folks manage to skirt Utah's ban on them adopting. Then, once I got pregnant, she reviewed Victor's and my parenting agreement. Now she leans in to see the cell-phone picture I'm showing off to friends who helped Walter come into being: a shot of him stretched out on a tree branch, eyes shining with a nine-year-old's pride at scaling the tree on his own and balancing on a branch eight or ten feet above the sidewalk.

"Great," I tell her, saying that she shows up in the book I'm writing to get the word out that people can find happiness through family contracts. She's more interested to hear that I've met Karen, got married, and folded her in as a third parent by amending the parenting agreement and taking advantage of DC's de facto parent statute. When I add that Walter's about to get a step-dad in the person of the tall Texan who's marrying Victor, and that Karen and I are hosting their post-wedding brunch just as they hosted our rehearsal dinner, she seems sick of my kvelling. But she perks up when she hears that the DC lawyer, like her, tried to talk us out of including the mushy emotional terms in the parenting agreement.

"I'd still give the same advice," she says, clearly unpersuaded by my story of happy-ever-after.

When pressed to explain why, she says that family contracts don't work out so well for most people, backing up her claim with a story about a client who thought he was a dad but the mom treated him like a donor, shutting him out from visits and decision making. She admits that they didn't come to a lawyer or even put their agreement in writing at the outset, reluctantly conceding that if they had sat down to voice what they expected to give and get, things might have turned out better. Reluctant to let this professional dispute overshadow the fact that we're there to honor our beloved friend, I don't point out that the lawyer never sees the couples and arrangements that work things out themselves, sticking together instead of falling apart.

I hear those stories just about every time I present material from this book at conferences or talk about it at a party, as well as tales of contracts and deals that do end up in court. For example:

A grandmother in one audience described her gay son's coparenting deal with a female friend that didn't make him as much a dad as grandma wanted, while a fellow panelist offered up his own much more collegial relationship with a lesbian couple and the toddler conceived with sperm he'd donated.

A birth mom I met detailed the agreements made with an adoption agency and with the daughter she reunited with some thirty years later.

A gay male couple copped to their deals for extracurricular intimacies.

A friend whose childhood was marred by her parents' acrimonious divorce entered a prenup with her husband-to-be to reduce the number of things that they could fight about, in the unhappy event of getting divorced themselves.

Some of these people worked with lawyers, some worked out arrangements on their own. Just like Plan A situations, some were cordial, some acrimonious. In any case, contracts and the agreements that law won't recognize shaped their parenthood and partnership.

This book has shared stories like these, and the law's view of them, to help people outside law schools better understand relationships and the way that family law sees them. The wonderful thing about contracts, and even nonbinding deals, is that they allow people to tailor the rules to their particular situation. For those of us who fall outside of convention in one way or another—and often, simultaneously, within other conventions—that knowledge can literally make or unmake a family.

Appendix

DISCLAIMER

The following form agreements are offered as samples, without any warranties or promises that they're legally enforceable, complete, well-written, balanced, or anything else. The coparenting agreement has worked for my family and could be altered to fit other people's circumstances. The open adoption agreement worked for another family. In both cases identifying information has been removed.

1. SAMPLE COPARENTING AGREEMENT
Parenting Agreement

We, _____ and _____, two unmarried individuals, have decided to conceive and raise a child together. _____ is presently pregnant and the child is due in _____. This agreement is made between _____ and _____ to express our understanding as to our intentions, rights and responsibilities as parents to our child and to each other. We fully realize that our power to make or enforce this contract may be limited by state law. With this knowledge, and in the spirit of love, cooperation, and mutual respect that has developed over the course of our _____ year friendship, we wish to state the following to be our agreement:

1) We agree that it is in our child's best interests that _____ shall be the primary legal and physical custodian of our child, having the

authority to make all major decisions regarding the child on her own. However, because it is also in our child's best interests to have two parents who love and care for him or her, and because it will often be easier to make both big and small decisions with the input of someone who loves our child, _____ intends to keep _____ abreast of issues as they arise with our child, and to consult with him prior to making any final decision on major matters (such as major medical procedures).

2) Both of us will be listed as parents on the birth certificate.

3) We agree that our child's last name will be _____. We further intend to agree on both first and middle names, _____ deferring to _____ on the choice of a middle name and _____ deferring to _____ on the first name.

4) Although we currently live in different cities, we intend that _____ will be an important part of our child's life and have significant visitation with the child. To achieve this end, we intend to make best efforts to live in the same city or town during the summers.

5) During the academic year we intend that _____ will travel to _____ at least once a month to visit _____ and our child. We intend that these visits will continue if either party moves to another location. Both on these visits, and during the summers, we will do our best to equitably share the responsibilities in nurturing, feeding, clothing, loving, raising, educating, and disciplining him or her.

6) As the child gets older, s/he may visit _____ or travel with _____ alone to events with his friends and family. Until s/he is old enough to travel on his or her own, _____ will accompany him or her on these trips. We intend to alternate paying for the child's trips up to two trips per year, with _____ paying for any trips beyond that. We further intend that, when visiting _____'s friends and family, unless we agree otherwise for a particular trip, we intend that each of us will pay for our own travel and that we will share accommodation and other expenses related to the visit.

7) We agree that _____ intends to make best efforts to spend our child's birthday with him or her, and to join _____ and the child for holiday celebrations. We recognize that we will want our child to know both sides of his or her family, and that traveling to visit them will be part of that process, and further that sometimes that travel will be at holiday times. However, we also recognize the toll that heavy traveling at the holidays entails and will use our best efforts to arrive at plans that facilitate connection but are not exhausting.

8) At our respective primary homes, we intend to each be responsible for our own housing and other living expenses and that _____ will be primarily responsible for the child's housing expenses. While _____ anticipates being responsible for many day-to day expenses of raising the child, _____ agrees to contribute a set amount each month for our child's food, clothing, medical and dental insurance and care, etc., in an amount to be determined by the parties and reevaluated annually. As to big ticket items, such as daycare, school tuition, summer camp, and major medical expenses, we agree to divide the expenses equally and, further, to confer with one another before incurring those expenses.

9) We agree to alter our estate plans (including wills, life insurance policies, retirement accounts, etc.) to make our child the beneficiary of at least 50 percent of our estates, leaving assets in trust for the benefit of our child and naming each other as the trustee/custodian of the assets for the child's benefit. We further agree to name one another as executors of our wills, and give one another both medical and financial powers of attorney, recognizing, however, that if and when either or both of us become partnered with a sweetie, s/he may want to give that person power of attorney for convenience and other considerations. We further agree to maintain life insurance on our respective lives for the benefit of our child with a death benefit of at least $200,000.

10) We agree to cooperate in selecting and naming a guardian for our child in our estate documents in the event neither of us is able to care for him or her.

11) We intend to each contribute $2,000 per year to an account for our child's college or post-secondary education. We agree to name each other as the successor trustee or custodian on these accounts.

12) Subject to the preceding paragraphs, we agree to be jointly responsibly for our child's financial support until s/he is twenty-one years old. We intend to renegotiate this to consider joint financial support until age twenty-five, depending on his or her educational needs and plan.

13) We agree to cooperate on taxes to ensure as equitable an outcome regarding tax deductions relating to our child as possible.

14) We will do our best to support a healthy, loving relationship between our child and the other parent, the other parent's romantic partner, and the other parent's immediate family. If one of us dies, we agree to allow and encourage our child to visit and communicate with the deceased person's family and partner.

15) We will do our best to support the romantic relationships of the other parent.

16) We expect that the logistics of living arrangements will be a complicated challenge, and we will attempt to be flexible in building an arrangement that works for all involved. For the first year and a half of our child's life, we will attempt to take parental leave from our jobs in order to live very close to each other and both actively participate in child care. In the summer, we will try to find and rent or purchase a duplex apartment or homes that are on the same street or within a few blocks. At the end of the child's first year, we will have a better sense of what type of living arrangement will work best for all involved and we will reevaluate at that time.

17) We agree that, assuming we own or rent separate apartments for summer housing and we are both present, the expenses of both rentals or mortgages shall be divided equally with a concomitant share of use.

18) We agree to take all steps necessary to maximize _____'s visitation and to help make visitation as easy as possible.

19) When we are living in the same city, visit one another in our home-towns, or travel together to another place, we will generally strive to share equally in the day-to-day care of our child.

20) We will both do our best to consider the impact on our child whenever making major life decisions for ourselves. We agree that if one of us decides to move out of our hometowns while our child is still a minor, s/he will discuss the move in detail with the other before making any major decisions. If we were to relocate to live closer to one another, then one parent decided to move, the parent who moves will continue to have rights and responsibilities in regard to visitation and child support as outlined in this agreement.

21) We agree that this agreement represents the intentions we have based on incomplete knowledge, prior to our child being born, and before either of us has been a parent. Accordingly, we agree to review this coparenting agreement as needed in order to jointly make changes to it when necessary as time passes. Any major changes to it will be in writing, signed by both of us.

22) We realize that the form of our friendship will change dramatically once our child is born, and we welcome this change. We have wanted to create a child out of the love and respect that exists in our friendship. We recognize that respect involves sitting comfortably with a difference of opinion on an important issue, and we express that mutual respect here as well as our intentions to protect and cultivate it as we face the challenges of being parents. We also intend to continue to give attention and nurturance to our friendship as it evolves and grows.

23) If any part of this agreement is not legally enforceable, we intend that the rest of it remains fully enforceable.

24) We agree to exercise good faith in navigating the new (to us) waters of being an opposite-sex gay couple raising a child together. As we understand that there will be misunderstandings and difficulties along the way in what we trust and hope will be an otherwise rewarding and loving relationship, we agree to engage in any dispute resolution procedures that will keep our nascent family unit intact and smoothly functioning. In particular, we agree to attend joint or family therapy should either one of us ask the other to do so and, if that is not successful, to resolve any disputes through mediation prior to resorting to more traditional and insidious means such as litigation.

All expenses related to therapy and mediation shall be shared equally by us.

25) Should one or both of us seek to legally enforce this agreement, we agree that this agreement should be construed under the laws of [State] in a court of competent jurisdiction in [State].

By signing below we signify that we have read and understood the above agreement and agree to its terms.

_____	_____
Name	Date
_____	_____
Name	Date

2. SAMPLE OPEN ADOPTION AGREEMENT

WARNING: The adoptive and birth families entered this agreement more than a decade ago, when it would not have been legally binding. It was adapted from the website of Open Adoption Insight. If you want a post-adoption contact agreement to be legally binding, make sure that your state allows it and that your agreement complies with all prerequisites for legal enforceability.

Our Understanding of Open Adoption

It is no accident that we have been brought together, for together we can accomplish what we could not do apart. Together we give this child the great necessities of life: the roots of security and the wings of opportunity. With hope in our hearts, we collectively offer a blend of security and nurture. It was love for children in general that put us on converging paths, and now it is our love for this unique child that unites us for the shared journey ahead.

We stand committed to our ideals. We believe that children have innate dignity. We are convinced that children are not possessions to be hoarded but rather gifts from God to be selflessly loved. We believe that children need security and stability, and we recognize that they innocently depend on the adults in their lives for these comforts. We believe relationships thrive in an atmosphere of honesty and mutual respect. We recognize that if any one of us is diminished, we all are.

Therefore we pledge to

1. Center on the child and elevate his or her interest above our own.
2. Be honest in all our interactions.
3. Take the time to consider situations from the perspective of others.
4. Protect the honor and reputation of the others in this relationship.
5. Consult each other before introducing new people to the arrangement.
6. Stay flexible and open to new possibilities.
7. Convey newly discovered medical information.
8. Be direct in the expression of feelings.
9. Consider mediation in the event of major misunderstanding or disagreement.
10. Consider sharing our experience for the benefit of others.
11. Send the birth parent letters and pictures once a month and arrange for visits on special occasions as well as phone contact on a regular basis.

We make this pledge as an expression of love, integrity, and goodwill.

_____	_____
Birth Parent(s)	Date
_____	_____
Adoptive Parent(s)	Date

3. SAMPLE COHABITATION AGREEMENT

Derived from Denis Clifford, Frederick Hertz, and Emily Doskow, *A Legal Guide for Lesbian and Gay Couples* (14th ed., 2007), and Ralph Warner, Toni Ihara, and Frederick Hertz, *Living Together: A Legal Guide for Unmarried Couples* (15th ed., 2013), both of which are copyrighted by Nolo.

Agreement to Share Property

_____ and _____ agree as follows:

1. Because we are sharing our home as a couple, this contract sets forth our rights and obligations toward each other. We intend to abide by this agreement in a spirit of cooperation and good faith.

2. All earned income received by either of us after the date of this contract and all assets acquired or property purchased with this income will belong in equal shares to both of us (regardless of how it is titled or held) with the following exceptions:

   _____

   _____

   Earned income includes contributions for retirement accounts, stock options, and other forms of compensation for our labor. Income from prior investments will not be considered earned income.

3. All real or personal property earned or accumulated by either of us prior to the date of this agreement (except jointly owned property listed in Attachment B of this agreement), including all future income this property produces, is the separate property of the person who earned or accumulated it and will not be transferred to the other except in writing. Attached to this agreement in the form of Attachment A, Separately Owned Property, and B, Jointly Owned Property, are lists of the major items of property each of us owns separately and both of us own jointly as of the date of this agreement.

4. Should either of us receive real or personal property by gift or inheritance, that property, including all future income it produces, belongs absolutely to the person receiving the gift or inheritance and cannot be transferred to the other except in writing.

5. In the event that either of us is seriously considering leaving or ending the relationship, that person shall take at least a three-day vacation from the relationship. We also agree to at least three counseling sessions if either one of us requests it.

6. In the event that we are unable to work out our disputes and we separate, either one of us may terminate this contract by giving the other two weeks written notice. We shall divide all jointly owned property equally. Each of us will retain our separate property, and neither shall

owe any post-separation support to the other, regardless of financial conditions.

7. Any dispute arising out of this contract will be mediated by a third person mutually acceptable to both of us. The mediator's role will be to help us arrive at a solution, not to impose one on us. If good faith efforts to arrive at our own solution to all issues in dispute with the help of a mediator prove to be fruitless, either of us may make a written request to the other that the dispute be arbitrated. In that case, our dispute will be submitted to arbitration under the rules of the American Arbitration Association, and one arbitrator will hear our dispute. The decision of the arbitrator will be binding on us and will be enforceable in any court that has jurisdiction over the controversy. By agreeing to arbitration, we each agree to give up the right to a jury trial.

8. This agreement represents our complete understanding regarding our living together and replaces all prior or contemporaneous agreements, written or oral. It can be amended, but only in writing, and any amendments must be signed by both of us.

9. If a court finds any portion of this contract to be illegal or otherwise unenforceable, the remainder of the contract is still in full force and effect.

Name   Date

Name   Date

Acknowledgments

Though all books create debts personal and professional, the braiding of personal and legal narratives in this book greatly increases my indebtedness to friends, family, colleagues, research assistants, and institutions. I cannot hope to list all the debts that piled up in the eight years during which this manuscript took shape, let alone repay them.

So many people from so many walks of life provided thoughtful advice and comments on book proposals and drafts of chapters and, in some cases, the entire manuscript. Thanks to the members of the DC feminist legal theory reading group as well as participants in faculty workshops, classes, and conferences at the University of Chicago, the University of Portland, the College of New Jersey, the University of Maryland, Tel Aviv University, the College of Law and Business in Tel Aviv, Florida State University, Western New England College, the meeting of the AALS Section on Sexual Orientation and Gender Identity Issues, and annual meetings of the Law and Society Association. The manuscript benefited from helpful comments from Lori Andrews, Rene Almeling, Carlos Ball, Heidi Bloom, Alex Boni-Saenz, Cynthia Bowman, Judith Branzburg, Naomi Cahn, Marybeth Caschetta, Mary Anne Case, Meryl Cohn, David Chambers, Adrienne Williams-Conover, Marybelle Cochran, Shula Darviche, Nancy Ehrenreich, Anne Ertman, Mary Jane Ertman, Carole Feld, Katherine Franke, Nora Galil, Fred Hertz, Sharon Kaczmarek, Kira Kilmer, Sam Korsak, Jennifer Levi, Larry Levine, Margot Lindsay, Naomi Mezey, Fernanda Nicola, Richard Posner, Nancy Polikoff, Dustin

Ryanders, Elizabeth Samuels, Elizabeth Schneirov, Jana Singer, Cathy Sledz, Judith Stacey, Susan Sterett, Samantha Watson, Carlie Wells, and Viviana Zelizer. For outstanding research support, both tireless and good-spirited, I thank Cameron Connah, Maxine Grosshans, Max Tondro, and especially Susan Herrick and Sue McCarty at the University of Maryland Carey Law School's Thurgood Marshall Law Library, as well as my research assistants Shadan Haghani, Caleb Karpay, Lauren Elfner, Nikita Floore, Saidah Grimes, Jaclyn Machometa, and Amelia Pleake-Tamm. Heidi Bloom and other kind and expert professionals at The Cradle provided both materials on the agency's history and connections to adoptive families that confirmed how well open adoption can work.

For help in shaping this mix of memoir and law into a format that could reach readers outside law schools, I thank Lisa Adams, Ian Ayres, Michael Aronson, Eric Ertman, Ted Fishman, Dorothy Roberts, and Alan Thomas. Without Debbie Gershenowitz I may not have made it to Beacon Press, where Gayatri Patnaik and Michael Bronski, editors extraordinaire of the Queer Ideas series, believed in this book, shaped it into its final format, and assembled a top-notch team at Beacon to edit and promote it.

Then there are the people without whom I would not have had this story to tell. Thanks to the gay parents who preceded us in the gayby boom, I could imagine a family grounded on friendship as well as romance. Because Karen Rothenberg, Jana Singer, David Super, and others spoke up for my writing on love and contracts, I have a permanent gig on the University of Maryland Carey Law School's fine faculty. Thanks to Carole and the late Pearl Feld, David Lash, Beth Becker, and the rest of the LA tribe, I'm now part of the mishpachah. Thanks to the University of Utah, I got a job in the midst of free-fall from one life to another, enabling me to find out that all things are possible, even insemination and giving birth as a single, white lesbian in Salt Lake City. Thanks to the Utah docs willing to be outstanding in their field by inseminating single and gay people, I have a son and a good story. Through the Unitarian ministers and congregations in Denver, Eugene, Provincetown, and Salt Lake City, the spirit of life spurred me to find my place in the family of things then sustained me en route. Thanks to All Souls Unitarian in Washington, DC, and its parenting covenant group, my son and I have a spiritual home.

Thanks to the Universities of Denver, Utah, and Maryland, generous financial and research support made possible the law review articles and book chapters that form the infrastructure of this book. Thanks to the generosity of Carole and Hanan Sibel, my research chair bought me time to sit still long enough to discern the two main themes running through my twenty years of scholarly writing.

Thanks are due to Richard McCann, who teamed up with Ruth Eisenberg to introduce me to Karen and on his own taught me to write in the first-person singular. For helping me refine that voice and determine the book's substance and structure, I am further indebted to the talented teachers and fellow students in courses at the Fine Arts Work Center, the Writer's Center, and Politics & Prose, as well as a Spiritual Memoir course I had the pleasure to facilitate with Kimberly Washington.

Finally, on the personal front: Thank you, Victor, for accepting my offer to inseminate and for being the most good-humored, impressive, and generous best friend and baby daddy a woman could want. Thank you Betsy Bahn, Melanee Cherry; Ertmans Andy, Anne, Eric, and Susie; Kit Gartland; Lisa Gonsalves; the late yet ever-fabulous Faye Jensen; Aviva Kempner; Laura Kessler; Cynthia Lane; Sylvia Lesser; Gerda Saunders; Pat Standley; Kathryn Stockton; Yofi Tirosh; Zvika Triger; and Shelley White for extraordinary inspiration and support as I lived the stories told in these pages. For priceless friendship through the years, I thank Nora Galil, Sam Korsak, Jennifer Levi, Amy Lyndon and Beth Lyndon-Griffith, the late great Kate Regan, and Renée Römkens. *Tusind tak*, as the Danes say, to my mother, Mary Jane Ertman, for everything—including coming around on the gay thing so fully that she changed that last line of the Shakespeare sonnet that she and my dad read at our wedding, reviewed every word of this manuscript, had her neighbors read it, and gave the title its final tweak. I also owe my father, Gardner Ertman, thanks for his paintings and the appreciation for all things light that flows through them, for opening his heart to my family by embracing Victor that year we all lived together, and for blessing my marriage to Karen.

Finally, I give thanks beyond words to the people under my roof. My son gave me a reason to write this book. Every day, he ushers me into a front-row seat to the future, as well as the gratifying, harrowing experience of life with your heart outside of your body as he bustles around the world. On top of all that, he's given me outstanding one-liners like "stranded on the island of what are we still doing here" to characterize the long process of writing this book. My wife, Karen Lash, has provided unfailingly wise editorial advice and other counsel on this book and the world beyond it, a continuing reminder never to give in to cynicism, an appreciation for all things pretty, and a steady, patient love I never even knew to wish for. Though they're no longer here to hear me say so, I must also thank Karen's late parents, Ed and Gloria Lash, for loving her so well that she could jump into being the third parent in this Plan B family with such confidence and style. That open-heartedness, which Victor and our son also possess, has given me the happiest ending I could have imagined.

Selected Sources

Books

Gritter, James L. *The Spirit of Open Adoption*. Washington, DC: CWLA Press, 1997

Hertz, Frederick, and Emily Doskow. *A Legal Guide for Lesbian and Gay Couples*, 16th ed. Berkeley, CA: Nolo Press, 2012.

Melina, Lois Ruskai, and Sharon Kaplan Roszia. *The Open Adoption Experience: A Complete Guidebook for Adoptive and Birth Families*. New York: Harper Perennial 1993.

Pepper, Rachel. *Ultimate Guide to Pregnancy for Lesbians*, 2nd ed. San Francisco: Cleis Press, 2005.

Savage, Dan. *The Kid: What Happened After My Boyfriend and I Decided to Get Pregnant*. New York: Plume Publishing, 1999.

Stoner, Katherine E., and Shae Irving. *Prenuptial Agreements: How to Write a Fair and Lasting Contract*, 4th ed. Berkeley, CA: Nolo Press, 2012.

Warner, Ralph, Tony Ihara, and Frederick Hertz. *Living Together: A Legal Guide for Unmarried Couples*, 15th ed. Berkeley, CA: Nolo Press, 2013.

Online Resources

Connections between singles looking for coparents

Modamily: http://www.modamily.com/landing/1/find-a-co-parenting-match.html

Coparents.com: http://www.coparents.com/

Coparent match.com: http://www.co-parentmatch.com/co-parent.aspx

My Adoption Advisor: Practical tools for would-be adoptive parents
http://www.myadoptionadvisor.com/

Cohabitation and marital agreements
 Nolo: Practical information and forms
 http://www.nolo.com/products/family-and-parenting.

Notes

Introduction

1. See, e.g., Martha M. Ertman and Joan Williams, eds., *Rethinking Commodification: Cases and Readings in Law and Culture* (New York: New York University Press, 2005); Martha M. Ertman, "Private Ordering Under the ALI Principles: As Natural as Status," in *Reconceiving the Family: Critical Reflections on the American Law Institute's Principles of the Law of Family Dissolution*, ed. Robin Fretwell Wilson (New York: Cambridge University Press, 2006), 284–304; Martha M. Ertman, "The Story of Reynolds v. U.S.: Federal 'Hell Hounds' Punishing Mormon Treason," in *Family Law Stories*, ed. Carol Sanger (New York: Foundation Press, 2007), 51–77; Martha M. Ertman, "Marriage as a Trade: Bridging the Private/ Private Distinction," *Harvard Civil Rights & Civil Liberties Law Review* 35 (1998): 79–132; Martha M. Ertman, "Commercializing Marriage: A Proposal for Valuing Women's Work Through Premarital Security Agreements," *Texas Law Review* 77 (1998): 17–112, http://digitalcommons.law.umaryland.edu /fac_pubs/389/; Martha M. Ertman, "Denying the Secret of Joy: A Critique of Posner's Theory of Sexuality," *Stanford Law Review* 45 (1993): 1485–524, http:// digitalcommons.law.umaryland.edu/fac_pubs/395/; Martha M. Ertman, "Race Treason: The Untold Story of America's Ban on Polygamy," *Columbia Journal of Gender and Law* 19 (2010): 287–366, http://digitalcommons.law.umaryland .edu/cgi/viewcontent.cgi?article=1605&context=fac_pubs; Martha M. Ertman, "What's Wrong with a Parenthood Market? A New and & Improved Theory of Commodification," *North Carolina Law Review* 82 (2003): 1–60, http://digital commons.law.umaryland.edu/fac_pubs/1325/.

2. Richard A. Posner, *The Problematics of Moral and Legal Theory* (Cambridge, MA: Belknap Press/Harvard University Press, 2002).

3. Robin West, "Sex, Reason, and a Taste for the Absurd," *Georgetown Law Journal* 81 (1993): 2417, http://scholarship.law.georgetown.edu/cgi/viewcontent .cgi?article=1658&context=facpub; Harville Hendrix, *Getting the Love You Want* (New York: Henry Holt, 1988), 124.

4. Progressive scholars too often neglect the power of law to remedy injustices. See Daphna Hacker, "Law and Society Jurisprudence," *Cornell Law Review* 96 (2011): 727–43.

5. Debora L. Spar, *The Baby Business: How Money, Science, and Politics Drive the Commerce of Conception* (Boston: Harvard Business School Press, 2006);

Anemona Hartocollis, "And Surrogacy Makes 3," *New York Times*, February 20, 2014, http://www.nytimes.com/2014/02/20/fashion/In-New-York-Some-Couples -Push-for-Legalization-of-Compensated-Surrogacy.html?_r=0.

6. See, e.g., Spar, *The Baby Business*; Naomi Cahn, *The New Kinship: Constructing Donor-Conceived Families* (New York: New York University Press, 2013); Marsha Garrison, "Law-Making for Baby-Making: An Interpretive Approach to the Determination of Legal Parentage," *Harvard Law Review* 113 (2000): 835–923, http://www.researchgate.net/publication/12470648_Law_making_for_baby_ making_an_interpretive_approach_to_the_determination_of_legal_parentage; Mary Lyndon Shanley, *Making Babies, Making Families: What Matters Most in an Age of Reproductive Technologies, Surrogacy, Adoption, and Same-Sex and Unwed Parents* (Boston: Beacon Press, 2001); Michael Sandel, *What Money Can't Buy: The Moral Limits of Markets* (New York: Allen Lane, 2012).

7. Dorothy E. Roberts, *Killing the Black Body: Race, Reproduction, and the Meaning of Liberty* (New York: Pantheon Books, 1997); Robert Pear, "Birth Control Mandate to Apply to Self-Insuring Religious Groups," *New York Times*, March 16, 2012, http://www.freerepublic.com/focus/news/2860276/posts; Erik Eckholm, "Ultrasound: A Pawn in the Abortion Wars," *New York Times*, February 25, 2012, http://www.nytimes.com/2012/02/26/sunday-review/ultrasound-a-pawn-in -the-abortion-wars.html?pagewanted=all.

8. Susan Frelich Appleton and D. Kelly Weisberg, *Adoption and Assisted Reproduction: Families Under Construction* (New York: Aspen Publishers, 2009), 154–55; Richard A. Posner and Elisabeth Landes, "The Economics of the Baby Shortage," *Journal of Legal Studies* 7 (1978): 323–48, http://organdonor incentives.org/wordpress/wp -content/uploads/2010/01/Economics-of-the-Baby-Shortage2.pdf.

9. Carol Sanger, "Bargaining for Motherhood: Postadoption Visitation Agreements," *Hofstra Law Review* 41 (2012): 309–40, http://www.hofstralawreview.org/wp -content/uploads/2013/09/BB.1.Sanger.final_.pdf.

10. US Department of Health and Human Services, *Postadoption Contact Agreements Between Birth and Adoptive Families*, https://www.childwelfare.gov/systemwide /laws_policies/statutes/cooperative.pdf (current through May 2011); Jeanne How-ard, *Untangling the Web: The Internet's Transformative Impact on Adoption* (New York: Donaldson Institute, 2012). For a compelling account of harms suffered under closed adoption, see Ann Fessler, *The Girls Who Went Away: The Hidden History of Women Who Surrendered Children for Adoption in the Decades Before Roe v. Wade* (New York: Penguin Press, 2006).

11. Wendy Wang et al., *Breadwinner Moms: Mothers Are the Sole or Primary Provider in Four-in-Ten Households with Children; Public Conflicted about the Growing Trend* (Washington, DC: Pew Research Center, 2013), www.pewsocialtrends .org/files/2013/05/Breadwinner_moms_final.pdf; Joan C. Williams, *Reshaping the Work-Family Debate: Why Men and Class Matter* (Cambridge, MA: Harvard University Press, 2010), 32–33, 120–21; Christopher Carrington, *No Place Like Home: Relationships and Family Life Among Lesbians and Gay Men* (Chicago: University of Chicago Press, 1999).

Chapter 2

1. "Report: Arnold Schwarzenegger Bought House for Baby Mama," *Boston Herald*, May 19, 2011.

2. *In re* Baby M, 537 A.2d 1227, 1249 (N.J. 1988).

3. Carol Sanger, "Developing Markets in Baby-Making," in *Contracts Stories*, ed. Douglas G. Baird (New York: Foundation Press, 2007), 127–59.

4. Ibid., 144–45.

5. Griswold v. Connecticut, 381 U.S. 479 (1965); Eisenstadt v. Baird, 405 U.S. 438 (1972); Roe v. Wade, 410 U.S. 113 (1973); Trimble v. Gordon, 430 U.S. 762 (1977); but see Lalli v. Lalli, 439 U.S. 259 (1978) (Powell, J. plurality opinion).

6. Sanger, "Developing Markets," 135. Race, class, and gender can greatly diminish choices. See *The Reproductive Rights Reader: Law, Medicine, and the Construction of Motherhood*, ed. Nancy Ehrenreich (New York: New York University Press, 2008).

7. Sanger, "Developing Markets," 145.

8. Ibid., 145, 146.

9. Elizabeth Bartholet, *Family Bonds: Adoption and the Politics of Parenting* (Boston: Houghton Mifflin, 1993), 193.

10. Centers for Disease Control and Prevention, Division of Reproductive Health, *Assisted Reproductive Technology Success Rates: National Summary and Fertility Clinic Reports* (Atlanta, GA: CDC, 2008), 30, 33.

11. Sanger, "Developing Markets," 136.

12. Ibid., 140.

13. "Luchina Fisher, Sarah Jessica Parker, Matthew Broderick Jump on Hollywood's Surrogate Trend," *ABC News*, April 30, 2009, http://abcnews.go.com/Entertainment /ReproductiveHealth/story?id=7465078; Angela Bassett et al., *Friends: A Love Story* (New York: Kimani Press, 2007), 320–46; Elaine Aradillas, "Sarah & Matthew Join a Roster of Celebs Using Surrogates," *People*, May 2, 2009, http:// www.people.com/people/article/0,,20276146,00.html.

14. RR v. MH, 689 N.E.2d 790 (Mass. 1998); *In re* Parentage of a Child by T.J.S. and A.L.S., 16 A.3d 386 (N.J. Super. Ct. App. Div. 2011), *aff'd*, 2012 WL 5233616 (N.J. 2012); *In re* Baby M., 537 A.2d 1227, 1249 (N.J. 1988). California, in contrast, enforced a gestational surrogacy contract in Johnson v. Calvert, 851 P.2d 776 (Cal. 1993).

15. Rene Almeling, *Sex Cells: The Medical Market for Eggs and Sperm* (Berkeley: University of California Press, 2011), 128–29.

16. Melanie Thernstrom, "My Futuristic Insta-Family," *New York Times Magazine*, January 2, 2011. [online version: http://www.nytimes.com/2011/01/02/magazine /02babymaking-t.html?scp=1&sq=melanie%20thernstrom&st=cse]

17. Ibid.

18. Susan Frelich Appleton and D. Kelly Weisberg, *Adoption and Assisted Reproduction* (New York: Aspen Publishers, 2009).

19. Naomi R. Cahn, *Test Tube Families: Why the Fertility Market Needs Regulation* (New York: New York University Press, 2009), 46–47; Gaia Bernstein, "The Socio-Legal Acceptance of New Technologies: A Close Look at Artificial Insemination," *Washington Law Review* 77 (2002): 1070.

20. Martha M. Ertman, "What's Wrong with a Parenthood Market?," *North Carolina Law Review* 82 (2003): 1–60; Debora L. Spar, *The Baby Business: How Money, Science, and Politics Drive the Commerce of Conception* (Boston: Harvard Business School Press, 2006), 3.

21. Rosanna Hertz, *Single by Chance, Mothers by Choice: How Women Are Choosing Parenthood without Marriage and Creating the New American Family* (New York: Oxford University Press, 2006), 57–60.

22. Almeling, *Sex Cells*, 122.

23. "Mitt Romney's Son Signed Contract Allowing Surrogate Mother of His Children to Have an Abortion Despite Father's Pro-Life Views," *Daily Mail* (UK), September 12, 2012, www.dailymail.co.uk.

24. Liza Mundy, *Everything Conceivable: How Assisted Reproduction Is Changing Our World* (New York: Alfred A. Knopf, 2007).

25. Michael Kamrava, O.A.H. No. 2010010877 (2010), available at Rong-Gong Lin II, "Michael Kamrava's Medical License Revoked," *Los Angeles Times*, June 1, 2011, http://documents.latimes.com/.

26. Judy Dutton, "Liquid Gold: The Booming Market for Human Breast Milk," *Wired*, May 17, 2011, http://www.wired.com/magazine/2011/05/ff_milk/all/1.

27. Keith R. Bradley, "Wet-Nursing at Rome: A Study in Social Relations," in *The Family in Ancient Rome*, ed. Beryl Rawson (Ithaca, NY: Cornell University Press, 1986), 241.

28. Naomi Cahn, "The New Kinship," *Georgetown Law Journal* 100 (2012): 368–89.

29. CDC Report, 3; Cahn, *Test Tube Families*, 1. African American, Latina, and Native American women have infertility rates much higher than white women. Dorothy Roberts, *Killing the Black Body* (New York: Vintage Books, 1999), 252. Carisa R. Showden, *Choices Women Make: Agency in Domestic Violence, Assisted Reproduction, and Sex Work* (Minneapolis: University of Minnesota Press, 2011), 109–10.

30. Cahn, *Test Tube Families*, 125.

31. Ibid., 1; Spar, *The Baby Business*.

32. For a recent account of at-home "turkey baster" insemination, see Lisa Schlesinger, "A Choice Not as Easy as It Looked," *New York Times*, June 2, 2013, http://www.nytimes.com/2013/06/02/fashion/My-Husbands-New-Son-Modern-Love.html?pagewanted=all.

33. Almeling, *Sex Cells*, 31.

34. Ibid., 71.

35. Ertman, "What's Wrong with a Parenthood Market?"

36. California Cryobank, www.cryobank.com.

37. Almeling, *Sex Cells*, 63; Jennifer Egan, "Looking for Mr. Good Sperm," *New York Times Magazine*, March 19, 2006, http://www.nytimes.com/2006/03/19/magazine/319dad.html.

38. Thernstrom, "My Futuristic Insta-Family," 28, 33.

39. A number of traditional surrogacy cases arose in the 1970s and '80s, most famously *Baby M*. In the wake of *Baby M*, many states passed statutes banning or otherwise regulating surrogacy, creating, along with decisions like *Baby M*, clarity so that couples using surrogacy could go to states like California, where it was legally recognized. See, e.g., Johnson v. Calvert, 851 P.2d 776 (Cal. 1993). Since then, the rare surrogacy dispute that makes it to court often involves odd circumstances. See, for example, JF v. DB, 897 A.2d 1261 (Pa. Super. Ct. 2006), *cert. denied* 909 A.2d 1290 (Pa. 2006) (intended parents did not arrive promptly at hospital because surrogate delayed telling them about the birth).

40. Pierce v. Society of Sisters, 268 U.S. 510 (1925); Griswold v. Connecticut, 381 U.S. 479 (1965).

41. See Bebe J. Anderson, "Lesbians, Gays, and People Living with HIV: Facing and Fighting Barriers to Assisted Reproduction," *Cardozo Journal of Law and Gender* 15 (2009): 455–60.

42. Centers for Disease Control and Prevention, *National Summary and Fertility Clinic Success Rates*, http://www.cdc.gov/art/NationalSummary_SuccessRates.htm. Updated July 24, 2012. Centers for Disease Control and Prevention, *National ART Surveillance*, http://www.cdc.gov/art/NASS.htm. Updated July 24, 2012.

43. Cahn, *The New Kinship*, 386 (citing Yaniv Heled, "The Regulation of Genetic Aspects of Donated Reproductive Tissue—The Need for Federal Regulation," *Columbia Science and Technology Law Review* 11 [2010]: 355–58); National Conference of State Legislators, *State Laws Related to Insurance Coverage for Infertility Treatment*, http://www.ncsl.org/IssuesResearch/Health/InsuranceCoverageforInfertility Laws/tabid/14391/Default.aspx. Updated March 2012.

44. *Baby Markets: Money and the New Politics of Creating Families*, ed. Michele Bratcher Goodwin (New York: Cambridge University Press, 2010), 250.

45. Michigan's Surrogate Parenting Act declares surrogacy contracts void and imposes penalties up to $10,000 and a year of prison, and even more serious penalties for hiring an underage or mentally disabled surrogate (fines up to $50,000 and up to five years in prison). Mich. Comp. Laws. Serv. §§ 722.855-722.859 (LexisNexis 2011). Virginia, in contrast, allows surrogacy but requires judges to pre-authorize the agreements. Va. Code Ann. § 20–160 (2011). For a breakdown by state, see Darra L. Hofman, "'Mama's Baby, Daddy's Maybe': A State-by-State Survey of Surrogacy Laws and Their Disparate Gender Impact," *William Mitchell Law Review* 35 (2009): 449–68.

46. T.F. v. B. L., 813 N.E.2d 1244, 1246 (Mass. 2004).

47. Ibid., 1254, 1246.

48. See, e.g., Doe v. XYZ Co., 914 N.E.2d 117 (Mass. App. Ct. 2009); Janssen v. Alicea, 30 So.3d 680 (Fla. Dist. Ct. App. 2010); *In re* paternity of M.F. and C.F., 938 N.E.2d 1256 (Ind. App. 2011).

49. Courtney G. Joslin, "Protecting Children (?): Marriage, Gender, and Assisted Reproductive Technology," *Southern California Law Review* 83 (2010): 1177–230.

50. Cal. Fam. Code 7613(b) (2012); D.C. Code § 16–909(e)(2) (2009).

51. Practice Committees of American Society Reproductive Medicine and Society for Assisted Reproductive Technology, "Recommendations for Gamete and Embryo Donation: A Committee Opinion," *Fertility and Sterility* 99 (2013): 47, 53. Other ASRM Ethics Committee Reports are available at http://www.asrm.org /EthicsReports/.

52. Mary E. Abusief et al., "Assessment of United States Fertility Clinic Websites According to the American Society for Reproductive Technology (ASRM)/Society for Assisted Reproductive Technology (SART) Guidelines," *Fertility and Sterility* 87 (2007): 88. In Rene Almeling's study, egg donors were paid, on average, $4,297 per cycle (Almeling, *Sex Cells*, 118).

53. These sites can be found at http://www.donorsiblingregistry.com; http://www .anonymousus.org; and http://www.cryokidconfessions.blogspot.com.

54. Cahn, *New Kinship*, 367.

55. Injuries still occur, for example, the six US women who contracted HIV from donor sperm between 1986 and 1989 (Almeling, *Sex Cells*, 30). Moreover, most lawsuits do not get recorded in a legal opinion because cases usually settle before trial.

56. Margaret Pomeranz, "The Kids Are All Right," *At the Movies*, Australian Broadcasting Corporation Online, September 1, 2010, http://www.abc.net.au /atthemovies/txt/s2985212.htm.

57. Colton Wooten, "A Father's Day Plea to Sperm Donors," *New York Times*, June 19, 2011, http://www.nytimes.com/2011/06/19/opinion/19wooten.html.

Chapter 3

1. N. R. Kleinfield, "Baby Makes Four, and Complications," *New York Times*, June 19, 2011.
2. Carlos Ball, *The Right to Be Parents: LGBT Families and the Transformation of Parenthood* (New York: New York University Press, 2012), 115.
3. Judith Stacey, *Unhitched: Love, Marriage, and Family Values from West Hollywood to Western China* (New York: New York University Press, 2011), 83.
4. Books documenting situations where everything mostly turns out fine include Rosanna Hertz, *Single by Chance, Mothers by Choice* (New York: Oxford University Press, 2008); Stacey, *Unhitched*; Susan Goldberg and Chloë Brushwood Rose, eds., *And Baby Makes More: Known Donors, Queer Parents, and Our Unexpected Families* (London, ON: Insomniac Press, 2009).
5. Kesler v. Weniger, 744 A.2d 794, 795–96 (Pa. Super. Ct. 2000).
6. Ibid., 796.
7. Brief of Appellee at 2, *Kesler*, 744 A.2d 794 (No. 00491 WDA 99).
8. *Kesler*, 744 A.2d at 796 (Pa. Super. Ct. 2000).
9. Johnson v. Superior Court [*Johnson I*], 95 Cal. Rptr. 2d 864 (Ct. App. 2000) and Johnson v. Superior Court [*Johnson II*], 124 Cal. Rptr. 2d 650 (Ct. App. 2002).
10. *Johnson II*, at 654.
11. *Johnson I*, at 868.
12. Rene Almeling, *Sex Cells: The Medical Market for Eggs and Sperm* (Berkeley, CA: University of California Press, 2011), 1, 59. Most sperm banks reject men who are shorter than 5'8" or chunky but make exceptions for donors in sought-after categories, like Jewish men, donors of color, and men willing to be contacted after the children turn eighteen (ibid., 55).
13. Ibid., 4, 80, 121.
14. *Johnson I*, at 868.
15. See Almeling, *Sex Cells*, 72. Recipients pay more for "washed" sperm that can be used for intrauterine insemination. As of January 2012, the California Cryobank charged between $355 and $615 for each vial of sperm from anonymous donors and between $455 and $715 for "open" donors willing to be contacted after the child turns eighteen. California Cryobank, "Services, Fees," http://www.cryobank.com/services/pricing. Accessed January 19, 2012.
16. *Johnson I*, at 873, 867.
17. Telephone interview with Walter Koontz, attorney for the Johnsons (November 18, 2011).
18. People v. Sorensen, 437 P.2d 495, 498 (Cal. 1968).
19. Ibid., 499.
20. See, e.g., Levy v. Louisiana, 391 U.S. 68 (1968); Trimble v. Gordon, 430 U.S. 762 (1977).
21. Naomi Cahn, "The New Kinship," *Georgetown Law Journal* 100 (2012): 388.
22. Cal. Fam. Code § 7613 (West Supp. 2012).
23. *Johnson I*, at 874.
24. Ferguson v. McKiernan, 940 A.2d 1236, 1239 (Pa. 2007).
25. Ibid., 1239, 1240; Brief of Appellee at 14, *Ferguson*, 940 A.2d 1236 (No. 16 MAP 2005).

26. Brief of Appellee at 4, *Ferguson*, 940 A.2d 1236 (No. 16 MAP 2005).

27. Brief for Appellant at 6, *Ferguson*, 940 A.2d 1236 (No. 16 MAP 2005).

28. *Ferguson*, 940 A.2d at 1245.

29. Ian R. Macneil, "The Many Futures of Contracts," *Southern California Law Review* 47 (1974): 691–816. Some family law scholars view marriage and family as relational contracts, sometimes using related terms like "covenant." See, e.g., Elizabeth S. Scott and Robert E. Scott, "Marriage as Relational Contract," *Virginia Law Review* 84 (1998): 1225–334; Margaret F. Brinig, *From Contract to Covenant: Beyond the Law and Economics of the Family* (Cambridge, MA: Harvard University Press, 2000).

30. Michael Serazio, "Seminal Case," *Houston Press*, March 10, 2005, http://www.houstonpress.com/2005-03-10/news/seminal-case/.

31. Ibid.; telephone interview with Sharon's attorney Peggy Bittick (November 28, 2011).

32. Brief of the Attorney General as Amici Curiae, at 2, *In re* Sullivan, 157 S.W.3d 911 (Tex. App. 2005).

33. Tex. Fam. Code § 160.702 (Vernon 2002), cited in *In re* Sullivan, 157 S.W.3d 911, 915 (Tex. App. 2005).

34. Tex. Fam. Code §§ 160.102(6), 160.301 ("The mother of a child and a man claiming to be the biological father of the child may sign an acknowledgment of paternity with intent to establish the man's paternity.") The Texas Attorney General read that language to allow sperm donors to contract back into legal fatherhood. Amicus Curiae Brief, *supra* note 32, at 7, 13.

35. Amicus Curiae Brief, *supra* note 32, at 13, 14.

36. Telephone interview with Peggy Sue Bittick, Sharon's attorney.

37. *In re* Sullivan, 157 S.W.3d 911, 922 (Tex. App. 2005).

38. T.F. v. B. L., 813 N.E.2d 1244, 1246 (Mass. 2004).

39. Charles Wilson, "Emily Herx, Teacher Claims She Was Fired from Catholic School for In Vitro Fertilization," *Huffington Post*, April 25, 2012, http://www.huffingtonpost.com/2012/04/25/catholic-school-ivf_n_1453524.html.

40. Marjorie McGuire Shultz, "Reproductive Technology and Intent-Based Parenthood: An Opportunity for Gender Neutrality," *Wisconsin Law Review* (1990): 322, 327.

41. I. Glenn Cohen, "Response: Rethinking Sperm Donor Anonymity: of Changed Selves, Non-Identity and One-Night Stands," *Georgetown Law Journal* 100 (2011): 443; see also John A. Robertson, *Children of Choice: Freedom and the New Reproductive Technologies* (Princeton, NJ: Princeton University Press, 1994); Judith F. Daar, "Regulating Reproductive Technologies: Panacea or Paper Tiger?" *Houston Law Review* 34 (1997): 609–64; Kimberly Mutcherson, "Making Mommies: Pre-Implantation Genetic Diagnosis and the Complications of Pre-Motherhood," *Columbia Journal of Gender and Law* 18 (2009): 313.

42. See, e.g., Naomi R. Cahn, *Test Tube Families: Why the Fertility Market Needs Regulation* (New York: New York University Press, 2009); Mary Lyndon Shanley, *Making Babies, Making Families: What Matters Most in an Age of Reproductive Technologies, Surrogacy, Adoption, and Same-Sex and Unwed Parents* (Boston: Beacon Press, 2001); Debora L. Spar, *The Baby Business: How Money, Science and Politics Drive the Commerce of Conception* (Boston: Harvard Business School Press, 2006); Michael J. Sandel, *The Case Against Perfection: Ethics in the Age of Genetic Engineering* (Cambridge, MA: Belknap Press, 2007); Liza

Mundy, *Everything Conceivable: How Assisted Reproduction Is Changing Our World* (New York: Alfred A. Knopf, 2007); Marsha Garrison, "Law-Making for Baby-Making: An Interpretive Approach for Determination of Legal Parentage," *Harvard Law Review* 113 (2000): 835–923.

43. Wash. Rev. Code §26.26.750 (2011).

44. Almeling, *Sex Cells*, 5.

45. Yuval Marin, *Equality for Same-Sex Couples: The Legal Recognition of Gay Partnerships in Europe and the United States* (Chicago: University of Chicago Press, 2010), 141; Nicole Atwill, "France: New Bioethics Law," *Law Library of Congress*, July 18, 2011, http://www.loc.gov/lawweb/servlet/lloc_news?disp3_l205402748_text; Executive Board of the German Medical Association, "Directive, Implementation of Assisted Reproduction," *Deutsches Ärzteblatt* 103 (2006): A1395. Available at http://www.bundesaerztekammer.de/downloads /Kuenstbefrucht_pdf.pdf.

46. Ellen Otzen, "Brits Opting for IVF 'Viking Babies,'" *BBC World Service*, December 23, 2009, http://bbc.co.uk/2/hi/health/8298465.stm.

47. David Blankenhorn, *The Future of Marriage* (New York: Encounter Books, 2007); David Blankenhorn, *Fatherless America: Confronting Our Most Urgent Social Problem* (New York: Basic Books, 1995); Elizabeth Marquardt, "When 3 Really Is a Crowd," *New York Times*, July 16, 2007, http://www.nytimes .com/2007/07/16/opinion/16marquardt.html?_r=0.

48. Cohen, "Response," 443, n. 58 (2012); Kermyt G. Anderson, "How Well Does Paternity Confidence Match Actual Paternity?" *Current Anthropology* 47 (2006): 513–20.

49. Ivy Singles Social Club of Washington, DC, http://www.ivysinglesdc.com/.

50. Buck v. Bell, 274 U.S. 200, 207 (1927).

51. Carrie apparently was raped by a family member, and the family institutionalized her to cover their shame. Victoria F. Nourse, *In Reckless Hands: Skinner v. Oklahoma and the Near-Triumph of American Eugenics* (New York: W. W. Norton, 2008), 24.

52. Skinner v. Oklahoma, 316 U.S. 535 (1942). The Court recognized eugenics' dangerous tendency to favor majorities, explaining that "[i]n evil or reckless hands, it can cause races or types which are inimical to the dominant group to wither and disappear" (ibid., 541).

53. Dorothy Roberts, *Killing the Black Body* (New York: Vintage Books, 1999), 108–9; Carisa R. Showden, *Choices Women Make: Agency in Domestic Violence, Assisted Reproduction, and Sex Work* (Minneapolis: University of Minnesota Press, 2011), 110. The AMA rejected the practice as unethical and unconstitutional. Board of Trustees, American Medical Association, "Requirements or Incentives by Government for the Use of Long-Acting Con-traceptives," *Journal of the American Medical Association* 267 (1992): 1818.

54. Courts struck down those measures as unconstitutional. Arkansas Dep't of Human Services v. Cole, 380 S.W.3d 429, 431 (Ark. 2011); Florida Dep't of Children & Families v. X.X.G., 45 So. 3d 79, 92 (Fla. Dist. Ct. App. 2010).

55. Cahn, *Test Tube Families*, 210.

56. Robert Pear, "Birth Control Mandate to Apply to Self-Insuring Religious Groups," *New York Times*, March 16, 2012, http://www.nytimes.com/2012/03/17/health /policy/obama-administration-says-birth-control-mandate-applies-to-religious

-groups-that-insure-themselves.html?_r=0 [*Note:* Online article has a different title]; Erik Eckholm, "Ultrasound: A Pawn in the Abortion Wars," *New York Times*, February 25, 2012, http://www.nytimes.com/2012/02/26/sunday-review/ultrasound-a-pawn-in-the-abortion-wars.html?pagewanted=all; Burwell v. Hobby Lobby Stores, 134 S.Ct. 2751 (2014).

57. Scholarly examinations of government interventions in repro tech include Lori B. Andrews, *The Clone Age: Adventures in the New World of Reproductive Technology* (New York: Henry Holt, 1999); Kimberly D. Krawiec, "Price and Pretense in the Baby Market," in *Baby Markets: Money and the New Politics of Creating Families*, ed. Michele Bratcher Goodwin (New York: Cambridge University Press, 2010), 41.

58. Cal. Fam. Code § 7613(b) (2012).

59. D.C. Code § 16–909(e)(2) (2009).

60. D.C. Code § 16–909(a-1)(2) (2009).

61. D.C. Code § 16–909(e)(1) (2009).

Chapter 4

1. Elisabeth M. Landes and Richard A. Posner, "The Economics of the Baby Shortage," excerpted in *Rethinking Commodification*, eds. Martha M. Ertman and Joan Williams (New York: New York University Press, 2005), 46–57; Margaret Jane Radin, "Contested Commodities," in *Rethinking Commodification*, 81–95.

2. Landes and Posner, "Economics of the Baby Shortage," 47.

3. See, e.g., Md. Code Ann., Cts. & Jud. Proc. § 5–641.

4. Viviana Zelizer, *Pricing the Priceless Child: The Changing Social Value of Children* (New York: Basic Books, 1985), 174.

5. Naomi Cahn, "Perfect Substitutes or the Real Thing?" in *Families by Law: An Adoption Reader*, eds. Naomi R. Cahn and Joan Heifetz Hollinger (New York: New York University Press, 2004), 19, 23.

6. Zelizer, *Pricing the Priceless Child*, 192–93.

7. Ibid., 190.

8. Ellen Herman, *Kinship by Design: A History of Adoption in the Modern United States* (Chicago: Chicago University Press, 2008), 37.

9. Ibid.

10. Compare Ind. Code § 35–46-1-9 (2013) with Md. Code Ann., Fam. Law § 5–3A-45 (2013); *In re* Adoption No. 9979, 591 A.2d 468 (Md. 1991). For an argument favoring the ban on paying birth-mother expenses, see Andrea B. Carroll, "Reregulating the Baby Market: A Call for a Ban on Payment of Birth Mother Living Expenses," *University of Kansas Law Review* 59 (2011): 290.

11. Quotes in this and succeeding paragraphs are from Ann Fessler, *The Girls Who Went Away* (New York: Penguin Press, 2006), 54, 57, 58, 61.

12. Ibid.

13. Ibid., 62–66; Elizabeth Samuels, "Surrender and Subordination: Birth Mothers and Adoption Law Reform," *Michigan Journal of Gender and Law* 20 (2013): 33–82.

14. Linda Gordon and Felice Batlan, "Aid to Dependent Children: The Legal History," *Social Welfare History*, http://www.socialwelfarehistory.com; Ricky Solinger, *Wake Up Little Susie: Single Pregnancy and Race before* Roe v. Wade (New York: Routledge, 1992).

15. E. Wayne Carp, *Family Matters: Secrecy and Disclosure in the History of Adoption* (Cambridge, MA: Harvard University Press, 1998), 209, 212.

16. Zelizer, *Pricing the Priceless Child*, 192–93.

17. Carp, *Family Matters*, 33.

18. Ibid., 32.

19. Patricia M. Collmeyer, "From 'Operation Brown Baby' to Opportunity," *Child Welfare* 74 (January/February 1995): 242.

20. "Medicine: The Cradle," *Time*, May 20, 1935, http://content.time.com/time /magazine/article/0,9171,754808,00.html (subscription required).

21. National Association of Black Social Workers, *Position Statement on Trans-Racial Adoption* (1972), http://pages.uoregon.edu/adoption/archive/NabswTRA .htm; Multiethnic Placement Act of 1994, Pub. L. No. 103–382, 108 Stat. 4056.

22. Cris Beam, *To the End of June: The Intimate Life of American Foster Care* (Boston: Houghton Mifflin Harcourt, 2013), 60–61; Multiethnic Placement Act of 1994, Pub. L. No. 103–382, 108 Stat. 4056.

23. Loretta Renn, "The Single Woman as Foster Mother," in *Studies of Children*, ed. Gladys Meyer (New York: Columbia University Press, 1948), 59, 60, 69–70, 71, 72–74, 75, 95, http://pages.uoregon.edu/adoption/archive/RennSWFM.html.

24. Jesse Green, *The Velveteen Father: An Unexpected Journey to Parenthood* (New York: Villard, 1999), 210, 211.

25. See "Timeline of Victories," National Center for Lesbian Rights, http://www .nclrights.org/about-us/mission-history/timeline-of-victories/ (acknowledging the landmark same-sex adoption case involving Annie Affleck and Rebecca Smith); Adoption of Tammy, 619 N.E.2d 315 (Mass. 1993); *In re* BLVB & ELVB, 628 A.2d 1271 (Vt. 1993); Susan M. Sterett, "Parents and Paperwork," in *Queer Mobilizations*, eds. Scott Barclay, Mary Bernstein, and Anna-Maria Marshall (New York: New York University Press, 2009).

26. Carlos A. Ball, *The Right to Be Parents: LGBT Families and the Transformation of Parenthood* (New York: New York University Press, 2012); *In re* Jacob and *In re* Dana, 660 N.E.2d 397 (N.Y. 1995); Ronald Smothers, "Accord Lets Gay Couples Adopt Jointly," *New York Times*, December 18, 1997, http://www.nytimes.com /1997/12/18/nyregion/accord-lets-gay-couples-adopt-jointly.html;Miss.CodeAnn. § 93–17–3(2); Utah Code Ann. § 78B-6–117(3). See also "NCLR Fact Sheet on Adoption by Lesbian, Gay and Bisexual Parents," http://www.nclrights.org/site /DocServer/adptn0204.pdf?docID=1221.

27. Quotes in this paragraph are from Dan Savage, *The Commitment: Love, Sex, Marriage and My Family* (New York: Dutton, 2005), 35, 36, 37.

28. Cahn and Hollinger, *Families by Law*, 2; Donaldson Institute and Princeton Survey Research Associates, *Benchmark Adoption Survey: Report on the Findings* (1997), ii, http://www.adoptioninstitute.org/old/survey/Benchmark_Survey_1997.pdf

29. Kathryn Joyce, *The Child Catchers: Rescue, Trafficking, and the New Gospel of Adoption* (New York: Public Affairs, 2013), 111, 131; Carp, *Family Matters*, 129; Cahn and Hollinger, *Families by Law*, 91; Averil Clarke, *Inequalities of Love: College-Educated Black Women and the Barriers to Romance and Family* (Durham, NC: Duke University Press, 2011), Appendix Table A16.

30. Cahn and Hollinger, *Families by Law*, 92; Beam, *To the End of June* , 61.

31. T.F. v. B.L., 813 N.E.2d 1244, 1246 (Mass. 2004).

32. Joan Heifetz Hollinger, "Analysis of the Proposed Uniform Adoption Act," in Cahn and Hollinger, *Families by Law*, 41.

33. Samuels, "Surrender and Subordination," 35.

34. Joan Heifetz Hollinger, "State and Federal Adoption Laws," in Cahn and Hollinger, *Families by Law*, 38.

35. Carol Sanger, "Bargaining for Motherhood," *Hofstra Law Review* 41 (2012): 324.

36. Quotes in this paragraph are from Hollinger, "Analysis of the Proposed Uniform Adoption Act," 41; and Joyce, *The Child Catchers*, 61, 111, 131.

37. Patricia J. Williams, *The Rooster's Egg* (Cambridge, MA: Harvard University Press, 1995), 218–25.

38. Quotes in this paragraph are from Joyce, *Child Catchers*, 122, 123.

39. Ibid., 56, 103–4, 117–18.

40. Bethany Christian Services, *Statement of Faith*, rev. ed. 2007, http://www.bethany .org/pdfs/stlouisstatementoffaith09.pdf.

41. Susan Newman, *Oh God! A Black Woman's Guide to Sex and Spirituality* (New York: One World/Ballantine, 2002), 32.

42. Jeanne A. Howard, *Untangling the Web: The Internet's Transformative Impact on Adoption: Policy and Practice Perspective* (New York: Donaldson Institute, 2012), 37.

43. Ibid.

44. Ibid., 38.

45. Jeanette Winterson, *Why Be Happy When You Could Be Normal?* (Toronto: Alfred A. Knopf Canada, 2011), 216–17, 226–29.

46. Howard, *Untangling the Web*, 46. Quotes in this paragraph are from Winterson, *Why Be Happy?*, 227, 229.

47. Amy Seek, "Open Adoption: Not So Simple Math," *New York Times*, May 7, 2010, http://www.nytimes.com/2010/05/09/fashion/09Lovehtml?pagewanted=all.

48. Ibid.; Annette R. Appell, "Controlling for Kin: Ghosts in Postmodern Family," *Wisconsin Journal of Law, Gender and Society* 25 (2010): 73–136.

49. Dan Bucatinski, *Does This Baby Make Me Look Straight? Confessions of a Gay Dad* (New York: Simon & Schuster, 2012), 230–31.

Chapter 5

1. E. Wayne Carp, *Family Matters: Secrecy and Disclosure in the History of Adoption* (Cambridge, MA: Harvard University Press, 1998), 52.

2. Ibid., 55.

3. Ellen Herman, *Kinship by Design: A History of Adoption in the Modern United States* (Chicago: Chicago University Press, 2008), 150.

4. Paul A. Rodrigues, "Adoption in the Sunshine," *Illinois Bar Journal* 99 (2011): 414.

5. Elizabeth Samuels, "Surrender and Subordination: Birth Mothers and Adoption Law Reform," *Michigan Journal of Gender and Law* 20 (2013): 43, 44, 78; Elizabeth Samuels, "The Idea of Adoption: An Inquiry Into the History of Adult Adoptee Access to Birth Records," *Rutgers Law Review* 53 (2001): 369.

6. Herman, *Kinship by Design*, 211; Ann Fessler, *The Girls Who Went Away* (New York: Penguin Press, 2006), 207–8.

7. Stickles v. Reichardt, 234 N.W. 728 30 (Wis. 1931)

8. Ibid., 730.

9. Ibid.

10. Ibid.

11. In re Adoption of a Child by D.M.H. and S.H., 641 A.2d 235, 246 (N.J. 1994).

12. Ibid., 237

13. Ibid., 245, 248

14. Utah Code Ann. § 78B-6–146 (2013).

15. Joan Heifetz Hollinger, *Adoption Law and Practice* (New York: Bender, 1988-2014), Appendix 13B.

16. U.L.A. Uniform Adoption Act Article 4 Comment.

17. Scholars have argued for expanding legal recognition of stepparents. Ayelet Blecher-Prigat, "Rethinking Visitation: From a Parental to a Relational Right," *Duke Journal of Gender and Law* 16 (2009): 1; David Chambers, "Stepparents, Biological Parents, and the Law's Perception of 'Family' After Divorce," in *Divorce Reform at the Crossroads*, eds. Steven D. Sugarman and Herma Hill Kay (New Haven, CT: Yale University Press, 1990).

18. Uniform Adoption Act Article 4 Comment.

19. Hollinger, "State and Federal Adoption Law" in *Families by Law: An Adoption Reader*, eds. Naomi R. Cahn and Joan Heifetz Hollinger (New York: New York University Press, 2004), 41.

20. Weinschel v. Strople, 466 A.2d 1301, 1305 (Md. Ct. Sp. App. 1983).

21. Ibid., 1303.

22. Kimberly D. Richman, *Courting Change: Queer Parents, Judges, and the Transformation of American Family Law* (New York: New York University Press, 2009).

23. William Blackstone, *Commentaries on the Law of England* (New York: Harper & Brothers, 1857), 451–53.

24. Michael Grossberg, *Judgment of Solomon: The d'Hauteville Case and Legal Experience in Antebellum America* (New York: Cambridge University Press, 1996).

25. Deborah Rhode, *Justice and Gender: Sex Discrimination and the Law* (Cambridge, MA: Harvard University Press, 1989), 154–56.

26. Groves v. Clark, 982 P.2d 446, 447 (Mont. 1999).

27. C.O. v. Doe, 757 N.W.2d 343 (Minn. 2008).

28. Henry Maine, *Ancient Law* (New York: C. Scribner, 1864), 5 (emphasis in original).

29. Vela v. Marywood, 17 S.W.3d 750, 755 (Tex. Ct. App. 2000).

30. Ibid., 754.

31. Ibid., 763.

32. Ibid., 764.

33. Quotes in this paragraph are from Carla M. v. Susan P., 2008 WL 3978346 (Cal. App. 2008). See also Vickie Bane, "I Want My Daughter Back," *People Magazine*, September 21, 2009, http://www.people.com/people/article/0,,20306373,00 .html; Sarah Werthan Buttenwieser, "A Story of Open Adoption, Closed—& Other Adoption Stories," *Valley Advocate* (Northampton, MA), September 20, 2009, http://www.valleyadvocate.com/blogs/home.cfm?aid=10547.

34. Carla M. v. Susan P., 2011 WL 2739649 (Cal. App. 2011).

35. Birth Mother v. Adoptive Parents, 59 P.3d 1233, 1236 (Nev. 2002), *cert. den'd*, 538 U.S. 965 (2003).

36. Cris Beam, *To the End of June: The Intimate Life of American Foster Care* (Boston: Houghton Mifflin Harcourt, 2013).

37. Ibid., 98, 11.

38. Joan Heifetz Hollinger and Naomi Cahn, "Forming Families by Law: Adoption in America Today," *Human Rights* 36 (2009): 16; Erika Lynn Kleiman, "Caring for Our Own: Why American Adoption Law and Policy Must Change," *Columbia Journal of Law and Social Problems* 30 (1997): 353.

39. Quote in this paragraph is from *In re* Adoption of Vito, 728 N.E.2d 292, 305 (Mass. 2000).

40. Carol Sanger, "Bargaining for Motherhood," *Hofstra Law Review* 41 (2012): 309–40.

41. Joseph Story, *Commentaries on Equity Jurisprudence*, vol. 2 (Boston: Hilliard, Gray and Co., 1886), § 1353; Sanger, "Bargaining for Motherhood," 309.

42. *In re* Adoption of Vito, 728 N.E.2d 292, 295 (Mass. 2000)

43. Ibid., 301.

44. Ibid., 304.

45. National Association of Black Social Workers, *Position Statement on Trans-Racial Adoption* (1972), http://pages.uoregon.edu/adoption/archive/NabswTRA.htm.

46. Christie Ward Gailey, "Ideologies of Motherhood and Kinship in U.S. Adoption," in *Ideologies and Technologies of Motherhood: Race, Class, Sexuality, Nationalism*, eds. Heléna Ragoné and France Winddance Twine (New York: Routledge, 2000), 11, 13–14.

47. Material in this paragraph is from Petula Dvorak, "In the District: A Same-Sex Adoption Story," *Washington Post*, August 2, 2012. http://www.washingtonpost.com/pb/local/in-dc-a-same-sex-couples-adoption-success-story/2012/08/02/gJQAP9O9RX_story.html.

48. Joan H. Hollinger, *Adoption Law and Practice*, vol. 3 (2012), §13-B.01.

49. Ibid.

50. Ibid.

51. Ibid., Appendix 13B.

52. Harold D. Grotevant and Ruth G. McRoy, *Openness in Adoption: Exploring Family Connections* (Thousand Oaks, CA: Sage Publications, 1998), 10.

53. Ibid., 16.

54. Ibid., 204.

55. Hollinger, *Adoption Law*, 13B.01.

56. Quotes in this paragraph are from Michaud v. Wawruck, 551 A.2d 738, 739 (Conn. 1988).

57. Ibid., 742.

58. Ibid.

Chapter 6

1. Nancy F. Cott, *Public Vows: A History of Marriage and the Nation* (Cambridge, MA: Harvard University Press, 2000), 31.

2. Cott calls the exchange "reciprocal economic contributions" (ibid., 30–31, 37).

3. Ibid., 30.

4. Interview by Mark Hall with Ken Burns, making of *Thomas Jefferson* documentary, PBS, January 21, 1997, http://www/pbs.org/jefferson/making/KB_00.htm.

5. Katherine M. Franke, "Becoming a Citizen: Reconstruction Era Regulation of African American Marriages," *Yale Journal of Law and the Humanities* 11 (1999): 252, 256, 262.

6. Cott, *Public Vows*, 35.

7. Annette Gordon-Reed, *The Hemingses of Monticello: An American Family* (New York: W. W. Norton, 2008).

8. Cott, *Public Vows*, 42.

9. Isabel Wilkerson, *The Warmth of Other Suns: The Epic Story of America's Great Migration* (New York: Random House, 2010), 60–62.

10. Cott, *Public Vows*, 46; Leyland Winfield Meyer, *The Life and Times of Colonel Richard M. Johnson of Kentucky* (New York: Columbia University Press, 1932): 322–23.

11. Smith v. DuBose, 3 S.E. 309 (Ga. 1887).

12. Ibid., 313. For an excellent discussion of whites providing for black "concubines" both before and after the Civil War, see Adrienne Dale Davis, "The Private Law of Race and Sex: An Antebellum Perspective," *Stanford Law Review* 51 (1999): 221–88.

13. Cynthia Grant Bowman, *Unmarried Couples, Law, and Public Policy* (New York: Oxford University Press, 2010), 22–23, 26.

14. Hewitt v. Hewitt, 394 N.E.2d 1204, 1205 (Ill. 1979).

15. Ibid., 1207.

16. Costa v. Oliven, 849 N.E.2d 122, 123 (Ill. App. 2006), *appeal den'd.*, 857 N.E.2d 670 (Ill. 2006).

17. Marvin v. Marvin, 557 P.2d 106, 110 (Cal. 1976).

18. The courts ultimately refused to let Michelle collect the money on the grounds that she and Lee never agreed that he would support her if they broke up, and even if they did, she benefited from their time together. (Marvin v. Marvin, 176 Cal. Rptr. 555 [Ct. App. 1981].)

19. Elaine Woo, "Michelle Triola Marvin Dies at 75; Her Legal Fight with Ex-lover Lee Marvin Added 'Palimony' to the Language," *Los Angeles Times*, October 31, 2009, http://www.latimes.com/local/obituaries/la-me-michelle-triola-marvin31-2009 oct31-story.html.

20. Long v. Marino, 441 S.E.2d 475 (Ga. App. 1994).

21. Bergen v. Wood, 18 Cal. Rptr. 2d 75, 76 (Ct. App. 1993).

22. Ibid., 77. "Consideration" is the legal term for the parties' motivation for making a promise. To be valid, a consideration should induce the other person to make a reciprocal promise (*Restatement [Second] of Contracts* §71 1981).

23. Bowman, *Unmarried Couples*, 97.

24. Ibid., 101.

25. Ibid., 99–100.

26. Sabrina Tavernise, "Married Couples Are No Longer a Majority, Census Finds," *New York Times*, May 26, 2011, http://www.nytimes.com/2011/05/26 /us/26marry.html.

27. 2010 Census. In addition, 8 percent of households are made up of single parents.

28. See, e.g., Gary S. Becker, *A Treatise on the Family* (Cambridge, MA: Harvard University Press, 1991); Richard A. Posner, *Sex and Reason* (Cambridge, MA: Harvard University Press, 1994).

29. Jodi Kantor, "The Obamas' Marriage," *New York Times Magazine*, November 1, 2009, http://www.nytimes.com/2011/05/26/us/26marry.html.

30. Becker, *Treatise*, 43.

31. William Poundstone, *The Prisoner's Dilemma* (New York: Doubleday, 1992), 125–26.

32. Viviana Zelizer, *The Purchase of Intimacy* (Princeton, NJ: Princeton University Press, 2005), 30–32; Becker, *Treatise*, 124.

33. Posner, *Sex and Reason*, 118.

34. Zelizer, *Purchase of Intimacy*, 22, 29.

35. *In re* Baby M, 537 A.2d 1227, 1249 (N.J. 1988).

36. Miller v. Miller, 42 N.W. 641 (Iowa 1889).

37. Ibid., 641. The detail about Mr. Miller's wandering appears in an earlier opinion in the same case (Miller v. Miller, 35 N.W. 464 [Iowa 1887]).

38. *Miller*, 42 N.W. at 642.

39. Marcel Mauss, *The Gift*, trans. Ian Cunnison (London: Cohen and West, 1954).

40. Richard Dawkins, *The Selfish Gene*, rev. ed. (New York: Oxford University Press, 1989), 212.

41. Fisher, *The Sex Contract: The Evolution of Human Behavior* (New York: William Morrow, 1982), 94, 99–100.

42. E. O. Wilson, *On Human Nature*, 25th anniversary ed. (Cambridge, MA: Harvard University Press, 2004), 83, 123, 139.

43. Ibid., 1–3.

44. Ibid., 158.

45. Shelley Taylor, *The Tending Instinct: How Nurturing Is Essential for Who We Are and How We Live* (New York: Times Books, 2002).

46. Ibid., 1–3, 52–69.

47. Ibid., 55.

48. Ibid., 76–77.

49. Ibid., 80–81.

50. Ibid., 41.

51. T. H. Holmes and T. H. Rahe, "The Social Readjustment Rating Scale," *Journal of Psychosomatic Research* 11 (1967): 213–18.

52. Taylor, *Tending Instinct*, 20–22.

53. Ibid., 21.

54. Ibid., 197; Martha Albertson Fineman, "The Vulnerable Subject: Anchoring Equality in the Human Condition," *Yale Journal of Law & Feminism* 20 (2008): 1–23.

55. Taylor, *Tending Instinct*, 10.

56. Ibid., 147.

57. Andrew Cherlin, *The Marriage-Go-Round: The State of Marriage and the Family in America Today* (New York: Random House, 2009), 27; Kathryn Edin and Tim Nelson, *Doing the Best I Can: Fatherhood in the Inner City* (Berkeley: University of California Press, 2013).

58. Gaia Bernstein and Zvi Triger, "Over-Parenting," *UC Davis Law Review* 44, no. 4 (2011): 1221.

59. Shelly Lundberg and Robert A. Pollock, "The American Family and Family Economics," *Journal of Economic Perspectives* 21 (2007): 3–26.

60. US Dept. of Labor, Bureau of Labor Statistics, *American Time Use Survey—2012 Results*.

61. Liana C. Sayer, "Time and Inequality: Trends in Women's and Men's Paid Work, Unpaid Work, and Free Time," *Social Forces* 84 (2005): 285.

62. Joan C. Williams, *Reshaping the Work-Family Debate: Why Men and Class Matter* (Cambridge, MA: Harvard University Press, 2010), 26.

63. Hannah Rosin, *The End of Men: And the Rise of Women* (New York: Riverhead Books, 2012); Lundberg and Pollack, "American Family," 7.

64. Ibid.; US Bureau of Labor Statistics, Annual Social and Economic Supplements, 1971–2010, Current Population Survey.

65. Taylor, *Tending Instinct*, 114–15.

66. Ibid., 115.

67. Jason DeParle, "Two Classes, Divided by 'I Do,'" *New York Times*, July 15, 2012, http://www.nytimes.com/2012/07/15/us/two-classes-in-america-divided-by-i-do .html?pagewanted=all&_r=0. [*Note:* Different dates for print and online versions.]

68. Taylor, *Tending Instinct*, 4.

69. Ibid., 30. One survey of 5,400 species of mammals showed that in most of them fathers do little other than stake out territories, compete with other males, and mate with females, with only a fraction of species benefiting from male caretaking of young. Sarah Blaffer Hrdy, *Mothers and Others: The Evolutionary Origins of Mutual Understanding* (Cambridge, MA: Belknap Press, 2009), 159.

70. Hrdy, *Mothers and Others*, 163, 128.

71. Taylor, *Tending Instinct*, 31, 83.

72. Hrdy, *Mothers and Others*, 169.

73. Ibid., 170.

74. Ibid., 171.

75. Elaine Sorensen and Chava Zibman, *Poor Dads Who Don't Pay Child Support: Deadbeats or Disadvantaged?* (Washington, DC: Urban Institute, 2001), 1.

76. Tamara Halle, *Charting Parenthood: A Statistical Portrait of Fathers and Mothers in America* (Washington, DC: Child Trends, 2002); Edin and Nelson, *Doing the Best I Can.*

77. Hrdy, *Mothers and Others*, 150; Jackie Goode, Claire Callender, and Ruth Lister, *Distribution of Income Within Families Receiving Benefits* (Washington, DC: Joseph Rowntree Foundation, 1998); see also Ann C. Foster and Craig J. Kreisler, "How Parents Use Time and Money," *Beyond the Numbers*, August 2012, http:// www.bls.gov/opub/btn/volume-1/pdf/how-parents-use-time-and-money.pdf.

78. Sondra E. Solomon, Esther D. Rothblum, and Kimberly F. Balsam, "Money, Housework, Sex and Conflict: Same-Sex Couples in Civil Unions, Those Not in Civil Unions, and Heterosexual Married Siblings," *Sex Roles* 52 (2005): 561–75; Liza Mundy, "The Gay Guide to Wedded Bliss," *Atlantic*, July 2013, 56, 61.

79. Nan D. Hunter, "The Future Impact of Same-Sex Marriage: More Questions than Answers," *Georgetown Law Journal* 100 (2012): 1855–79.

80. Mundy, "Gay Guide," 62–63.

81. See, e.g., Leigh Goodmark, *A Troubled Marriage: Domestic Violence and the Legal System* (New York: New York University Press, 2012).

Chapter 7

1. Cynthia Grant Bowman, *Unmarried Couples, Law, and Public Policy* (New York: Oxford University Press, 2010); Gary J. Gates and Frank Newport, *Gallup Special Report: New Estimates of the LGBT Population in the United States,*

February 2013. Available at http://williamsinstitute.law.ucla.edu/research/census
-lgbt-demographics-studies/gallup-lgbt-pop-feb-2013/.

2. U.S. v. Windsor, 133 S.Ct. 2675 (2013); Erik Eckholm, "Gay Marriage Opponents
   Set to Continue Court Battle," *New York Times*, October 8, 2014, http://
   www.nytimes.com/2014/10/09/us/opponents-of-same-sex-marriage-geared-to
   -continue-battle-in-courts.html?_r=0.
3. Posik v. Layton, 695 So. 2d 759, 760 (Fla. Dist. Ct. App. 1997).
4. Ibid., 761.
5. Ibid.
6. Ibid.
7. Crooke v. Gilden, 414 S.E.2d 645 (Ga. 1992).
8. Bowman, *Unmarried Couples*, 52.
9. Martha Ertman, "Marriage as a Trade: Bridging the Private/Private Distinction,"
   Harvard Civil Rights-Civil Liberties Law Review 36 (2001): 84; Cynthia Starnes,
   "Divorce and the Displaced Homemaker: A Discourse on Playing With Dolls,
   Partnership Buyouts and Dissociation Under No-Fault," *University of Chicago
   Law Review* 60 (1993): 108.
10. American Law Institute, *Principles of the Law of Family Dissolution: Analysis
    and Recommendations* (St. Paul, MN: American Law Institute Publishers, 2002),
    § 6.03.
11. Tara Siegel Bernard and Ron Lieber, "The High Price of Being a Same-Sex
    Couple," *New York Times*, October 3, 2009.
12. "Navratilova Speaks on Suit," *New York Times*, July 26, 1991.
13. Sandra Faulkner and Judy Nelson, *Love Match: Nelson vs. Navratilova* (New
    York: Birch Lane Press, 1993).
14. Cochran v. Cochran, 106 Cal. Rptr. 2d 899, 902 (Ct. App. 2001).
15. Ibid., 906.
16. Ibid.
17. Featherston v. Steinhoff, 575 N.W.2d 6 (Mich. App. 1998), *appeal denied* 589
    N.W.2d 774 (Mich. 1998).
18. Ibid., 8.
19. Ibid., 10.
20. Bowman, *Unmarried Couples*, 159 (citing 2008 Population Survey by the US
    Census Bureau). These numbers do not include kids whose parents are in same-
    sex couples.
21. Ibid., 159.
22. Deposition of Ann T. Young, September 13, 1999, p. 11; Deposition of Howard
    McLane, pp. 3–4.
23. McLane v. Musick, 792 So. 2d 702 (Fla. Dist. Ct. App. 2001).
24. Deposition of Howard McLane, p. 31.
25. Ibid., 43–46, 49.
26. Ibid., 43–46, 49.
27. Ibid., 52.
28. Ibid., 29.
29. *Restatement (Second) of Contracts* (1981), §§ 4, 69.
30. Whorton v. Dillingham, 248 Cal. Rptr. 405, 407 (Ct. App. 1988).
31. Ibid., 409.
32. Ibid.

33. Katharine Silbaugh, "Turning Labor into Love: Housework and the Law," *Northwestern University Law Review* 91 (1996): 1–86.

34. Author communication with attorneys for Howard McLane and Donnis Whorton, January 2014.

35. McLane v. Musick, 792 So. 2d 702, 705 (Fla. Dist. Ct. App. 2001).

36. Byrne v. Laura, 60 Cal. Rptr. 2d 908 (Ct. App. 1997).

37. It was not a contract to make a will, which must be in writing, because Flo could have predeceased Skip (ibid., 915).

38. Ibid., 912.

39. Ibid.

40. Ibid.

41. Ibid., 913–14.

42. Ibid., 914.

43. Cynthia Grant Bowman, "A Feminist Proposal to Bring Back Common Law Marriage," *Oregon Law Review* 75 (1996): 709–80; see also Marsha Garrison, "Is Consent Necessary?" *UCLA Law Review* 52 (2005): 887–88.

44. Martha Albertson Fineman, *The Neutered Mother, the Sexual Family and Other Twentieth Century Tragedies* (New York: Routledge, 1995); Tamara Metz, *Untying the Knot: Marriage, the State, and the Case for Their Divorce* (Princeton, NJ: Princeton University Press, 2010), 14, 137–38; Alice Ristroph and Melissa Murray, "Disestablishing the Family," *Yale Law Journal* 199 (2010): 1236–79.

45. Naomi Cahn and June Carbone, *Red Families v. Blue Families: Legal Polarization and the Creation of Culture* (New York: Oxford University Press, 2010), 118.

46. Ibid., 39–40; Ralph Richard Banks, *Is Marriage for White People? How the African American Marriage Decline Affects Everyone* (New York: Penguin Press, 2011), 6–10.

47. Bowman, *Unmarried Couples*, 224.

48. Nancy D. Polikoff, *Beyond (Straight and Gay) Marriage: Valuing All Families under the Law* (Boston: Beacon Press, 2008).

49. Ibid., 5.

50. Banks, *Is Marriage for White People?*, 7; Carol Stack, *All Our Kin* (New York: Basic Books, 1974); Kathryn Edin and Laura Lein, *Making Ends Meet: How Single Mothers Survive Welfare and Low-Wage Work* (Russell Sage Foundation: New York, 1997) .

51. Bowman, *Unmarried Couples*, 93–96.

52. Ibid., 97, only measuring cross-sex couples, based on 2008 Census data; 2010 Census data on children.

53. Andrew Cherlin, *The Marriage-Go-Round: The State of Marriage and the Family in America Today* (New York: Random House, 2009), 155.

54. Bowman, *Unmarried Couples*, 143; Shachar Lifshitz, "Married Against Their Will? Toward a Pluralist Regulation of Spousal Relationships," *Washington and Lee Law Review* 66 (2009): 1565.

55. American Law Institute, *Principles*, § 6.03, § 6.06.

56. Bowman, *Unmarried Couples*, 133–34, 168; Cherlin, *Marriage-Go-Round*, 17.

57. Kathryn Edin and Tim Nelson, *Doing the Best I Can: Fatherhood in the Inner City* (Berkeley: University of California Press, 2013).

58. William N. Eskridge Jr., "Family Law Pluralism: The Guided Choice Regime of Menus, Default Rules, and Override Rules," *Georgetown Law Journal* 100 (2012): 1881–987.

59. Arielle Kuperberg, "Reassessing Differences in Work and Income in Cohabitation and Marriage," *Journal of Marriage and Family* 74 (2012): 703–4.

60. Bowman, *Unmarried Couples*, 139–40; Gabrielle Gotta et al., "Heterosexual, Lesbian, and Gay Male Relationships: A Comparison of Couples in 1975 and 2000," *Family Process* 50 (2011): 353–76.

61. Bowman, *Unmarried Couples*, 142.

62. Kuperberg, "Reassessing Differences in Work and Income in Cohabitation and Marriage."

63. Stephanie Koontz, *Marriage: A History: From Obedience to Intimacy, or How Love Conquered Marriage* (New York: Viking, 2006).

64. *Restatement (Second) of Contracts*, §§ 4, 19, 110 (1981).

Chapter 8

1. Homer H. Clark Jr., *The Law of Domestic Relations in the United States*, 2nd ed. (St. Paul, MN: West Publishing, 1988), 263–64.

2. See, e.g., Hernandez v. Robles, 855 N.E.2d 1 (N.Y. 2006).

3. United States v. Windsor, 133 S.Ct. 2675 (2013).

4. Feminists disagree about whether highlighting marriage's contractual elements is good for women. Compare Carole Pateman, *The Sexual Contract* (Stanford, CA: Stanford University Press, 1988), 154–88, with Linda R. Hirshman and Jane E. Larson, *Hard Bargains: The Politics of Sex* (New York: Oxford University Press, 1999), 94.

5. Robert H. Mnookin and Lewis Kornhauser, "Bargaining in the Shadow of the Law: The Case of Divorce," *Yale Law Journal* 88 (1979): 950–97.

6. Patricia Brady, "Martha Washington Creates the Role of First Lady," Gilder Lehrman Institute of American History, http://www.gilderlehrman.org/history -by-era/early-republic/Essays/Martha-Washington-Creates-Role-First-Lady.

7. John Heilemann and Mark Halperin, *Game Change: Obama and the Clintons, McCain and Palin, and the Race of a Lifetime* (New York: Harper, 2010), 67, 68, 73.

8. Henry Wiencek, *An Imperfect God: George Washington, His Slaves, and the Creation of America* (New York: Farrar, Straus and Giroux, 2003), 84–86.

9. Married Women's Property Acts, starting in the mid-nineteenth century, gave married women the right to form contracts and own property. Nancy F. Cott, *Public Vows* (Cambridge, MA: Harvard University Press, 2000), 52–55.

10. Peggy Pascoe, *What Comes Naturally: Miscegenation Law and the Making of Race in America* (New York: Oxford University Press, 2009), 242–43.

11. Loving v. Virginia, 388 U.S. 1 (1967).

12. United States v. Windsor, 133 S.Ct. 2675 (2013); Erik Eckholm, "Gay Marriage Opponents Set to Continue Court Battle," *New York Times*, October 8, 2014, http://www.nytimes.com/2014/10/09/us/opponents-of-same-sex-marriage -geared-to-continue-battle-in-courts.html?_r=0.

13. Mildred Loving, "Loving for All," remarks prepared for delivery on June 12, 2007, the fortieth anniversary of the Supreme Court decision. Available at http:// www.freedomtomarry.org/page/-/files/pdfs/mildred_loving-statement.pdf.

14. Viviana Zelizer, *The Purchase of Intimacy* (Princeton, NJ: Princeton University Press, 2005), 134; Jane E. Larson, "'Women Understand So Little They Call My Good Nature "Deceit"': A Feminist Rethinking of Seduction," *Columbia Law Review* 93 (1993): 374–472.

15. Hattin v. Chapman, 46 Conn. 607, 608 (1879).

16. Md. Code Ann., Fam. Law § 3–102 (2006); Elaine Marie Tomko, "Rights in Respect of Engagement and Courtship Presents When Marriage Does not Ensue," annotation, *American Law Reports*, 5th ed., vol. 44 (1996), 1.

17. Zelizer, *Purchase of Intimacy*, 134–45. ("[G]enerally speaking, courts treat engagement rings as quintessential conditional gifts, returnable to the donor almost regardless of the circumstances that ended the engagement" (ibid., 145).

18. Robert A. Pratt, "The Case of Mr. and Mrs. Loving: Reflections on the 40th Anniversary of *Loving v. Virginia*," in *Family Law Stories*, ed. Carol Sanger (New York: Foundation Press, 2008), 22.

19. "By the Numbers: The 10 Most Expensive Celebrity Divorces," *Forbes*, April 12, 2007, http://www.forbes.com/2007/04/12/most-expensive-divorces-biz-cz_lg_ 0412celebdivorce_slide_4.html?thisSpeed=undefined; Jane Lewis, "Profile: Ivana Trump," *MoneyWeek* (London), December 12, 2005, http://www.moneyweek.com /news-and-charts/profile-ivana-trump; Uniform Marriage and Divorce Act § 307 (1970) (amended 1971 and 1973) 9A U.L.A. 132 (Supp 2012).

20. Simeone v. Simeone, 581 A.2d 162, 165 (Pa. 1990).

21. "Ain't Love Expensive," *Sunday Telegraph* (Sydney), October 9, 2000; "Beyonce and Jay-Z's $25 Million Prenup!," *The Rundown*, May 5, 2008, http://www .therundown.tv/headlines/say-what/beyonce-and-jay-zs-25-million-prenup/; Donna Bertaccini, "Lovers Seek Lawyers as Divorce Booms," *BBC*, November 8, 2004, http://news.bbc.co.uk/2/hi/business/3992381.stm; Margaret Littman, "Is a Prenup Expiration Date an Ex-Wife's Best Revenge?" *Chicago Tribune*, March 27, 2002, http://articles.chicagotribune.com/2002-03-27/features/0203270022_ 1_prenuptial-agreements-jane-welch-clauses.

22. Jay Busbee, "Details of Elin Woods' Newly Written Prenup Emerge," *Yahoo Sports*, December 3, 2009, http://sports.yahoo.com/golf/blog/devil_ball_golf/ post/Details-of-Elin-Woods-newly-rewritten-prenup-em?urn=golf,206529; Steve Helling, "Tiger Woods and Elin Nordegren's Divorce Is Final," *People*, August 23, 2010, http://www.people.com/people/article/0,,20414961,00.html.

23. *In re* Marriage of Dawley, 551 P.2d 323, 329 (Cal. 1976).

24. Louise Rafkin, "If 'Forever' Doesn't Work Out: The Same-Sex Prenup," *New York Times*, April 1, 2012, http://www.nytimes.com/2012/03/25/fashion/weddings/ same-sex-marriage-and-prenuptial-agreements.html?pagewanted=all.

25. Perkinson v. Perkinson, 802 S.W.2d 600 (Tenn. 1990).

26. Diosdado v. Diosdado, 118 Cal. Rptr. 2d 494 (Ct. App. 2002); *In re* Marriage of Cooper, 769 N.W.2d 582 (Iowa 2009); *In re* Marriage of Mehren and Dargan, 13 Cal. Rptr. 3d 522 (Ct. App. 2004).

27. Kelm v. Kelm, 623 N.E.2d 39 (Ohio 1993).

28. Pyeatte v. Pyeatte, 661 P.2d 196 (Ariz. Ct. App. 1983).

29. Ashby v. Ashby, 227 P.3d 246 (Utah 2010).

30. AZ v. BZ, 725 N.E.2d 1051 (Mass. 2000); Kass v. Kass, 696 N.E.2d 174 (N.Y. 1998).

31. *In re* Marriage of Meiers, 2005 WL 1983707 (Cal. App. 2005) (No. B172440).

32. *In re* Marriage of Weiss, 49 Cal. Rptr. 2d 339 (Ct. App. 1996); *In re* Marriage of Nuechterlein, 587 N.E.2d 21 (Ill. App. Ct. 1992).

33. Avitzur v. Avitzur, 446 N.E.2d 136 (N.Y.), *cert. denied* 464 U.S. 817 (1983); Becher v. Becher, 706 N.Y.S.2d 619 (Sup. Ct. 2000).

34. Odatalla v. Odatalla, 810 A.2d 93 (N.J. Super. Ch. Div. 2003); Aziz v. Aziz, 488 N.Y.S.2d 123 (Sup. Ct. 1985); Chaudry v. Chaudry, 388 A.2d 1000 (N.J. Super. Ct. App. Div. 1978).

35. Uniform Premarital Agreement Act (1983), 9C U.L.A. 35 (2001). About half of the states have adopted the UPAA. As of mid-2014, two states have adopted its 2012 update, the Uniform Premarital and Marital Agreements Act.

36. McGuire v. McGuire, 59 N.W.2d 336, 341 (Neb. 1953).

37. Mary Anne Case, "Enforcing Bargains in an Ongoing Marriage," *Washington University Journal of Law and Policy* 35 (2011): 227–36.

38. Friends, family, colleagues, and students told me about some of these deals. Others are from Amy Chua, *Battle Hymn of the Tiger Mother* (New York: Penguin Press, 2011), 7; Ralph Richard Banks, *Is Marriage for White People? How the African American Marriage Decline Affects Everyone* (New York: Penguin Press, 2011), 51–54; Paula Szuchman and Jenny Anderson, *Spousonomics: Using Economics to Master Love, Marriage, and Dirty Dishes* (New York: Random House, 2011), 10, 34.

39. US Census Bureau, Number, Timing and Duration of Marriage and Divorces: 2009, May 2011, 12, http://www.census.gov/prod/2011pubs/p70-125.pdf.

40. Ibid., 5.

41. Bowman, *Unmarried Couples*, 234–35.

42. Betsey Stevenson and Justin Wolfers, "Marriage and Divorce: Changes in Their Driving Forces," *Journal of Economic Perspectives* 21, no. 2 (2007): 27–52.

43. Ai-jen Poo, "Making the Care Economy a Caring Economy," in *The Shriver Report: A Woman's Nation Pushes Back from the Brink*, ed. Maria Shriver (New York: Palgrave Macmillan, 2014), 78–81.

44. Dorothy E. Roberts, "Spiritual and Menial Housework," *Yale Journal of Law and Feminism* 9 (1997): 51–80.

45. Betty Friedan, *The Feminine Mystique* (New York: W. W. Norton, 1963); Patricia Hill Collins, *Black Feminist Thought: Knowledge, Consciousness, and the Politics of Empowerment* (New York: Routledge, 2000), 54.

46. Premilla Nadasen, "Expanding the Boundaries of the Women's Movement: Black Feminism and the Struggle for Welfare Rights," *Feminist Studies* 28 (2002): 271, 286; Laura T. Kessler, "Transgressive Caregiving," *Florida State Law Review* 33 (2005).

47. Andrew Cherlin, *The Marriage-Go-Round: The State of Marriage and the Family in America Today* (New York: Random House, 2009), 9. Jonathan Goldberg-Hiller, *The Limits to Union: Same-Sex Marriage and the Politics of Civil Rights* (Ann Arbor: University of Michigan Press, 2004).

48. Martha M. Ertman, "Marriage as a Trade: Bridging the Private/Private Distinction," *Harvard Civil Rights-Civil Liberties Law Review* 36 (2001): 79, 80–81.

49. Lawrence v. Texas, 539 U.S. 558 (2003).

50. Gary J. Gates, *Same-Sex and Different Sex Couples in the American Community Survey, 2005–2011*, Williams Institute, available at http://williamsinstitute.law.ucla.edu/research/census-lgbt-demographics-studies.

51. U.S. v. Windsor, 133 S.Ct. 2675 (2013); Eckholm, "Gay Marriage Opponents Set to Continue Court Battle."

52. Lawrence v. Texas, 539 U.S. 558, 578 (2003); Goodridge v. Dep't. of Pub. Health, 798 N.E.2d 941 (Mass. 2003); Varnum v. Brien, 763 N.W.2d 862 (Iowa 2009);

"Gay Marriage Around the World," *Pew Research Religion and Public Life Project*, December 19, 2013 (listing the countries that allow gay marriage). Available at http://www.pewforum.org/2013/12/19/gay-marriage-around-the-world -2013.

53. Jana B. Singer and Jane C. Murphy, *Resolving Family Conflicts* (Burlington, VT: Ashgate, 2008), xiv.

54. Gay and Lesbian Advocates and Defenders, "Protecting Families: Standards for LGBT Families." Available at http://www.glad.org/protecting-families.

55. Ian Ayres, *Carrots and Sticks* (New York: Bantam Books, 2010), 15.

56. stickK, http://www.stickk.com/about.php.

57. Jana B. Singer, "Dispute Resolution and the Post-Divorce Family: Implication of a Paradigm Shift," *Family Court Review* 47 (2009): 363.

58. Pauline H. Tesler, "Collaborative Family Law," *Pepperdine Dispute Resolution Law Journal* 4 (2004): 317–36.

59. Pauline H. Tesler and Peggy Thompson, *Collaborative Divorce: The Revolutionary New Way to Restructure Your Family, Resolve Legal Issues, and Move on with Your Life* (New York: ReganBooks, 2006), 106–9, 158–62.

60. Ibid., 167, 172.

61. Ibid., 259, 266.

62. Ibid., 263.

63. Singer and Murphy, *Resolving Family Conflicts*, xxiii–xxiv.

Chapter 9

1. Joan Williams, "Is Coverture Dead? Beyond a New Theory of Alimony," *Georgetown Law Journal* 82 (1994): 2227–90; Martha M. Ertman, "Commercializing Marriage: A Proposal for Valuing Women's Work Through Premarital Security Arrangements," *Texas Law Review* 7 (1998): 31.

2. Uniform Marriage and Divorce Act § 307 (1970) (amended 1971 and 1973), 9A U.L.A. 132 (Supp. 2012).

3. Some states do not enforce alimony-limiting agreements. Barbara A. Atwood and Brian H. Bix, "A New Uniform Law for Premarital and Marital Agreements," *Family Law Quarterly* 46 (2012): 321.

4. Nancy F. Cott, *Public Vows: A History of Marriage and the Nation* (Cambridge, MA: Harvard University Press, 2000), 11.

5. Katharine B. Silbaugh, "Marriage Contracts and the Family Economy," *Northwestern University Law Review* 93 (1999): 135.

6. *Restatement (Second) of Contracts* (1981), § 2 cmt. e; § 77 cmt. a.

7. Flechas v. Flechas, 791 So. 2d 295 (Miss. Ct. App. 2001).

8. Ibid., 298; Brief of Appellant at 5, *Flechas*, 791 So. 2d 295 (Miss. Ct. App. 2001) (No. 00-CA-00223), 2000 WL 34429904.

9. Flechas, 791 So.2d at 301 (Miss. Ct. App. 1998).

10. Ibid., 302

11. Cynthia Starnes, "Divorce and the Displaced Homemaker: A Discourse on Playing With Dolls, Partnership Buyouts and Dissociation Under No-Fault," *University of Chicago Law Review* 60 (1993): 67–140.

12. *In re* Marriage of Bonds, 5 P.3d 815 (Cal. 2000).

13. "Judge Who Heard Barry Bonds' Child Support Case Has Withdrawn from the Case," *Jet*, September 26, 1994.

14. See, e.g., *In re* Estate of Hollett, 834 A.2d 348 (N.H. 2003); Bloomfield v. Bloomfield, 764 N.E.2d 950 (N.Y. 2001); Krejci v. Krejci, 667 N.W.2d 780, 788–89 (Wis. Ct. App. 2003); Uniform Premarital Agreement Act § 6(a)(2) (1983).

15. Murray Chass, "Giants Make Investment: $43 Million in Bonds," *New York Times*, December 6, 1992; *Bonds*, 83 Cal. Rptr. 2d at 787–88; "Barry Bonds Career Stats," Major League Baseball.com, http://mlb.mlb.com/team/player .jsp?player_id=111188.

16. *In re* Marriage of Bonds, 5 P.3d 815, 838 (Cal. 2000)

17. Ibid., 817.

18. Ibid., 837.

19. Cal. Fam. Code. § 1615 (2004).

20. Atwood and Bix, "A New Uniform Law for Premarital and Marital Agreements."

21. Borelli v. Brusseau, 16 Cal. Rptr. 2d 16 (Ct. App. 1993); Wendy L. Hillger, Note, "Borelli v. Brusseau: Must a Spouse Also be a Registered Nurse? A Feminist Critique," *Pacific Law Journal* 25 (1994): 1414–16.

22. *Borelli*, 16 Cal. Rptr. 2d at 17–18.

23. Ibid., 19.

24. Ibid., 20 (citations omitted).

25. Ibid.

26. A number of scholars have critiqued *Borelli v. Brusseau*. See, e.g., Kaiponanea T. Matsumura, "Public Policing of Intimate Agreements," *Yale Journal of Law and Feminism* 25 (2013): 180–81; Silbaugh, *Marriage*, 124.

27. See, e.g., Holler v. Holler, 612 S.E.2d 469 (S.C. Ct. App. 2005).

28. *Borelli*, 16 Cal. Rptr. 2d at 22.

29. Ibid., 24.

30. "Costs of Care," National Clearinghouse for Long Term Care Information, US Department of Health and Human Services. Available at http://www.longtermcare .gov/LTC/Main_Site/Paying/Costs/Index.aspx.; "Occupational Employment Statistics: Maids and Housekeeping Cleaners," Bureau of Labor Statistics, US Department of Labor, March 27, 2012, http://www.bls.gov/oes/current/oes372012 .htm; "Occupational Employment Statistics: Childcare Workers," Bureau of Labor Statistics, US Department of Labor, March 27, 2012. http://www.bls.gov/oes /current/oes399011.htm; "Taxi Fares in Major U.S. Cities," Schaller Consulting. Updated January 2006. http://www.schallerconsult.com/taxi/fares1.htm.

31. Diosdado v. Diosdado, 118 Cal. Rptr. 2d 494, 495 (Ct. App. 2002).

32. Ibid., 497 (quoting *In re* Marriage of Bonds, 5 P.3d 815 (Cal. 2000)).

33. *In re* Marriage of Mehren and Dargan, 13 Cal. Rptr. 3d 522 (Ct. App. 2004).

34. Barbara Bennett Woodhouse, with comments by Katharine T. Bartlett, "Sex, Lies, and Dissipation: The Discourse of Fault in a No-Fault Era," *Georgetown Law Journal* 82 (1994): 2525–70.

35. Dawbarn v. Dawbarn, 625 S.E.2d 186 (N.C. App. 2006).

36. Ibid., 189- 190.

37. *In re* Marriage of Goldman, 554 N.E.2d 1016 (Ill. App. Ct. 1990).

38. Ibid., 1018.

39. Ibid., 1019.

40. Ibid., 1020.

41. Ibid., 1019.

42. Ibid., 1023.

43. Avitzur v. Avitzur, 446 N.E.2d 136 (N.Y. 1983); Hurwitz v. Hurwitz, 215 N.Y.S. 184 (N.Y. App. Div. 1926).
44. Victor v. Victor, 866 P.2d 899 (Ariz. Ct. App. 1993); Mayer-Kolker v. Kolker, 819 A.2d 17 (N.J. App. 2003).
45. Odatalla v. Odatalla, 810 A.2d 93 (N.J. Super. C. Ch. Div. 2002).
46. Ibid., 95, 96.
47. Ibid., 98.
48. Aleem v. Aleem, 947 A.2d 489 (Md. 2008); Soleimani v. Soleimani, 2012 WL 3729939 (Kan. Ct. App. 2012).

Index